D1469462

Henrietta Green's
NEW COUNTRY
KITCHEN

Henrietta Green's
NEW COUNTRY KITCHEN

The best produce · The best recipes

Special photography by Jess Koppel

Conran Octopus

*To Coco, my god-daughter — in the
hope that she will grow up to be a keen
and informed cook.*

*First published in 1992 by
Conran Octopus Limited
37 Shelton Street
London WC2H 9HN*

*Text copyright © 1992 Henrietta Green
Special photography copyright © 1992 Jess Koppel
Design and layout copyright © 1992 Conran Octopus Limited*

*The right of Henrietta Green to be identified as the author of
this work has been asserted by her in accordance with the
Copyright, Designs and Patents Act 1988.*

*All rights reserved. No part of this book may be reproduced,
stored in a retrieval system or transmitted in any form or by any
means, electronic, electrostatic, magnetic tape, mechanical,
photocopying, recording or otherwise, without the prior
permission in writing of the publisher.*

*Both metric and imperial quantities are given in the recipes.
Use either all metric or all imperial, as the two are not interchangeable.
Unless stated otherwise, all spoon measures given are level.*

*Art Director   Mary Evans
Design   Paul Welti
Project Editor   Denise Bates
Editor   Lewis Esson
Editorial Assistant   Lynne Drew
Picture Research   Jessica Walton
Production   Julia Golding
Home Economist   Lyn Rutherford
Photographic Stylist   Róisín Nield
Illustrations   Lynne Robinson*

*British Library Cataloguing in Publication Data
Green, Henrietta
Henrietta Green's New Country Kitchen.
I. Title
641.555*

ISBN 1 85029 366 X

Typeset by Servis Filmsetting Limited
Printed in China

Contents

Introduction

Whenever I tell anyone that I am a food writer, he or she invariably replies 'Then you must be a good cook'. Without wishing to blow my own trumpet, I suppose I am; but what I really aspire to is to be an excellent shopper.

Not everyone can shop well, some people are just not interested. They find it boring and a waste of time; their ideal is to rush into the nearest supermarket, grabbing from the nearest shelves and loading their trolley sky-high while praying that the contents will see them through the week. And, knowing the busy pressurized lives most of us lead, who can blame them?

But shopping really is the key to successful cooking, as without good produce you do not stand a chance. Not so long ago cooking was a complicated process; hours were spent in the kitchen creating elaborate dishes, transforming ingredients with intricate preparations and tucking them up in blankets of rich sauces. So what did the initial quality matter if the taste was so heavily disguised?

Nowadays the trend has moved away from this complicated approach and back to the more robustly flavoured food that we generally think of as cooking from the country. Our appetites crave fresher, purer flavours, simpler dishes such as those which you will find in *New Country Kitchen*, where the true nature of the ingredients shines through. The actual preparation and cooking may be simpler but, and it is a very large but, in order to achieve the right balance and effect and to wheedle and coax out the flavours, the ingredients have to be of the best possible quality – which neatly brings us back to shopping.

In order to shop well you need to know how and what to buy. I have spent years championing quality produce and have acquired a reputation for an understanding and discernment of the cornucopia of ingredients found in this country and elsewhere. I have visited endless farms, nurseries, factories and smaller speciality producers; wherever I go I talk about the produce in an attempt to get to grips with how and to what standards it is grown or produced. So many different factors can affect eating quality and I believe that only when armed with a knowledge of the roots of a product can you reach a better understanding of its nature. To this end, I explain in this book the different grades, cuts, varieties and standards of the produce generally available in this country so that anyone can make an informed choice when buying.

Most of us are well served by supermarkets; they are remarkably convenient and although they have done sterling work in raising their standards and expanding their range of varieties, too often their produce, aimed at a mass market, is bland and lacks strength of flavour. So I generally prefer to shop in my smaller local shops; it is not that small is necessarily better, but you can usually get more helpful, personal and flexible service. If you give advance notice a good butcher will cut and trim his meat to your specifications, a fishmonger will order the fish you need and fillet it, giving you the bones for a stock; a delicatessen will discover the right cheese and a keen greengrocer will buy in those special herbs. Search out the shops where service is paramount and remember, if you are not happy with the quality, do not be afraid to say so and stand your ground. After all, it is you the customer who must be satisfied.

Other sources of good food are farm shops, which often stock unusual varieties of vegetables and local butter and cream straight from the farm, pick-your-own farms, where you can be sure of the freshness and, of course, street markets. But do not be put off by the inevitable grumpy dragons manning the stalls who tell you 'not to touch'. Examine the produce and if it is blemished, complain. Another useful tip is to scour the back pages of magazines for mail order suppliers where you can find such interesting delicacies as smoked eels, first rate kippers, free-range geese for Christmas and even oysters delivered in prime condition by overnight carrier. In spite of what the supermarkets would have you believe, buying from small specialist suppliers is not necessarily more expensive.

If you think that this all sounds like hard work, believe me, it is worth it in the end. I have already said that I think the right shopping is as important as the cooking; sometimes I even spend more time on shopping than on the actual food preparation.

All my recipes reflect this new approach to food where the produce is of paramount importance. Just as you would always expect food straight from the farm to be fresh and in peak condition, so I urge you to seek out this quality when you are cooking from *New Country Kitchen*. My style is for strong vibrant flavours and – as the saying goes – you can't make a silk purse out of a sow's ear. Neither can you make fine meals from poor quality ingredients.

The Recipes

Soups

Starters

Light Dishes

Vegetables and Salads

Fish and Shellfish

Beef, Lamb and Pork

Poultry and Game

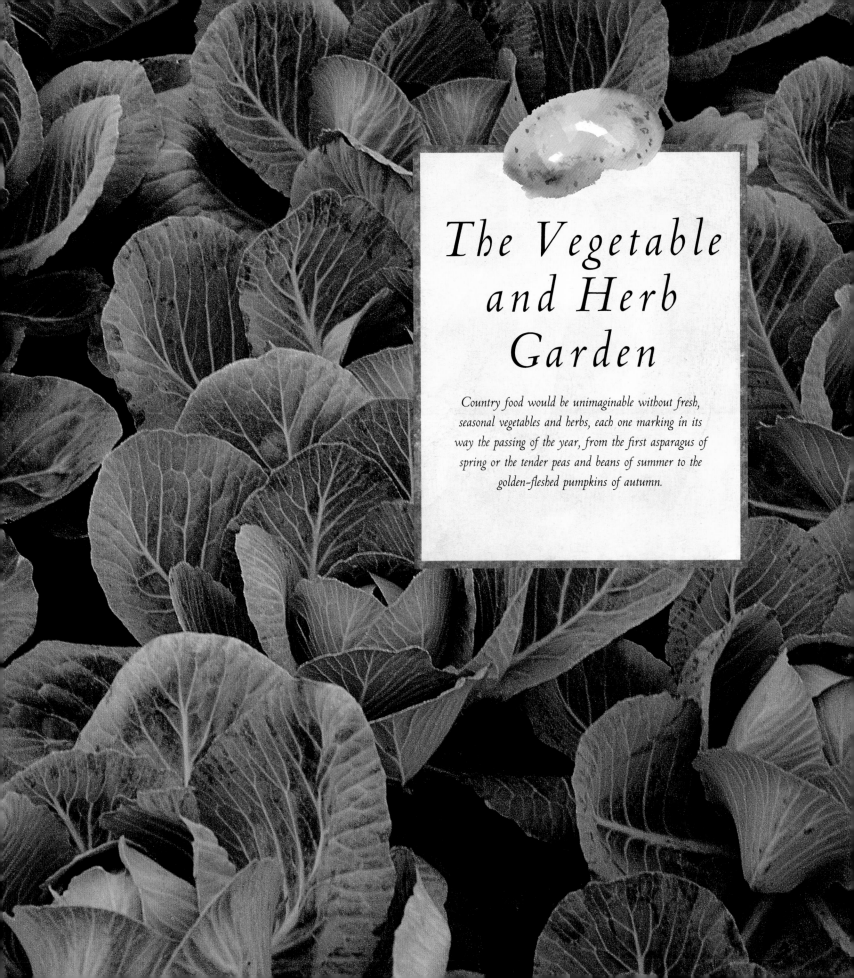

The Vegetable and Herb Garden

Country food would be unimaginable without fresh, seasonal vegetables and herbs, each one marking in its way the passing of the year, from the first asparagus of spring or the tender peas and beans of summer to the golden-fleshed pumpkins of autumn.

Vegetables

In spite of the temptation presented by the glorious array of imported vegetables on sale throughout the year, as a general principle I try to buy fresh home-grown vegetables in season. Not only does it make sense financially, as they are bound to be cheaper, but it is when they are at their best. The only frozen vegetable I buy is sweetcorn. I cannot see the point of any other frozen vegetables; and the only tinned vegetables I keep are pulses, for emergencies, and tomatoes.

Vegetables are categorized by the part of the plant we eat; there are roots and tubers, leaf vegetables, stalks and stems and vegetable fruits and seeds.

Homegrown produce hangs for sale on a garden fence.

Vegetable Stock

Many recipes call for a vegetable stock, and this may be made with almost any vegetable — even the water used in the cooking of vegetables may be added.

MAKES ABOUT 1.1 L/2 PT

2 carrots
2 stalks of celery, with their leafy tops
1 whole leek, including the green leaves
2 tomatoes
1 onion
small bunch of parsley
15 g/$\frac{1}{2}$ oz butter
1 tbsp oil
bay leaf
2–3 black peppercorns
strip of lemon zest

Coarsely chop all the vegetables and the parsley.

Melt the butter with the oil in a large pan over a medium heat. Add the vegetables and sauté them for 3–5 minutes, until soft.

Add the bay leaf, peppercorns and the lemon zest along with water to cover (about 1.1 1/2 pt). Bring to the boil. Cover, lower the heat and simmer gently for about 1 hour.

Leave to cool and strain through a sieve before use.

What price perfection?

Fresh vegetables are essential for a balanced diet and over the last few years we have come to expect them to be perfectly formed, regularly shaped and free from any blemish. In order to achieve these high standards, farmers and growers are forced to wage chemical warfare with herbicides, insecticides and fungicides. The trouble is that the chemicals are absorbed into the vegetables and, as a result, we are absorbing them into our bodies; it is no longer even enough just to wash or peel them. Although the experts find it difficult actually to pin-point the harmful effect they may have on our health, I cannot think of anyone who claims that they are beneficial.

Now I do not want to be an alarmist, but it is a situation that is escalating as the quantities used are increasing. Unless things change, it may soon get out of control. The first thing to realize is that pesticide residue is the price we pay for perfect vegetables, so we should think about changing our views on exactly what it is we want. We should also realize that not even all the chemicals permitted by law are necessarily safe; scientific testing is improving, and the government is having to knock several off their approved list. We, the consumers, should demand to know what is being used. Equally, we should demand that more money is spent on developing biological pesticides, whereby insects rather than chemicals are introduced to control other insects.

Pesticide residues are everywhere in the ecosystem, so much so that minimal amounts are even found in organically grown vegetables – vegetables grown to a sustaining system, without the use of chemicals and where the land is revitalized.

Several of our major supermarket chains are

Growing your own vegetables is one way of knowing what they have been treated with.

doing sterling work monitoring pesticide residues, but they should be encouraged to publish their findings. The more vigilant we are, the safer our vegetables will become.

One thing I do want to make clear is that when I mention lowering the standards of vegetables, I am only talking about their eye appeal – this does not mean that I would ever recommend buying old wrinkled vegetables which have been bruised by bad handling. Vegetables should be fresh and pert, plump and full; as they get old and tired they start to lose their moisture, so they sag and wrinkle.

Roots and Tubers

Most of the root vegetables are in season during the winter and are well suited to winter dishes, such as soups, stews, gratins and braises.

SWEDES, for instance, can be added to stews or peeled and roasted with meat, or boiled and then mashed with lashings of cream, butter and black pepper. Although most people think of them as pale orange, they can be any colour from purple to white and it makes little difference to their flavour. The larger the swede, the more likely it is to be coarse and woody in texture, so choose them medium size and make sure that they are firm to the touch with unbroken and unblemished skins.

In cooking, swedes and WINTER or MAINCROP TURNIPS are almost interchangeable, although the former tends to a coarser flavour. The latter are obviously available during the winter months, always need peeling and can be round, flattened or cylindrical. They are usually yellow or white in colour, with or without a green or purple stripe at the top. SPRING or YOUNG WHITE TURNIPS, on the other hand, are far smaller and sweeter; with their nutty flavour and a crisp texture they often only need to be lightly scrubbed and can be boiled, poached or steamed in a matter of minutes. If you are lucky enough to buy them with their leafy tops still attached, do not throw away the greens: steam them, toss them in a good olive oil slightly sharpened with lemon juice and serve them as a salad.

The young leaves of SCORZONERA and SALSIFY, also known as 'vegetable oyster' or 'oyster plant' as its roots are said to taste like oysters, are also eaten in salads in the same way. In Italy they even add *barba di becco*, the white crunchy-textured salsify shoots. Gener-

ally, however, it is the long white fleshy roots of the vegetables that are eaten and these can be boiled, baked or made into soups.

PARSNIPS make the most amazing velvety soup (see page 16) as do JERUSALEM ARTICHOKES. Buy these crisp-fleshed roots with as few knobbly bits as possible – they will not affect the taste but they make peeling much more difficult – and, as soon as you have peeled them, drop them into water acidulated with lemon juice or vinegar, otherwise they will discolour. Then boil them in a mixture of milk and vegetable stock, flavoured with parsley, peppercorns and a bay leaf. Once they are soft, whizz them in a food processor until smooth.

CELERIAC should also be soaked in acidulated water once it has been peeled. This is especially

Turnips promise robust winter stews and creamy purées.

important if you are making *céleri rémoulade*, that favourite dish of French *traiteurs* in which blanched shredded celeriac is tossed in a pungent mustard mayonnaise. Do not be put off by the scabby appearance of the root, as underneath its pock-marked skin lies a treasure trove of nutty juiciness which I sometimes use when cooking instead of celery. Avoid the large knobs as they can be tough, woody and sometimes even woolly in texture.

HORSERADISH is a very misshapen root and is not always easy to come by: when you see it fresh, snap it up. It will keep for ages in the refrigerator, if you peel and grate it and put it in a jar with a little wine vinegar.

CARROTS and POTATOES, the most popular root vegetables which are dealt with in more detail later, should be stored in a cool dark place — but remember that the refrigerator is too cold for potatoes!

Gratin of Mixed Root Vegetables

Make sure that your vegetables are all fresh and firm: if they are flabby they will break down while baking. Slice them into pieces of a uniform size so they will all take about the same time to cook.

SERVES 8

4 garlic cloves
15 g/½ oz butter
450 g/1 lb Cara or Pentland Squire potatoes, thinly sliced
115g/4 oz carrots, thinly sliced
225 g/8 oz celeriac, thinly sliced
225 g/8 oz parsnip, thinly sliced
115 g/4 oz swede, thinly sliced
1 tsp grated nutmeg
350 ml/12 fl oz double cream
salt and freshly ground black pepper

Preheat the oven to 200C/400F/gas6.

Cut one of the garlic cloves in half and rub the cut ends all over the inside of a large ovenproof gratin dish, then grease it with the butter. Finely chop the remaining garlic.

In a large bowl, toss the potatoes, carrots, celeriac, parsnip, swede and chopped garlic to mix them together. Season with plenty of salt and pepper and the grated nutmeg.

Arrange half the vegetables in a layer so they overlap slightly, pour over a little of the cream, then arrange another layer on top and pour over the remaining cream so that the vegetables are well covered.

Bake in the preheated oven for about 40 minutes, or until the vegetables are tender but not too soft and the top has turned a golden brown.

Parsnips

Although some supermarkets sell parsnips washed and bagged, I never trust them in this state. Somehow wrapping them in plastic makes them go flabby and even causes them to sprout. It is far better to buy them still covered with earth: it may make more work, but they will probably be fresher. Choose the plump shapes, as you will get more slices of a similar size, and avoid those which are too enormous and fat as they will almost certainly have a woody central core which you will have to throw away.

Parsnips should always be peeled and they may be baked in slices, roasted with meat or boiled and then whizzed in a food processor with copious quantities of cream (or crème fraîche for a sharper flavour), butter and pepper for a meltingly delightful purée. They may also be very thinly sliced, using a mandoline grater or the slicing disk of a food processor, and deep-fried in oil to make the most unusual 'chips'.

Curried Parsnip Soup

SERVES 6

1 tbsp coriander seeds
1 tsp cumin seed
1 dried red chilli
1 tsp ground turmeric
pinch of fenugreek
55 g/2 oz butter
1 onion, finely chopped
1 large garlic clove, chopped
2 parsnips, chopped
1 tbsp flour
1 l/1¾ pt chicken stock (see page 106)
150 ml/¼ pt double cream
small bunch of chives, chopped
salt and freshly ground black pepper

Grind the coriander, cumin and chilli together in a food processor or pound them in a mortar with a pestle. Mix them together with the turmeric and fenugreek and, as you will not need all this mixture for the recipe, store all but 1 tablespoon immediately in a small airtight jar for further use.

In a large saucepan, melt the butter over a low heat and add the onion, garlic and parsnip. Cover the pan and cook gently for 10 minutes.

Then stir in the flour and the tablespoon of spice mixture. Cook for a further 2 minutes, stirring from time to time. Pour in the stock and leave to simmer for about 15 minutes, or until the parsnip is tender.

Whizz in a food processor until smooth and add some water or a little extra stock to dilute it to a good soup consistency. Return the soup to the pan and gently reheat it. Then add the cream and adjust the seasoning.

Serve scattered with chives.

Carrots

Carrots are rich in Vitamin A and have a high sugar content. They may be classified according to shape, maturity and size: the early small and slender Amsterdam, with its smooth skin; the Nantes which is broader and longer than the Amsterdam, but is also used for forcing or as an early crop; the stumpy conical Chantenay, which is a maincrop type grown for summer eating; the large late-maturing Berlicum, which is used for winter storage; and the large long Autumn King, with its tapered shape, which is also used for winter storage.

Early carrots mature relatively quickly and are eaten as soon as they do, whereas maincrop carrots take longer to grow and are either eaten fresh or stored for use in winter. Their taste is much more a factor of their degree of maturity and the type of soil in which they were grown than their shape and variety. Ideally they should be grown in a rich but light soil for a clean sweet flavour; and because the maincrop carrot is slower growing, it tends to have a fuller-bodied flavour and a denser texture which stand up well to slow cooking in braises and stews.

Larger carrots should always be peeled and, when choosing them, avoid any with pitted surfaces or which seem to weigh heavy for their size – a sure sign of a woody centre. With small young carrots you need not bother with peeling as their skin is so soft; a light scrub or scrape under running water should be enough to clean them. They may then be eaten raw or steamed or cooked in stock or butter in a matter of minutes.

Glazed Carrots with Sauternes

The best carrots for this dish are any of the maincrop varieties as they hold together well and have such a sharp colour which glistens under the rich glaze.

If it seems an extravagance to use such a special wine as a Sauternes for cooking, try any of the cheaper sweet dessert wines such as Vin Santo, Beaumes-de-Venise or Loupiac. The remainder of the bottle may also be chilled and served with the last course.

SERVES 4

30 g/1 oz butter
450 g/1 lb carrots, cut into 2.5 cm/1 in sticks
150 ml/¼ pt chicken stock (see page 106)
150 ml/¼ pt Sauternes, or other dessert wine
salt and freshly ground white pepper

Melt the butter over a medium heat in a large saucepan which has a tight-fitting lid. Stir in the carrots to coat them with the butter.

Add the stock and wine. Season, cover the pan and cook the carrots for about 20 minutes, or until tender.

After 15 minutes or so, remove the lid to check the liquid. As you want it to be thick and syrupy, you may need to simmer the pan uncovered for the final 5 minutes in order to reduce the sauce. However, do make sure the carrots do not catch or burn. Otherwise replace the lid and simmer for the last 5 minutes.

Beetroot

Beetroot is classified as a salad root and most people buy it ready boiled for salads, which strikes me as a terrible shame for several reasons. First of all, I dislike beetroot in a salad; its velvety texture is quite wrong for mixing with salad leaves. Far more importantly, if trimmed and cooked, you miss out on the stalks and leaves which can be lightly poached in water, then cooled and dressed in vinaigrette for a salad. Also, when the beetroots are commercially cooked, vinegar is sometimes added in the misguided belief that it sharpens their flavour.

If you do buy them raw, choose even-sized beetroots – neither too big nor too small – which have an unbroken skin and which feel firm to the touch and show no sign of wrinkling.

Beetroot Gratin

SERVES 4

6 beetroots, each weighing about 115 g/4 oz
85 g/3 oz finely grated Parmesan
175 ml/6 fl oz double cream
3 tbsp fresh breadcrumbs
salt and freshly ground black pepper
butter, for greasing

Carefully wash the beetroots, making sure the skins are not punctured. Cut off their roots and leaves, leaving only about 5 cm/2 in of stalk at either end to make sure they bleed as little as possible while cooking.

Put them in a saucepan, pour over enough water to cover and bring to a simmer over a medium heat. Continue to simmer for about 40 minutes.

Preheat the oven to 190C/375F/gas5 and lightly grease a gratin dish with butter.

Drain the beetroots in a colander and leave to cool. Peel them either by rubbing off their skins or, if particularly thick, with a sharp knife. Cut them into slices about 6 mm/$\frac{1}{4}$ in thick.

Sprinkle 30 g/1 oz of the Parmesan over the bottom of the prepared gratin dish. Arrange half of the beetroot on the bottom of the dish, season and sprinkle over another 30 g/1 oz of the Parmesan. Then repeat the process once more. Pour over the cream, so that it covers the beetroot, and scatter the breadcrumbs on top.

Bake for about 15 minutes, or until the juices start to bubble at the side of the dish. Serve immediately.

With such a wide range of potatoes available, from tiny Jersey Royals to the red-skinned Desirées, choosing the right variety for the cooking method is crucial opposite.

Potatoes

The potato comes from the same botanical family as Deadly Nightshade and what we eat are the tubers which form on the plant's underground stems. These tubers are vital for the plant's survival and reproduction, as it is there that it stores carbohydrates and water.

Potatoes consist mostly of carbohydrate and fibre and also contain vitamins A and C, iron and calcium. It is their cell structure and the proportion of starch to dry matter that affects the texture when cooked: 'waxy' potatoes, with a lower starch content, boil and deep-fry beautifully but are hopeless for baking or mashing; 'floury' potatoes, on the other hand, are ideal for purées, as they collapse on boiling. So, whether you are boiling, steaming, baking or roasting, it is important to choose the right variety of potato.

British potatoes fall into three categories: 'earlies' from the beginning of June, 'second earlies' on sale from July to September and 'maincrop', ready to be harvested from September onwards. The colour of the skin can vary from a pale thin cream through a rosy pink to a dark conker-brown, and their flesh can be anything from a milky white to a deep yellow.

Earlies, or 'new' potatoes, herald the start of summer and are firm and waxy with a strong earthy taste. When they are first lifted, they have a very high dry-matter content which makes them perfect for boiling. As they mature, the starch content rises and the waxy texture disappears; they become softer as they cook and their skin thickens. To make sure you are buying a true early, rub its skin with your finger: it should flake off readily as it has, to use the technical jargon, no 'skin set'.

True earlies are best boiled and certainly need no peeling, as their skins are part of their pleasure. The most common British varieties are Home Guard, Arran Comet, Ulster Sceptre, Pentland Javelin and Maris Bard (also a good baker when mature). Starting in

April, you can also buy imported earlies from places like Jersey, Egypt and Morocco.

Second earlies include Wilja, which is particularly good for sautéing, and Estima, which is an adequate all-rounder.

The best-known maincrop potatoes include: red-skinned Desirée, with its high dry matter content and light yellow flesh, which is ideal for boiling and makes reasonably good chips; Maris Piper for excellent chips; Pentland Squire, with a texture well suited to mashing; Cara, recognizable by its spotted pink skin, which is a good all-rounder and ideal for baking as it fluffs up superbly; and King Edward (known as Kerr's Pink in Scotland) which roasts well and makes good chips. Incidentally, one of the most useful EC regulations to have been introduced recently is that all potatoes have to be identified by name in the shops. This should help considerably when shopping.

Other interesting maincrop varieties include the Pink Fir, which has all the nutty taste and firm texture of an early; the French Ratte and Belle de Fontenay, which are both equally good plainly boiled and served hot or cold in salads, especially if you dress them when still warm; Golden Wonder, which is a good baker; and Record, which is the potato for roasting.

Whether each variety has its own inherent taste is a matter of some controversy as so many factors affect flavour — such as soil, climate, weather pattern, farming practices and the degree of maturity — that it is impossible to isolate any predominant factor. When buying potatoes, choose the variety and size appropriate for the method of cooking. Always make sure they are fresh and firm, with unbroken skin (except for earlies) and never buy any with green areas or sprouting roots; it means that they have been left lying around in the light too long and are becoming toxic.

PAPER BAG POTATOES

Paper Bag Potatoes

As the potatoes for this recipe should be quite small, I sometimes use young earlies, such as Jersey Royal. However, the best results are obtained using mature Maris Bard or baby maincrop King Edward or Record. I always leave the skin on, as it firms up while the flesh softens to a creamy whip. You can use any mixture of fresh herbs and even add a little lemon zest; just make sure your mixture is not too overpowering or it will drown the taste of the potatoes.

SERVES 4–6

24 small potatoes, scraped
1 tbsp finely chopped flat-leaf parsley
1 tbsp finely chopped fresh rosemary
1 tbsp finely chopped fresh thyme
large pinch of sea salt
55 g/2 oz butter, diced

Preheat the oven to 180C/350F/gas4.

Arrange the potatoes on a large sheet of greaseproof paper and scatter over the herbs. Sprinkle with the sea salt and dot with the butter. Fold the paper over loosely, so that the potatoes are not wrapped too tightly. Then fold the edges over, pressing them down and tucking them in to make a sealed parcel. Bake in the preheated oven for 45 minutes.

Lift the parcel out, taking care not to tear it, and put it on a serving plate. Cut the parcel just before serving, so the heady aroma can be fully appreciated.

Henrietta's Roast Potatoes

At the risk of sounding conceited, I really do think I make the best roast potatoes ever. To be fair, they are not really roast potatoes in the classic sense, with a crisp outside and a silky soft centre; mine are crisp right through, more like huge crunchy chips which explode as you take your first bite — but that is how I like them.

For the right effect, it is very important what fat and potatoes you use. When I am not worrying too much about my fat intake, I go for a goose or duck fat; otherwise it must be olive oil. As for the potato, a firm maincrop is best, such as Desirée, King Edward or Record (if you can find them, as they mostly end up as crisps).

SERVES 4–6

675 g/1½ lb potatoes (see above), peeled and quartered
2 tbsp flour
3 tbsp duck or goose fat (see page 117) or olive oil
sea salt and freshly ground black pepper

Preheat the oven to 200C/400F/gas6.

In a saucepan over a medium heat, boil the potatoes in lightly salted water for about 5 minutes or until just parboiled, that is to say just slightly soft. Drain them and leave to cool slightly.

Sift the flour into a paper bag and add a generous pinch of salt and black pepper. Put the potatoes into the bag a few at a time and give it a good shake so the potatoes are well coated in the seasoned flour.

Put them in a roasting dish large enough to spread them out in a single layer, dot or pour over 2 tablespoons of the fat or oil and then give the pan a good shake.

Roast on the top shelf of the preheated oven for a minimum of 2 hours, turning the potatoes now and again so that they cook evenly. Baste them with the remaining fat or oil if they look in danger of drying up.

If you are roasting meat or poultry at the same time, you can use the fat from that to baste them. Should you want to cook the meat or poultry at a lower temperature, it will not affect the potatoes. Just start them off at 200C/400F/gas6 for about 30 minutes, then turn the oven down to the required temperature. However, you must make sure that you have allowed enough time for them to become fully crisp.

The Onion Family

No kitchen can ever afford to be without the onion and its relations, such as garlic, shallots and leeks. Essential to most savoury dishes, they lend a sweet sharpness, an extra bite and a considerable depth of flavour.

The best ONIONS for cooking are the fat juicy Spanish onions, with their caramel-coloured papery skin, or the smaller sharper-flavoured English onions. Red onions, usually imported from France or Italy, seem to lose their hazily sweet taste, their texture and sadly even their colour if cooked for any length of time, so it is wiser to restrict their use to salads or *gremoladas* (see page 136) so that their full flavour can shine through. White onions also have a milder flavour and I rarely use them. However, what I do find immensely useful are the baby white pearl onions; their shape and size make them delightful in stews, braises and sauces and they are never too overpowering. Pickling onions are of a similar size and, if you buy them when still quite young and fresh, can be substituted for pearl onions; but be careful as older ones are tougher and harsher in flavour.

When buying onions, they should be firm to the touch, unblemished and quite dry. If you leave them in the light too long, they will go soft and sprout vibrant green shoots; if this happens throw away the onion, but save the shoots and use them as you would chives.

SPRING ONIONS, the most gentle of all onions, are particularly handy if you want to cook something very quickly, as they will soften and lose the raw edge of their flavour in minutes. WELSH ONIONS look like spring onions, but they have a far stronger bite.

SHALLOTS can be used instead of onions, but they should always be stewed rather than being fried in butter as frying makes them bitter. They come in three varieties distinguished by colour: those tinged with red or pink are the mildest, the shiny golden brown ones are slightly stronger and the grey brown are the most pungent of all.

GARLIC is grown in this country, but it really needs relentless sun to give it any real intensity of flavour. Dried garlic comes in various sizes and colour and, as with shallots, the pinker the clove the milder the flavour. Fresh garlic first comes into season in the spring and lasts until the early summer. Plumper and less astringent than dried garlic, its cloves are a chalky white and its stems a delicate pale green. Garlic should never be kept too long as it tends to dry out or sprout green shoots in the middle of the cloves, which can then become quite bitter.

LEEKS may either be boiled, poached, sautéed or stir-fried, to be eaten as a vegetable, or added to stocks, soups and stews for extra flavour. For some inexplicable reason, I have developed an irrational prejudice against fat leeks and prefer to buy them thinner, even though it means more work cleaning them. It is a good idea to buy untrimmed leeks, then you can tell exactly how fresh they are; if their tops have faded from their natural bright green to an unsightly yellow and are dry and papery, it means they are on the way out. Equally, check their centres as, sometimes at the end of their season in early summer, they may have a thick woody core which makes them useless for anything but stocks. Baby leeks are sweeter and milder in flavour and really need nothing more than a short sharp steam to bring out their sweet succulence.

Onion Marmalade

Some recipes for onion marmalade result in quite a thin mixture which may be dished out in quite large quantities to be eaten as a vegetable. The version given here is very dense, bold and sweet. It should probably be thought of more as a chutney, and served quite sparingly. It goes well with Homemade Sausages (see page 150), Game Terrine (see page 174), a chunk of farmhouse Cheddar or even with plainly grilled lambs' liver. It may be eaten hot, straight from the pan; or cooled, packed into a sterilized jar and kept for weeks.

Spanish onions are best for this recipe as they soften down easily and absorb the alcohol while still holding their shape.

SERVES 8

3 tbsp olive oil
675 g/1½ lb onions, thinly sliced
140 g/5 oz caster sugar
3½ tbsp sherry vinegar
2 tbsp crème de cassis
250 ml/8 fl oz red wine
sea salt and freshly ground pepper

Heat the oil in a large wide-based pan over a medium heat. Add the onions and cook them for about 15 minutes, until they are golden brown.

Stir in the sugar and season. Turn down the heat to low, cover the pan and cook, stirring occasionally, for a further 10 minutes, or until the onions have softened and turned a slightly deeper brown. If at any time they look in danger of burning, add a teaspoon of water.

Stir in the vinegar, cassis and wine and cook uncovered, stirring regularly, for a further 30 minutes, or until the onions have absorbed most of the liquid and reduced to the consistency of jam.

The distinctively French way of transporting onions.

Roast Garlic

For some, the idea of eating a whole head of garlic seems a rather curious idea. However, once you have plucked up the courage to try it, you will realize just how good it is. The curious thing is that roast garlic does not really taste like garlic at all; it is far creamier and softer than you could possibly imagine. It goes wonderfully well with roast lamb, chicken and other roast meats.

The best garlic to use comes from plump heads as the fuller the clove, the juicier the result. Either use fresh garlic or, if you prefer it more pungent, dried heads. Forget about the smaller heads with tiny cloves as extracting the purée can be so fiddly that you will probably lose patience.

SERVES 6

6 heads of garlic
olive oil, for brushing

Preheat the oven to 180C/350F/gas4.

Using a pastry brush, paint each head of garlic all over with olive oil. Cut out 6 small squares of greaseproof paper and wrap up each garlic head in one.

Bake them in the preheated oven for about 35 minutes, or until soft.

To extract the purée simply slit the skin of a clove with a knife and ease out the pulp or press down on it to squeeze it out.

If you are roasting a joint of lamb, simply scatter one unwrapped head per person at the base of the joint and roast them in the pan juices for the last 35 minutes of cooking time.

ROAST GARLIC

Brassicas

European members of the brassica family include a wide range of vegetables. Some of the cultivated varieties, such as cauliflower and broccoli, were known to have been eaten by the Ancient Greeks and Romans, and cabbage was certainly grown by the Saxons and Celts, so they must number amongst the green vegetables with the longest culinary tradition.

Unless you are buying 'spring greens' or loose-leafed young cabbage, always choose CABBAGE with a firm, compact heart and fresh outer leaves which show no sign of frost or insect damage. The variety and type you buy depends to some extent on the time of the year, although rather ironically 'spring cabbage' has now come to mean young cabbage and is available all year round. Savoy, that most elegant of cabbages with its fine-veined crinkly leaves, is only in season from September to March. With a flavour milder than the smooth-leaved winter cabbage, it can be shredded raw

for salads and makes a welcome change to the ubiquitous coleslaw, made with the crunchy but dull Dutch white cabbage.

RED CABBAGE, essentially a winter vegetable, is now also grown all the year round and can be braised for hours for a rich, earthy flavour as well as being pickled or turned into a robust warm salad.

Red cabbage apart, no cabbage should ever be cooked for very long – the actual time will depend on the variety and how thickly it has been shredded. As a general rule, however, it only needs just enough time to soften the texture whilst still retaining the crunchiness. It can be poached in stock or water, sautéed in butter, steamed or stir-fried.

The BRUSSELS SPROUT is the one member of the brassica family I try to avoid, as I find its flavour bland and don't really care for its texture. However, the thousands of kitchen gardens and allotments sporting fine examples of the species are living proof that not everyone agrees with me. Choose them when still tightly formed and pale to deep green; as with all the

A firm, creamy white head is a sure sign of freshness in a cauliflower.

brassicas, if the leaves are yellowing it means they are not fresh. Be sure to cook them briefly to preserve what texture they have.

I much prefer the nuttier flavour of KALE and CURLY KALE, both loose-leaf plants which may be cooked exactly as cabbage. Again the leaves should be firm, free of blemishes and a good clear and even colour. The best CAULIFLOWERS to buy are those with firm creamy-white unmarked tight heads; as they age, they droop, turn a greyish yellow and the florets separate and fall apart.

Unlike cauliflower, SPROUTING BROCCOLI produces several clusters of flowering heads instead of a single one; these can vary in colour from a velvety soft green to a deep purple. What we nowadays commonly term BROCCOLI, or CALABRESE, produces spears of deep green which are actually made up of clusters of flower buds. The stalks should be tender, so watch out for any signs of woodiness as this makes them tough to eat. If the flower buds have started to run to yellow, they are way past their best. Both sprouting broccoli and calabrese need only a gentle heat when cooking and, if possible, their heads should be cooked in steam rather than by direct contact with water or stock.

KOHLRABI, sometimes called TURNIP-ROOTED CABBAGE, also turns woody if left to grow too long, so choose the smaller sweeter ones. It should be peeled and sliced and can be eaten raw or lightly boiled like cabbage. It also makes a good substitute for turnip with its sweet, if less fiery, flavour.

Warm Red Cabbage Salad

Choose a firm red cabbage. One way of testing is to press on it gently; if it retains an imprint of your fingers, it means it is old and flabby and not worth buying.

To prepare any cabbage, pull away the loose outer leaves and any of the top leaves that may have been marked. Cut it in half and then cut away the base of the stem in a deep 'V' shape to get rid of the core. Going with the grain, shred it to whatever thickness you want, then rinse it in a colander and drain it thoroughly.

SERVES 4

55g/2 oz walnut halves
2 tsp walnut oil
2½ tbsp olive oil
1 garlic clove, finely chopped
1 red onion, thinly sliced
2½ tbsp balsamic vinegar
1 small red cabbage, weighing about 450 g/1 lb, finely sliced
115 g/4 oz semi-soft goats' cheese, cubed
1 firm red apple, cored and thinly sliced
1 tbsp finely chopped fresh parsley
½ tsp finely chopped fresh marjoram
salt and freshly ground black pepper

Preheat the oven to 180C/350F/gas4.

In a bowl, toss the walnut halves in the walnut oil and season. Lay them out on a baking tray and roast in the preheated oven for 5–7 minutes, or until they begin to smell nutty. Remove them from the oven and leave to cool.

Heat the olive oil in a wide sauté pan over a moderate heat. Add the garlic and onion and sauté gently for about 2 minutes. Then stir in the vinegar and cook for a further 30 seconds. Add the cabbage and continue cooking, stirring continuously, for about 3 minutes or until the cabbage is just wilted. Season well with salt and pepper and a little more vinegar, if necessary, to sharpen the flavour.

Stir in the goats' cheese carefully, so as not to crush or break it up, along with the apple, parsley, marjoram and walnuts. Toss briefly and remove from the heat.

Serve immediately.

Fruiting Vegetables

These vegetables form a rather loose collection; what they do have in common, however, is that what we eat is the fruit containing the seeds. If the fruit is under-ripe, it will be too firm and lacking any inherent flavour; but if it is over-ripe, the seeds or pips will be too large and tough and the flesh pappy.

Over-ripe VEGETABLE MARROWS are particularly unpleasant as their seeds grow to an inordinately large size and their skin turns hard and bitter. Unfortunately, there is no sure-fire way of avoiding geriatric marrows, although weighing them in your hands can be a guide. They should feel full, but not over-heavy for their size. Their actual freshness is a different matter; look for a bright, slightly glossy skin with no hint of yellowing, and avoid any which are bruised or badly marked.

COURGETTES are baby marrows, developed from the French marrow especially for cutting when very small. Courgettes may be no bigger than a finger or up to 22.5 cm/9 in long, and their colour anything from a deep dense or pale mottled green to a canary yellow. Their skin should be taut and glossy and should always be left unpeeled. Either cut them in half lengthwise, brush with oil and grill; or cut them across into slices and steam, fry, sauté or poach them.

PUMPKINS and SQUASHES generally do need to be peeled before cooking. There are a number of varieties, but I particularly like the nutty SUMMER SQUASH, or PATTY PAN, which when small and young may be cooked in its skin. WINTER SQUASHES have a firmer, more floury texture and are well endowed with vegetable protein and carbohydrates, making them excellent for vegetarians. Like all the members of the family, they can be turned into terrific chutneys and soups.

CAPSICUMS or SWEET PEPPERS may also be yellow or deep dark purple, although the most common colours are red or green. I have never understood the attraction of eating these raw as, although crunchy and succulent, they have no length or depth of flavour. I much prefer them grilled or roasted, when their sweetness starts to caramelize and they have far more body. Buy them when firm and fleshy and avoid any with wrinkled or broken skins. Always remove their seeds and any white pith before use.

The closely related CHILLI PEPPERS, of which there are literally hundreds of varieties, add bite to a wide variety of dishes. Remember that the thinner the chilli, the hotter it is likely to be.

AUBERGINES, like peppers, are not grown very successfully in Britain. However, as you see them in practically every supermarket and greengrocer, they almost count as one of our own vegetables. Usually purple, there are now pale green, pinky mauve and white varieties ranging from the size of a lime to that of a small melon. Even if they are very large, I never bother to peel or salt them, although some people say it is essential for removing their bitterness. Again they should be glossy and look blown up like a balloon; once they begin to sink and their skin starts to wrinkle, they are no longer worth buying.

SWEETCORN or CORN ON THE COB comes from the maize plant. Mature plants are sold on the cob and these may be bought still wrapped in the pale green leaves of the husk. For the freshest possible cobs, check that the leaves are still supple, the silk moist and the corn plump and tightly packed. To strip it, pull back the leaves and silk then cut the cob at its base. To cook it, plunge it into boiling water and simmer for 8–10 minutes, depending on its size. Baby sweetcorn kernels, always sold stripped, only need a couple of minutes boiling or they can even be eaten raw.

Golden orange pumpkin adds a welcome touch of colour to autumn dishes.

Courgette and Corn Chowder

If I can, I like to mix green and yellow courgettes for this soup for an extra dash of colour. When they are in season I sometimes also use summer squashes, such as Butter, Little Gems or Patty Pans, for their varied skin colours. I sometimes even mix in a couple of boldly striped ones for extra interest.

Corn is one of the very few vegetables I recommend buying frozen. The idea of going to all the trouble of boiling fresh cobs and shredding them for the kernels, only to add them to a soup, seems a little unnecessary. Unlike most frozen vegetables, moreover, frozen corn has a very good taste and texture.

SERVES 4

1.1 l/2 pt milk
350 g/12 oz frozen sweetcorn kernels, defrosted
30 g/1 oz flour
1 small onion, finely chopped
1½ tbsp finely chopped fresh coriander
1½ tbsp finely chopped fresh mint
3 large basil leaves, finely chopped
6 coriander seeds
piece of cinnamon stick, about 5 cm/2 in long
225 g/8 oz courgettes (see above), diced
2 tomatoes, skinned and chopped
juice of 1 lime
salt and freshly ground black pepper

Put about 150 ml/¼ pt of the milk along with 225 g/ 8 oz of the corn into a food processor and sift in the flour. Whizz until smooth, then strain the mixture into a large saucepan.

Add the remaining milk, the onion, ½ tablespoon each of the coriander and mint, the basil, coriander seeds and cinnamon. Slowly bring to the boil over a low heat, stirring continuously.

Add the courgettes, half the prepared tomatoes and the remaining sweetcorn to the pan. Simmer for about 10 minutes, or until the courgettes are tender.

Stir in the remaining chopped tomato and the lime juice (if this curdles the milk, do not worry as it gives the soup a 'chowder' look). Remove the cinnamon stick, season and garnish with the remaining herbs.

Stewed Cucumbers

The most common cucumber in the shops is the long and smooth 'indoor' cucumber which is grown in a greenhouse or under a frame. Juicy and crisp, it is the best kind to use for cooking as its skin may be eaten. This allows a contrast of taste and texture between the sweet melting flesh and the slightly bitter harder skin. If you find this too overpowering, peel the skin off lengthwise in alternating strips, rather than removing it all.

The shorter, fatter and hardier 'ridge' or 'outdoor' cucumber, with its crunchier texture and bumpy skin, has a stronger flavour and should always be peeled, whether you are cooking it or serving it raw. Baby ridge cucumbers are sometimes wrongly sold as gherkins. True gherkins need to be salted and pickled before they can be eaten.

SERVES 4

2 long smooth cucumbers
45 g/1½ oz butter
2 onions, chopped
125 ml/4 fl oz chicken stock (see page 106)
3½ tbsp dry white wine
½ tsp ground mace
15 g/½ oz flour
salt and freshly ground white pepper

To prepare the cucumbers, trim off the ends and cut them in half lengthwise. If you don't like the seeds, scoop them out with a teaspoon. Cut the cucumber

COURGETTE AND CORN CHOWDER left, GRISSINI (SEE PAGE 192) centre, LETTUCE AND CHERVIL SOUP (SEE PAGE 41) right.

halves into 2.5 cm/I in lengths and divide these again into quarters or sixths, depending on how fat the cucumbers are.

Melt 30 g/I oz of the butter in a heavy-based pan over a medium heat. Add the onions and cook them gently for about 5 minutes, or until they are soft but have not changed colour.

Add the cucumbers and cook for another couple of minutes, then pour in the stock and wine and season with salt and pepper and mace. Bring to the boil, cover, reduce the heat and cook gently for about 10 minutes.

Meanwhile, mash the remaining butter with the flour to make a thick paste. Remove the pan from the heat and stir in the paste, a little at a time. Return the pan to the heat and, stirring continuously, simmer for a further couple of minutes until the sauce thickens. Adjust the seasoning and serve.

Tomatoes

Tomatoes are usually a disappointment unless ripened naturally in the sun; those grown commercially in greenhouses are all too often woolly, watery and lacking in flavour and sweetness. There are any number of varieties, from the commercially popular – but all too easily dismissed – Moneymaker to the large beefsteak, striped Tigerella and tiny cherry. Plum tomatoes from Italy and Marmande tomatoes from France are sometimes imported into this country and should be snapped up when available, as their glorious rich flavour will remind you of how a tomato should taste. Otherwise you will have to resort to the cunning trick of always sprinkling tomatoes with a little sugar. When buying tomatoes, choose those which are plump and firm, with an evenly coloured skin, and which weigh heavy in the hand.

When you are using tomatoes for cooking, you may want first to peel off their skins. This can be simply done by cutting small crosses in their bases and then pouring some boiling water over them. Leave them in the water for a couple of minutes, then drain and refresh them in cold water. You will then find that the skins peel off easily.

For some sauces, canned tomatoes will work just as well. For the best possible flavour and texture, however, try to get some fresh Italian plum tomatoes. Recently yellow-skinned tomatoes, in varying shapes and sizes, have found their way into our shops; you may want to buy them as a novelty, but you will find that their exciting colour has no match in their taste.

Green Tomato, Raisin and Mint Chutney

Among all the thousands of chutneys this is one of my favourites, as it has a sharp clean flavour that, unlike many others, is neither too cloying or sweet.

This recipe is also a useful way of using up unripe or green tomatoes which are too hard and bitter to be eaten raw and fail to ripen, even if left on a sunny window sill or wrapped in brown paper bags.

As with all chutneys, make sure the ingredients are of a good quality and free of any bruises or blemishes.

MAKES FOUR 575 ML/1 PT JARS

1.5 k/3½ lb green tomatoes, cut into dice
450 g/1 lb onions, finely chopped
450 g/1 lb raisins
450 g/1 lb demerara sugar
250 ml/8 fl oz cider vinegar
100 g/3½ oz fresh root ginger, peeled and finely sliced
1 tsp cayenne
½ tsp salt
55 g/2 oz coarsely chopped fresh mint leaves

Put all the ingredients except the mint in a large saucepan or preserving pan and bring to a simmer over a medium to low heat. Then leave to simmer, uncovered, for about 1 hour, stirring occasionally with a wooden spoon, taking care not to crush or break up the vegetables or to let the mixture bubble too fiercely.

Stir in the mint and simmer for a further 15 minutes, or until the vegetables are just tender but not too soft.

Have ready 4 warm dry sterilized 575 ml/I pt glass jars and pack the chutney loosely into the jars. Cover with waxed paper discs and leave to cool overnight.

The following morning, seal and label the jars and store them in a cool dark place to mature for about a month before you even think of trying the chutney.

Peas and Beans

These vegetables are all members of the legume family – plants which bear their seeds in pods that split open when ripe.

There are numerous varieties of GARDEN PEAS; best known are the large wrinkled marrowfat, which are commonly used for canning and freezing, and the small smooth, incredibly sweet petit pois. As both are grown for the peas inside their pods, choose pods which are a clear bright green, full and swollen, but still quite soft as hard pods are an indication of over-mature peas. As a general guideline, to obtain a given weight of shelled peas, you need to buy $2\frac{1}{2}$ times the weight of peas in the pod. Once podded, the peas should be eaten as soon as possible, as they quickly loose their sweetness.

As the name suggests, every bit of the MANGE-TOUT PEA or EDIBLE PODDED PEA may be eaten. Again there are different varieties – sugar pea, sugar-snap, snow pea. The best ones to buy are the small- to medium-sized pods which are crisp and bright green; mange-tout peas are flat-podded, with just a hint of tiny weeny peas showing through the paper-thin pods, while sugar snaps are rounder and plumper. If they are still very young, you should not even need to top and tail them. When fresh, the pods are crisp and a vibrant green; as they age, they start to flop and lose their intensity of colour.

Both the ordinary and edible podded pea can be simmered in water, stewed in butter (with a little chopped lettuce for added sweetness) or stir-fried in butter, olive oil or stock.

The ASPARAGUS PEA is actually from a different branch of the family, but has the same sweetness and tenderness. Once their pods are over 2.5 cm/1 in long, they are too tough and stringy to eat. However, their tendrils are particularly tasty; if you can collect enough they are delightful in a salad.

In this country, the most popular GREEN BEAN is the scarlet RUNNER BEAN. Depending on the variety, they can be anything from 15 cm/6 in to 60 cm/24 in long and any colour from shades of pink, yellow or green to mottled green, green marked with a purplish black or even entirely black (although they do turn green when cooked). FRENCH BEANS are the preferred green beans on the Continent; small, thin and round, they too can be any colour. Both sorts of bean should be firm and supple, with as little string around the edges of the pods as possible (several stringless varieties are grown). To prepare green beans, top and tail them and cut them to the required size; for larger runner beans, I suggest you shred them before cooking them in boiling water until tender or sautéing them in butter. Baby BROAD BEANS are so soft that you can eat every bit of them – pod, skin and all. However, larger broad beans must be shelled and, ideally, podded (see Pasta with Spring Vegetable Sauce overleaf).

Dried peas and beans, or PULSES, are also very important and feature in several recipes. We have a few of our own in this country, including yellow and green SPLIT PEAS, LENTILS and BROAD BEANS. Most other pulses, however, like BORLOTTI and CANNEL-LINI BEANS, FLAGEOLETS and CHICK PEAS, cannot cope with our dreary climate and have to be imported. Some need soaking prior to cooking, whereas others may be cooked immediately (instructions are usually given on the packet). One thing it is important to remember is not to salt the beans until after they have been boiled, as it makes them much tougher.

Pasta with Spring Vegetable Sauce

One of the nicest pasta sauces is made with sweet and tender baby vegetables, which hardly need any cooking time at all. If you can find them, use baby broad beans and just toss them whole into the sauce; otherwise buy 2½ times the weight of larger pods, avoiding any which have badly marked pods or which are very swollen as this means the beans inside will probably be too large and consequently be too tough. Their skins can also be quite tough, and this ruins the effect of the soft buttery bean inside; so you should remove them as explained below.

You could also use mange-tout peas instead of shelled garden peas. In fact, when I make this sauce I tend to use whatever sweet-flavoured and tender baby vegetables I can find. So I suggest you make up your own mixture according to availability and merely think of this recipe as a guide.

It is, however, essential to use the right shape of pasta. Noodles made in flat wide ribbons, like tagliatelle, are probably the best as they are the right shape to trap the small vegetables on their surface; if you use thin and round pasta, like spaghetti, the vegetables will just slide to the bottom.

SERVES 4

285–350 g/10–12 oz dried pasta (see above)
55 g/2 oz shelled broad beans
6 tbsp extra-virgin olive oil
3 spring onions, trimmed and cut into 2.5 cm/1 in lengths
2 baby leeks, trimmed and cut into 2.5 cm/1 in chunks
4 tbsp coarsely chopped flat-leaf parsley
3 green peppercorns
2 tbsp chicken stock (see page 106) or water
3 tbsp white wine

6 baby carrots
55 g/2 oz mange-tout peas
55 g/2 oz shelled baby peas
30 g/1 oz baby spinach leaves
1 tsp balsamic vinegar
sea salt and freshly ground black pepper

Cook the pasta in a large saucepan of lightly salted water until just tender but still firm to the bite.

While the pasta is cooking, pod the broad beans, put them in a saucepan, cover with lightly salted water and bring to the boil over a medium heat. Simmer for 3–4 minutes. Drain and refresh them immediately under cold running water. When they are cool enough to handle, skin the beans with your hands by gently slitting them open with the nails and carefully pressing them out with the fingers.

Meanwhile start making the sauce: heat 3 tablespoons of the oil in a large heavy-based sauté pan over a medium to low heat. Add the spring onions, leeks, 2 tablespoons of the parsley and the peppercorns and cook gently for 2–3 minutes. Pour in the stock and white wine and simmer for 1 minute. Then stir in the carrots, mange-tout peas and shelled baby peas and poach the vegetables for a further 2–3 minutes. Add the prepared broad beans, then drop the baby spinach leaves into the pan and leave them just long enough to wilt.

Using a slotted spoon, transfer the vegetables to a warm bowl. Turn up the heat to medium, add the remaining oil and balsamic vinegar and simmer for about 3–4 minutes to allow the sauce to reduce slightly. Season to taste.

Drain the pasta well, tip it into a large serving bowl and add the vegetables. Pour over the sauce, sprinkle with the remaining parsley, give the pasta a good toss and serve.

PASTA WITH SPRING VEGETABLE SAUCE

Stalks, Stems and Leaves

CARDOONS, rarely seen in the shops, are one of the most underrated of vegetables. A member of the thistle family and closely related to the globe artichoke, it is the stalk rather than the flower heads or choke which is eaten. The stalks are cut when still young and tender, lightly blanched and eaten like celery in soups, salads and stews.

SEAKALE, another rare delicacy, is in season only briefly in early spring. The baby leaf stalks are grown under cloches or earth banks, to emerge pallid and frail. They should be lightly boiled or steamed and eaten with a Hollandaise Sauce (see page 128). Later, in April, come HOP SHOOTS or 'bines' which are thinned from the hop plants. These must be cut before they grow thick and hairy, and are cooked simply in the same ways as seakale. Both of these types of young shoots taste like asparagus and I always think of them as overtures for the main work.

ASPARAGUS has a short season in Britain, from May to late June. The shoots or 'spears' are cut at between 15–25 cm/6–10 in in length; they may be as fat as a big toe or as thin as a little finger, as with the reed-thin baby asparagus called 'sprue'. The best spears are firm and taut, fleshy with not a hint of woodiness, and with the tips still tightly closed. In this country and the USA green stems are preferred, whereas milky white asparagus with tips tinged with purple is eaten on the Continent. This is not a question of variety, but rather of the way the asparagus is grown. The former are left to sprout in beds, whereas the latter are earthed up in soil banks to blanch them and prevent the stalks from turning green. Some people find the pale white ones too astringent and prefer the slightly grassier

White asparagus, generally favoured on the Continent, is blanched to keep the stalks white.

flavour of the green; whereas others think that only the white ones are worth eating.

The ideal way to cook asparagus is in a tall asparagus pan, so that it stands upright allowing the stalks to boil in water while the tips are gently steamed. Failing that, lay the spears flat and either simmer in a large pan or steam them in a steamer. Serve them hot with melted butter or Hollandaise Sauce (see page 128), or cold with vinaigrette.

Delicate tender WHITE CELERY is also grown in the dark to blanch it, while crisper GREEN CELERY is left uncovered. Just to confuse the issue, however, there are now several self-blanching varieties. The celery head should be neat and hold tightly together. The stalks should be resilient and firm; if they droop and bend they are no longer fresh. Watch out for stalks which are too thick, as they may be tough and stringy.

If possible, buy celery untrimmed with its leaves still attached, as not only are these a good indication of the freshness of the plant (they start to go blotchy and lose their colour within days), they are very useful chopped as an additional flavouring in stocks, soups and stews. Raw celery can be eaten in salads or served to accompany cheese, or it may be braised or baked *au gratin* and served as a vegetable.

FLORENCE or BULB FENNEL, not to be confused with the herb fennel, is a short stocky plant with an edible swollen leaf base. It has a slight aniseed taste and a crisp texture when fresh, but rapidly goes rubbery and chewy with age. The bulbs are usually sold trimmed of their feathery tops and they should be a snowy white with green-tinged stalks. Buy them when plump and firm, with the layers tightly wrapped around each other, and avoid any which are soft to the touch. They may also be chopped and eaten raw in salads; alternatively whole or halved bulbs may be braised or stewed, or brushed with oil and grilled or roasted.

SPINACH is an invaluable leaf vegetable which is rich in vitamins A and C and in minerals. The tiny baby leaves or 'pousses' can be added raw to salads; larger older leaves should be washed thoroughly and cooked with only the water clinging to them, until they reduce to a pulp. As spinach cooks down almost to nothing, allow about 170 g/6 oz per person. Make sure the leaves are bright to dark green, firm rather than wilting and free of slime and insect damage. Some people like to tear off their stalks, but I never bother, particularly as they add texture.

SPINACH BEET, although often confused with spinach, is actually a close relative of the beetroot which is grown solely for its leaves. With a stronger flavour and slightly thicker, more luscious leaves than spinach, it may be prepared and cooked in the same ways.

CHARD is another member of the beet family and is easily distinguished by its glossy leaves and thick white ribbed stems. Tasting like seakale or asparagus, these stems are sometimes stripped down and steamed on their own. The Ruby chard has deep red stems and leaf ribs; Swiss chard, or perpetual spinach, grows happily throughout the year and, if left to go to seed, will produce tight seed heads which are delightful in a salad. Buy chard when the leaves are bright and evenly coloured, with soft tender stems; if left too long in the ground they toughen and become far too stringy. Prepare and cook the leaves like spinach.

Roast Vegetables with Thyme

Once you have cut the fennel bulb, it will start to discolour and turn brown; so, unless you are using it immediately, soak it in acidulated water. Choose the firm, crisp elongated male bulbs for this recipe as they are easier to pack into a gratin dish than the rounder more curvaceous female bulbs.

Beefsteak or plum tomatoes are much better for roasting than our more vapid varieties. Not only do they taste better but, because of their texture, they will hold together better.

SERVES 6–8

6 fennel bulbs
6 beefsteak tomatoes
pinch of sugar
7 garlic cloves
4 tbsp olive oil
5 tbsp white wine
2 small dried chillies
4–6 small sweet red onions
3 celery stalks, trimmed and cut into 15 cm/6 in lengths
3–4 sprigs of thyme
2 sprigs of rosemary
sea salt and freshly ground black pepper

Preheat the oven to 180C/350F/gas4.

Trim the tops of the fennel and, if necessary, peel off a layer of the outer leaves. Using a sharp knife, cut them in half lengthwise and, making a deep 'V', cut away the central core. Wipe the tomatoes, cut small crosses in their tops and, if they do not look very sweet, sprinkle them with a pinch of sugar.

Cut the garlic cloves in half and rub one of the cut ends all over the insides of a deep ovenproof gratin dish. Using a pastry brush, lightly paint the inside of the dish with oil. Then pour in the wine and add the chillies. Arrange the fennel, tomatoes, onions, and celery in a single layer, tucking in the remaining garlic. Brush the tops of the vegetables with the remaining oil, tuck in the sprigs of herbs and season.

Bake in the preheated oven for about 45 minutes or until the vegetables are tender, occasionally basting them with their juices and brushing them with extra olive oil, if necessary, to stop them from going too brown. Serve with roast meat or fish.

Globe Artichokes

Globe artichokes probably originated in the Mediterranean region and are thought to have been eaten as long ago as Roman times. Several varieties are now cultivated including the fat pale-green, tightly formed Camus de Bretagne, which are imported into this country from Brittany, and Violettes de Provence, the tiny, violet-tipped artichokes grown in the South of France, Italy and Spain which are so small and soft that every part of them can be eaten. They may be deep-fried or baked whole, or even served raw.

With the larger artichokes only certain parts may be eaten, namely the base of the leaves and the heart – once the spiky choke on top of it has been removed. Always choose artichokes when fresh and firm, with their leaves closely layered together. If their tips are going brown, they are past their best and the leaf base will be rather tough. Sometimes, however, you can buy artichokes in this state very cheaply: simply cut off the leaves and just cook their hearts. Although restaurants go to an inordinate amount of trouble trimming the leaf tops and removing the choke, I never bother.

Recently in a restaurant in Brittany, I came across 'artichoke crisps' which were quite superb and well worth copying. The chef had simply sliced the raw heart very finely on a mandoline grater and then deep-fried the slices in groundnut oil.

Globe Artichokes with Broad Beans

SERVES 4

4 globe artichokes
1 large lemon, halved
1 tbsp olive oil
3 sprigs of parsley
3 peppercorns
140 g/5 oz broad beans in their pods
2 hard-boiled eggs, shelled
150 ml/¼ pt extra-virgin olive oil
2 tsp finely chopped fresh summer savory
1 tsp drained and finely chopped capers
sea salt and freshly ground black pepper

Rub the artichokes all over with the cut halves of a lemon. Pack the artichokes in a saucepan, right side up, and fill it with just enough water to come up to the tips of their leaves – you do not want to drown them. Add the ordinary olive oil along with the parsley sprigs, peppercorns and a generous pinch of salt.

Bring the water to the boil over a medium heat and simmer for about 35–45 minutes, depending on the size of the artichokes. To test if they are cooked, break off a leaf and check the texture of the fleshy tip; it should be soft and yielding while the rest of the leaf is still firm. When they are ready, strain them through a colander and turn them upside down to allow any water inside to drain away.

Meanwhile make the sauce: pod the broad beans, put them in a saucepan and cover with lightly salted water. Bring to the boil and simmer over a medium heat for 3–4 minutes. Drain and refresh them immediately under cold running water. When they are cool enough to handle, skin by gently slitting them open with the nails and carefully pressing them out with the fingers.

Cut one of the eggs in half, remove and reserve the yolk, then coarsely chop the other whole egg with the remaining white.

Sieve the reserved yolk into a bowl and slowly beat in the extra-virgin olive oil, a few drops at a time, to make a thickish mixture. (You are not making a mayonnaise, so do not worry if the emulsion is not perfect.)

Then stir in the juice from the lemon halves, along with the chopped egg, summer savory and capers. Fold in the skinned broad beans carefully, so as not to break them up, and season the mixture.

Arrange the drained artichokes on a serving plate and gently separate the top leaves to make a small opening. Remove the hairy choke. Spoon some of the sauce into the artichokes and leave to cool. Then serve with the rest of the sauce in a bowl.

GLOBE ARTICHOKES WITH BROAD BEANS

Salad Vegetables

When thinking of a salad, most people start with lettuce. Thankfully, however, the range of salad leaves available has increased over the last few years beyond the dreams of gastronomy. Where once we had to make do with lank vapid Butterheads, we now have a whole range of differently coloured and textured plants.

LETTUCES are generally classified into several different types, categorized by shape and structure. ROUND LETTUCES include the loose Butterhead, the crisp and sweet-flavoured Webb's Wonderful, the equally crisp but sadly flavourless Iceberg, the Four Seasons, with its red-tinged leaves, and the sturdy Buttercrunch. LONG LETTUCES are recognizable by their long upright, tightly bunched leaves, like the well-known Cos; others are the tiny and aptly named Little Gem and the compact-hearted St Albans. LOOSE-HEARTED LETTUCES have no heart and include the reddish brown oak leaf, the red Lollo Rosso and the

pale-green Lollo Biondo, both of which have crinkly, curly leaf tips. SALAD BOWL, or CUT-AND-COME-AGAIN LETTUCES, grow in small groups of leaves, some of which may be pulled off while the plants are still in the ground and they will grow back again.

Another interesting salad plant is CHICORY, which has a sharp bitter-sweet flavour with an interesting edge and depth. Italy boasts the widest range, including such stunning hardy red varieties as the long pointed Treviso Rosso, Verona Flamba and the variegated Sottomarina. Although we call the round compact red chicory RADICCHIO, this is a misnomer; in Italy it is the generic name for all red chicories. Then there is Witloof, also known as Brussels chicory or Belgian endive, with bud-like shoots that are forced and blanched to give them their succulent texture and pure white leaves tipped with the palest of yellow green. ENDIVES are often confused with chicories and, as they belong to the same family and taste almost the same, it is not surprising. There are two main types of endives: the curly-leaf frisée and the broad-leaf Batavian endive or escarole.

Then there are the SINGLE-LEAF SALAD PLANTS,

Lollo Rosso lettuce

such as LAMB'S LETTUCE or CORN SALAD (*mâche* in France), a low-growing plant with roundish, silky-textured leaves which are slightly nutty in taste; pungent ROCKET with a spicy taste which can turn quite overpowering in larger older leaves; peppery WATERCRESS which should never be touched when the leaves have wilted or turned yellow; and the similarly tasting LAND CRESS or WINTER CRESS; and PURSLANE with its juicy and mild-flavoured leaves and stems. Last and, as far as I am concerned least, comes MUSTARD AND CRESS which I honestly think is a waste of time, with its stringy stalks and itsy-bitsy leaves – the only use I have ever made of it is to snip it into egg sandwiches, and I would never dream of putting it in a salad.

RADISHES are classified as salad roots and they can be round or cylindrical, red, red-striped, white or white-and-red. Although they are usually eaten raw, I was recently served them lightly blanched as a vegetable and they made interesting if slightly curious eating. I eat them on their own, spread lavishly with a sweet unsalted butter. I also like to let a few radish plants go to seed, then add the seed pods to a salad while they are still small and tender; this way I get the benefit of a radish flavour without the interruption of its texture. Like the other salad root, BEETROOT (see page 17), I would never dream of adding them to a salad. Beetroot stains everything it touches and – to my mind – has entirely the wrong texture for mixing in with leaves. If I am going to make a salad with beetroot, it will be on its own, or perhaps with a little grated bulb fennel.

Lettuce and Chervil Soup

You can usually tell just how fresh a lettuce is by the pertness of its leaves. Another means, which is more reliable when buying the loose-hearted soft-leaved lettuces, is to turn the lettuce upside down and examine the base of its stem: if it is still chalky white and exuding a milky substance, it has been cut within a few hours. It soon dries up, however, and the base starts turning brown, getting darker as it ages.

Cos lettuces seem to retain their firmness and shape longer than most other lettuces, but once their leaves start to separate and pull apart or turn brown at the edges, it will have lost the sweet flavour that makes it so good for this soup. Several cookbooks suggest that you can use tired lettuces for cooking, but do not be tempted.

SERVES 4–6

30 g/1 oz butter
1 large onion, finely chopped
1 garlic clove, finely chopped
225 g/8 oz cos lettuce leaves, broken into pieces
small bunch of chervil
15 g/½ oz flour
1 l/1¾ pt chicken stock (see page 106) or water
150 ml/¼ pt double cream
1 egg yolk
salt and freshly ground black pepper

In a large saucepan, melt the butter over a medium heat. Add the onion and garlic and cook for 5 minutes to soften. Stir in the lettuce leaves and the chervil, reserving a few sprigs for garnish, and cook for a minute or two.

Sprinkle over the flour and, using a wooden spoon, stir it into the mixture. Cook for a further minute, then gradually add the stock and simmer for 5 minutes.

Whizz in a food processor until smooth, return to the pan and slowly reheat the soup. If you prefer your soup ultra-smooth, pass it through a sieve. Depending on how thick it is, you may need to add a little extra stock or water.

Meanwhile, whisk the cream and egg together in a bowl. Remove the soup from the heat and slowly add the cream mixture, stirring constantly. Season and gently bring the soup back to just below the boil.

Serve sprinkled with the sprigs of chervil.

Wilted Green Salad with Prosciutto

For a green salad like this with a warm dressing, use leaves that wilt easily, such as lamb's lettuce, rocket, Ruby red or Swiss chard, baby spinach or ordinary spinach torn into small pieces, dandelion leaves, Batavian endive, oak leaf lettuce or flat-leaf parsley.

SERVES 6

2 tbsp red wine vinegar
1 large shallot, finely chopped
1 garlic clove, finely chopped
6 tbsp extra-virgin olive oil
255–350 g/9–12 oz of mixed leaves (see above)
12 thin slices of prosciutto, cut into slivers
sea salt and freshly ground black pepper

Pour the vinegar into a wok, add a generous pinch of salt and stir until dissolved. Add the shallot and garlic. Simmer over a medium heat for a couple of minutes.

Then stir in the olive oil, add plenty of black pepper and heat the sauce for a couple of minutes, or until it is warmed through.

Tip in the mixed leaves and toss and stir them for a couple of minutes, or until they are just wilted but have not gone entirely limp. Using a slotted spoon, transfer the leaves to a large salad bowl and scatter over the prosciutto. Then pour the dressing left in the wok over the top. Serve at once.

Putting together a salad

Salads are a very personal matter, as what they are made up of must depend on your taste and sense of colour. I like my salads leafy, with a good contrast of sweet and bitter and crisp and soft. I always keep a bag in the refrigerator full of different leaves, wrapped in damp paper or packed in polythene to keep them fresh, and I pick and choose from them to make an assortment. Nowadays, most supermarkets do this for you with their ready-trimmed mixed and washed salad – but it is not nearly so much fun.

I usually start with a full-flavoured lettuce, such as Little Gem or Webb's Wonderful, tearing the leaves by hand into bite-size pieces as I do not believe in cutting them with a knife.

Then I may add some frisée for texture, chicory for bitterness and Treviso Rosso for colour. There are plenty of other leaves and herbs that I also like to include, though not altogether at the same time: chives or, for a more delicate flavour, their purple flowers; salad burnet; chervil for its nuttiness; flat-leaf parsley for a hint of chlorophyll; hyssop flowers for their colour; sorrel for its lemony bite; nasturtium leaves or rocket for a dash of pepper; purslane for its texture; and baby spinach leaves – the list is endless, and none of my salads are ever alike.

Allow a total of about 45–55 g/1½–2 oz per person, and tear the leaves by hand into similar bite-size pieces. Once I have made up my mix, I wash it in cold water and then use an invaluable rotary salad drier to get off the water.

Basic Vinaigrette

1 tsp Dijon mustard
5 tbsp extra-virgin olive oil
1 tbsp white wine vinegar
sea salt and freshly ground black pepper

In a bowl, beat the mustard with a few drops of the olive oil until smooth.

Then slowly whisk in the rest of the oil and the vinegar until it is thick and creamy.

Season to taste.

Variations

1 Replace the vinegar with the juice of I lemon.
2 Add I finely chopped shallot.
3 Add I tablespoon of finely chopped herbs, such as flat-leaf parsley, chives or tarragon.

Tomato, Honey and Garlic Dressing

5 tbsp tomato juice
l tsp runny honey
l small garlic clove, crushed
l tsp balsamic vinegar
5 tbsp extra-virgin olive oil
2 basil leaves, finely chopped
sea salt and freshly ground black pepper

In a large bowl, whisk the tomato juice with the honey, garlic and vinegar. Gradually whisk in the oil until the ingredients are mixed together.

Season and stir in the basil.

Yoghurt Dressing

5 tbsp Greek yoghurt
l tsp Dijon mustard
5 tbsp extra-virgin olive oil
juice of $\frac{1}{2}$ lemon
l tbsp finely chopped fresh coriander
sea salt and freshly ground black pepper

In a large bowl, beat the yoghurt with the mustard until smooth. Gradually whisk in the oil and lemon juice until the dressing is thick and smooth.

Season and stir in the coriander.

From left to right: *TOMATO, HONEY AND GARLIC DRESSING, HERB VINAIGRETTE, YOGHURT DRESSING, GREEN SAUCE (SEE OVERLEAF).*

Herbs

Fresh herbs are essential in cooking, for their taste, smell and colour. Every keen cook should have a herb garden or, at the very least, a sunny window ledge packed with pots. When cutting or plucking sprigs or leaves from a herb plant, try to use either the tips, side shoots or lateral leaves, to encourage new growth.

Most of the supermarket chains now stock a good range of cut fresh herbs. Because of the evaporation of their volatile oils, however, they start to loose intensity of flavour after a few hours, even if they are kept chilled. Nevertheless, they are still better than most dried or frozen herbs, if admittedly more expensive.

Always buy cut herbs when they look perky, and avoid any which show signs of wilting or if the leaves are changing colour. If they are in transparent sleeves, check for condensation on the lids as this means that they are losing moisture and are past their prime. When

The flowers of herbs such as chives can be used in salads or salad dressings for extra colour.

you get them home, wrap the herbs in damp paper and keep them in the refrigerator. Bunches of parsley can be stood in a jug of fresh water in a cool place out of direct sunlight. (Change the water every couple of days as this keeps the herbs fresher and prevents that appalling smell of stale parsley water.)

Some herbs, particularly the woody-stemmed perennials like thyme, rosemary, bay, hyssop, fennel and sage, do dry quite successfully. The soft-stemmed herbs which mostly die back during the winter or need re-seeding, such as parsley, mint, basil, tarragon, chervil and coriander, should really only be used fresh, although they may sometimes be frozen successfully.

To chop herbs, I find the quickest way is to snip them with a pair of scissors, either directly into the food or into a small mug (for the herbs with larger leaves, just fold the leaves up and then snip them into tiny pieces) – it is a lot less work.

There are several superb combinations of herbs and other foods, which work because they are complementary and balance each other's flavours: examples include eggs with sorrel, chicken with tarragon, lamb with rosemary, peas with mint, tomatoes with basil, broad beans with summer savory, rhubarb with sweet cicely (to alleviate some of its tartness), dill with salmon and mackerel with fennel. Nevertheless, I am all in favour of cooks experimenting for themselves, as this is the only way that their repertoire of herbs can be broadened.

I also think that cooks should use varying amounts of herbs, according to their feel for them and the taste they prefer. This is why I do not always specify the amount exactly – a 'large bunch' means a handful to one and a few sprigs to another. I have deliberately left it vague and urge you to achieve the balance you like rather than follow my instructions blindly. The pungency of herbs also varies according to the time of year, so amounts can never be exactly prescribed.

With few exceptions, however, I do insist (although it goes without saying that you are free to ignore my prejudice) on using flat-leaf rather than moss-curled, or curly-leaf, parsley. I know that moss-curled parsley is grown in this country all year round and is very British, but I just do not like its grainy coarse texture and its overwhelming flavour. It should only really be used with very bold-flavoured and coarse or chewy-textured ingredients, as in Jambon Persillé (see page 155). Flat-leaf parsley is far softer and subtler and enhances the flavour of food rather than overwhelming it.

I personally never use dried herbs, bay leaves apart; and if I cannot get the fresh herb I need for a particular recipe, I will substitute another fresh herb of a similar flavour. If you choose to use dried herbs, however, keep them in a warm dry place away from the light. Also remember that they fairly rapidly lose any flavouring power they had, so buy them from shops with a rapid turnover and replace them on a regular basis.

Green Sauce

This is a very powerful sauce of Italian origin and is usually served with plainly boiled meats, such as beef or tongue or sausages. You could also use it to dress hard-boiled eggs or the flesh of a chicken after it has been boiled for stock (see page 106), or even to give a boost to a mild soft cheese.

SERVES 4

6 anchovy fillets
4 tbsp finely chopped fresh flat-leaf parsley
8 small gherkins, finely chopped
30 g/1 oz capers, drained and finely chopped
1 small garlic clove, finely chopped
grated zest and juice of ½ lemon
6 tbsp extra-virgin olive oil
sea salt and freshly ground black pepper

Roughly chop the anchovies into small pieces and pound them to a smooth paste in a mortar with a pestle.

Put the paste into a large bowl along with the parsley, gherkins, capers, garlic and lemon zest and juice. Stir the ingredients together.

Whisk in the olive oil a little at a time. Check the seasoning (because of the anchovies you may not need any salt but add plenty of pepper).

Leave to stand for at least 30 minutes before serving.

The Dairy

Whether from the cow, sheep or goat, milk is the essential component of all dairy products, producing rich cream and yoghurt and golden yellow butter. And countless local cheese-making skills transform it into literally hundreds of different cheeses.

Milk

Milk is not only one of our most complete foods in itself but it is also used as the basis of all dairy produce. While we in the West generally drink and process milk from the cow, ewe and goat, it is the milk of the buffalo and yak which finds favour in India and Tibet respectively, and in Northern Africa the milk from the camel is used.

The composition of milk varies according to the type and breed of animal, as well as its condition and diet. Among the nutrients it contains are calcium (a daily pint will supply the average requirement for most people), fat, protein (principally casein, lactoglobulin and lactalbumin), vitamins A and B2, and carbohydrate in the form of the sugar lactose.

Once collected, fresh cows' milk is subjected to various treatments: most milk sold in Britain is pasteurized to kill off any harmful bacteria. The exact process varies, but generally involves heating the milk to a temperature of 72C/161F for 15 seconds only and then rapidly cooling it. The milk may then be homogenized by forcing it through a fine aperture, which has the effect of breaking down the fat globules and distributing them evenly throughout the milk.

Milk may also be skimmed to reduce its fat content. This was once done by hand: after the milk had been left to stand overnight the dairymaid would skim off the cream which had risen to the surface using a wooden skimmer. Now the process is highly mechanized and the milk is spun in a centrifuge to separate off the heavier fat globules.

In Britain, fresh cows' milk is graded according to its fat content and processing: CHANNEL ISLAND or GOLD TOP has a legal minimum of 4.9% fat and is the only milk to come from specified breeds, in this case Jersey and Guernsey cows. Because they are much smaller animals producing less milk than the more common Friesian, the butterfat content of their milk is much higher as it is more concentrated. Gold top is pasteurized but never homogenized; the cream rises to form the very marked cream line you see in the bottles.

SILVER TOP or WHOLE MILK has a fat content of 3.9% and is pasteurized but never homogenized. RED TOP, on the other hand, is exactly the same except it has been homogenized. Either of these may be used when milk is required in cooking.

SEMI-SKIMMED MILK, sold in bottles with a red and silver striped top, is both pasteurized and homogenized and has a fat content between 1.5–1.8%. SKIMMED MILK undergoes the same processing, but it has a fat content of less than 0.3%. It is sold in bottles with silver and blue tops. Both grades of skimmed milk can be used for cooking, but they have a tendency to burn unless heated over a low heat; also, because of their low energy and fat-soluble vitamin A content, they are not thought sufficiently nutritious for babies and young children.

Anyone who wants to use low-fat milk but needs to increase their calcium intake should buy one of the various brands of CALCIUM-ENRICHED MILK available. Equally, if anyone has difficulty digesting milk, they could try ACIDOPHILUS MILK which is made by re-introducing the natural bacteria lactobacillus acidophilus killed off during pasteurization, which makes milk easier to digest.

BUTTERMILK was traditionally a by-product of butter-making, but it is now commercially made by adding a buttermilk culture to skimmed milk. The result is a light milk with a slightly acidic taste, useful for baking scones and bread and in salad dressings.

Guernsey cows, whose milk goes to produce creamy gold top milk.

In spite of a recent attempt by the government to ban the sale of RAW (unpasteurized) fresh milk on the grounds that it constituted a health hazard, you can still buy it direct from a few licensed farms. In fact, because by law it is subjected to scrupulous testing, it does not present a risk and is favoured by the cognoscenti as it is thought to be fuller-flavoured and more beneficial. When bottled, unpasteurized milk is easily recognized by its green top. ORGANIC MILK — usually sold raw but also available pasteurized — is from animals reared according to the principles of organic farming. Ironically there are no regulations governing fresh EWES' and GOATS' MILK, as they are comparatively new to the market; however as the government is in the throes of drawing them up, it is just a question of time.

Fresh milk should be kept in the refrigerator; whole milk will last for about five days and skimmed milk for about three days.

The life of fresh milk can also be prolonged by certain industrial processes: LONG LIFE or UHT (Ultra Heat Treated) milk, available whole, semi-skimmed and skimmed, is homogenized then heated to a very high temperature (132C/270F) for 1 second only, rapidly cooled and aseptically packed in polythene and foil-lined containers. It has a shelf-life of about six months, but should be treated as fresh milk once opened. STERILIZED MILK lasts unopened for about two months: sold either in glass bottles with a crown cap or plastic bottles with a blue cap, it is homogenized, bottled, sealed and heated to at least 100C/212F for about 30 minutes and then cooled. As the process caramelizes the milk's sugars giving it a sweet sticky flavour, it is ideal for baked rice pudding and other such nursery foods.

Both CONDENSED MILK and EVAPORATED MILK are concentrated by high heat, and DRIED MILK or MILK POWDER is made from spray-dried (usually skimmed) milk and may be reconstituted by adding water to it.

Cream

Originally cream was skimmed by hand from the milk; now it is generally produced by industrialized centrifugal separation. Like milk, most cream is pasteurized, either fresh or UHT, and may also be homogenized. It is graded according to its legally defined minimum fat content. The higher the fat content the less likely it is to curdle when cooked and, provided it has not been homogenized, the easier it is to beat air into it.

DOUBLE CREAM, with a high fat content of 48%, can safely be added to hot soups, stews and sauces and whips into sharp well-defined peaks; do not over-whip it as it goes grainy. EXTRA DOUBLE CREAM or DOUBLE CREAM THICK has the same fat content as double cream but it is heavily homogenized to produce an even distribution of the butterfat globules, giving it a thicker texture but making it impossible to whip. WHIPPING CREAM, with 35% fat, will whip to at least double its volume. SPOONING CREAM has the same fat content as whipping cream, but will not whip as it is heavily homogenized.

SINGLE or POURING CREAM may or may not be homogenized for a more even blend. As it only has a fat content of 18%, it is more likely to curdle when added to a hot liquid. To prevent this happening always stir it in a little at a time and never re-heat it. It cannot be whipped, as the optimum fat content for whipping is 35–40%. If the fat content is lower, there are not enough globules to enclose the air bubbles and form foam. If, however, the fat content is too high, the fat globules come into contact with each other too quickly and form butter granules before enough air has been incorporated and the cream goes grainy, as sometimes happens with double cream.

Creams vary greatly in consistency and fat content, with golden yellow clotted cream the richest of all.

The best way to whip cream is to put it in a chilled bowl and use a balloon whisk to aerate it rather than a rotary beater, which actually wears away the fat membrane and causes the cells to 'glue'. HALF CREAM is very light, with a fat content of 12%, and is useful for coffee or for pouring over breakfast cereals.

CLOTTED CREAM is the richest of all creams as it has a 55% fat content. It is different from all others in that it is made by cooking rather than by centrifugal separation: whole milk, usually from Jersey, Guernsey or South Devon herds, is heated to about 108C/226F and left to cool for a minimum of $4\frac{1}{2}$ hours. The thick wrinkly cream crust is then skimmed off.

CRÈME FRAÎCHE is made by adding a lactic bacteria culture to a rich cream to thicken it and give it a distinctive light acidic flavour without souring it. Its fat content can vary, and depends on the cream used.

To make crème fraîche
Simply mix 1 tablespoon of yoghurt or cultured buttermilk into every 3 tablespoons of whipping cream and slowly bring it to about 24C/75F over a low heat, stirring constantly. Then remove it from the heat, cover and let it stand in a warm place for a few hours, by which time it should taste just like the real thing. It can be used exactly as you would double cream (except it does not whip) and will keep in the refrigerator for a week or two.

SOUR CREAM is homogenized single cream which has been soured by the addition of a bacterial culture. SMETANA, an Eastern European sour cream, is traditionally made with a mixture of sour cream enriched with sweet cream, although what we buy here is cultured sour cream mixed with skimmed milk.

Yoghurt

Yoghurt is a soured milk which is thought to have originated among the nomadic tribes of Eastern Europe. Their yoghurt was very rich and acidic and an entirely natural product in the sense that it was not manufactured. Whole milk was left to ferment and, as there was no temperature control and it was often left too long, it would occasionally separate and turn very sour indeed.

The yoghurt made now, either domestically or imported into this country, is far milder. It is usually made with skimmed cows' milk with added skimmed milk powder, or with goats' or ewes' milk. First the milk is pasteurized, then it is inoculated with a starter culture and incubated until the right amount of milk sugar turns to acid and it thickens. It is then cooled to prohibit further growth.

The milk may be incubated in one of two different ways; either it is continually stirred in large tanks to give the resulting yoghurt a thick creamy consistency (stirred-type), or it is poured into pots or cartons and then left undisturbed. This latter treatment results in a junket-like set texture. In order to extend its shelf-life, yoghurt may be pasteurized to inhibit further bacterial growth (long-life); LIVE or ACTIVE YOGHURT contains live bacteria and, if it is stored at room temperature or above, will quickly become sour. SPECIAL-CULTURE YOGHURTS are made when the milk is injected with bifidus and acidophilus bacteria to make a lighter, more delicate yoghurt, which is said to be easier to digest.

The fat content of yoghurt depends on the milk from which it is made: VERY-LOW-FAT or SKIMMED MILK YOGHURT should have a fat content of less than 0.5%; LOW-FAT will contain 0.5–2.0%; GREEK-STYLE YOGHURT is a stirred yoghurt which can have a fat content ranging from 1.8–17%, so it is wise to

Goats' milk is used to make yoghurt as well as various cheeses.

check the label first. LABNA is Greek-style yoghurt which has been strained to remove some of the whey, resulting in a rich creamy yoghurt with a more pronounced and concentrated flavour.

To stabilize yoghurt

As with cream in cooking, the higher the fat content of yoghurt, the easier it is to add it to a hot liquid without fear of curdling. To be on the safe side you can stir a little of the hot liquid into the yoghurt first and then add that back to the liquid. Alternatively, if you are using a low-fat version you should stabilize it first: for every 575 ml/I pt of yoghurt you need either I lightly beaten egg white and a pinch of salt or I teaspoon of cornflour mixed in I tablespoon of water. Then mix either of these in the yoghurt and simmer it for 10 minutes over a low heat, stirring constantly.

Butter

Butter is made by churning cream and it takes about 9 1/18 pt of milk to make 450 g/1 lb of butter, which must, by law, contain no less than 80% milk fat. Its taste and texture depend on the quality of milk and the method used to make it.

There are three different types: LACTIC BUTTER is pale yellow with a sweet fresh flavour and a creamy texture. The best that I have ever tasted comes from Isigny in Normandy. The cream is skimmed off whole milk and then may or may not be pasteurized, a purée culture of lactic bacteria is added and it is left to ripen for about 16 hours. The cream is then churned so that the globules of fat form and the buttermilk is eliminated. The butter may then sometimes be lightly salted so that it will keep for up to four weeks.

SWEET CREAM BUTTER is most commonly made in this country or imported from Holland and Denmark. Pasteurized cream is churned without being ripened and, to improve its keeping qualities, it may be salted with a minimum of 2% salt (Welsh butter with its very salty taste has about 5% salt), or slightly salted with 1% salt. It is then stored at a cool temperature for a few weeks to mature. Sometimes, after a few weeks and just before it goes off to market, it is churned again and a lactic bacteria culture is added with a little water to make it taste like a lactic butter.

FARMHOUSE BUTTER, as you might expect, is made on the farm rather than in an industrial creamery. In France it is made from full cream, but in Britain it is almost always made from whey, a by-product of cheese-making. The whey is churned into butter and, as it contains some of the cultures used to make cheese, the butter tends to have a slightly cheesy taste. If improperly made, an excess of moisture may also make it slightly watery. Real farmhouse butter, as opposed to butter which is simply described as such, is really worth seeking out. However, it has a comparatively short shelf-life and is best eaten within a couple of weeks of purchase. It is often for sale around the countryside in better local or farmhouse shops.

All butter should be kept in the refrigerator, well wrapped to prevent any contamination of flavours.

I prefer to cook with unsalted butter, as it has a clearer taste and, when melted, makes less scum and does not catch so easily.

To clarify butter

In order to get rid of the sediment when using it in cooking, you can first clarify butter: melt it over a low heat and leave it to cook gently for a few minutes, making sure it does not turn brown. When it has separated, remove it from the heat, leave it to stand for a few minutes and then pour it through a sieve lined with a damp piece of muslin or paper towel. It can then be heated to a very high temperature without burning and will keep in the refrigerator for a couple of weeks.

CONCENTRATED BUTTER has a very high butter-fat content (about 96%) as most of its moisture has been removed. It too will heat to a high temperature and is excellent for shallow-frying.

There are also a number of margarines, butter spreads, butter substitutes, vegetable and low- or no-fat spreads sold as butter substitutes. I prefer the real thing and, when watching my diet, would rather do without butter than resort to any of these.

Flavoured Butters

Butter flavoured with herbs, spices, sugars or other ingredients may be served with grilled meat or fish or puddings. Best made with a slightly softened unsalted butter, flavoured butters are easy to prepare and can be mixed well in advance.

Roll the butter mixture into a sausage shape, wrap this in foil and store it in the freezer. Then, when you want to use the butter, you can simply slice off attractively shaped discs.

Lime Butter

SERVES 4

55 g/2 oz unsalted butter
zest and juice of 1 lime
sea salt and freshly ground black pepper

Whizz the butter until smooth in a food processor along with the lime zest.

With the machine still running, add the lime juice and season to taste.

Turn the butter out of the bowl, place it on a sheet of greaseproof paper and shape it into a ball. Then roll it out into a sausage shape about 10 cm/4 in long and wrap it in foil.

Store in the freezer until required.

Variations

1 Make a chilli butter by replacing the lime zest and juice with a small pinch of chilli paste, a pinch of cayenne and 1 teaspoon of lemon juice.

2 Make a mustard butter by replacing the lime zest and juice with 1 tablespoon of grainy French mustard and the juice of half a lemon.

3 Make a herb butter by adding a small bunch each of flat-leaf parsley, chervil and tarragon to the food processor, whizzing them until finely chopped and then processing the butter until smooth.

4 Make a sweet butter by adding 1 tablespoon of caster sugar, 1 or 2 soft ripe strawberries and 2 teaspoons of vodka to the butter.

Sauce Beurre Blanc

Best made with a good unsalted butter for a sweet creamy flavour, this classic French sauce is remarkably easy to make, provided you only beat the butter into the pan in small amounts and never let it get too hot.

SERVES 4

55 g/2 oz shallots, finely chopped
2 tbsp white wine vinegar
3 tbsp dry white wine
115 g/4 oz unsalted butter, chilled
few drops of lemon juice
salt and freshly ground white pepper

Put the shallots, vinegar and wine into a small heavy-based saucepan. Simmer over a medium heat until reduced to about 1 tablespoon of syrupy liquid. Remove the pan from the heat while you cut the butter into small pieces.

Using a balloon whisk, start to beat the pieces of butter into the pan one at a time. Turn the heat down to low, return the pan to the heat and continue adding and whisking in the butter.

If the sauce looks like it is getting too hot and the butter starts to melt into a clear liquid, simply remove the pan from the heat and carry on whisking off the heat.

When all the butter is incorporated, add the lemon juice and season to taste.

Serve immediately or keep warm off the heat in a double boiler or in a bowl balanced over a saucepan filled with warm water.

Cheese

Turning milk into cheese has always struck me as one of the wonders of food production. That such a wide diversity of tastes, textures, shapes and colours can be made from milk is nothing short of a miracle.

In fact cheese-making dates back to the earliest days of European and Asian civilization, when primitive farmers first discovered an efficient means of preserving milk for those seasons when the animals were dry. Once the milk was collected, they would leave it to curdle in the sun, then beat it with branches and sprinkle it with salt. The cheese was finally matured by either further drying in the sun or storing it in caves. Over the centuries cheese-making has become very refined and sophisticated and numerous techniques now exist.

To start at the beginning, nothing has such a strong influence on the cheese as the milk from which it is made. Most cheeses are made from cows', ewes' or goats' milk although, in some parts of the world, mares', yaks', reindeers' and buffaloes' milk (as for mozzarella) are used. The milk can either be whole, skimmed or semi-skimmed; it may also be fresh, raw or pasteurized and left to mature overnight or longer.

To explain the process of cheese-making as simply as possible, I have divided it into three basic stages.

First the milk must be prepared, so a starter and rennet are added: the starter introduces the bacteria essential for the milk to ripen and the rennet causes the milk to curdle so it separates out into curds and whey. The curds are what the cheese is made of, so the whey must be drained away. (Although a few cheeses, such as ricotta, are actually made from the whey.)

Then begin the processes specific to the actual making of cheese. These can include cutting, milling or

The art of cheese-making, combined with individual local conditions, has produced over the centuries an extraordinary variety of cheeses.

kneading the curds, 'cheddaring' them (a process specific to Cheddar by which they are turned and stacked), heating them slightly, ladling them into moulds, leaving them to drain naturally, salting them or leaving them to soak in brine for a saltier flavour, injecting them with mould for a blue cheese or pressing them for a semi-hard or hard cheese.

Finally there comes the process of ripening. Some cheeses are eaten fresh, within a day or so of being made; others may be aged for as long as three years. Again depending on the cheese, the atmosphere in which they are matured may be damp or dry – in a cellar, cave or drying room – and the cheese may be turned daily or every two weeks or so to ensure that it ripens evenly. It may also be pierced, so a mould may develop within it; washed or brushed for a rind finish or for a bloom of mould to develop on its exterior; or even wrapped in a cloth or sealed in wax or fat.

Throughout the world countless different cheeses are made. They may be loosely divided into the following categories.

FRESH-MILK or UNRIPENED SOFT CHEESES, such as fromage frais, ricotta, Petit Suisse, curd cheese, cottage cheese or cream cheese.

The number of varieties of soft unripened cheeses is so large that it can be rather confusing knowing which is which and for what they are best suited.

Fromage frais is similar to our curd cheeses and both can be eaten on their own or used in cooking. When made with whole milk, it is known as full-fat fromage frais or curd cheese and has a minimum 20% fat content; the medium-fat version contains 10–20%. Low-fat, skimmed milk and even 0%-fat soft cheese are available, but these generally don't cook well.

Cream cheese is a soft cheese made with double cream and cottage cheese and is the result of slowly heating the curds before washing and draining them. Again, the fat content will vary according to the milk and/or cream used.

You can also find fresh goats' milk cheeses, sold either as individual cheeses or cut from whole logs, either plain or rolled in ash to develop their flavour or mixed with fresh chopped herbs. As the latter have a high water and low acid content, they can be a source of listeria; so it is generally considered safer to buy those made with pasteurized milk and to avoid them altogether if pregnant, very young or old, or otherwise with an immune system not in full working order.

Then there are the creamy RIPENED SOFT CHEESES, covered with a downy rind (or, to put it more technically, coated with a bacteria culture). Camembert and Brie are probably the most famous examples: some people like to eat these while they are still quite hard and chalky; others prefer them melting and runny. If you are buying a cut piece, first check how ripe it is by looking at the inside; it will have a layer of soft creamy paste in the middle, sandwiched between

Farmhouse Cheddar must be matured for many months before being sold.

two layers of firmer cheese – the width of the central band is an indication of the ripeness of the cheese. For a whole cheese, press its sides gently: they should be soft and yielding. A good cheese should also smell sweet with a hint of hay; if it is tinged with ammonia it is probably over the top.

SOFT RIND-WASHED CHEESES have rinds which range in colour from pale beige to a deep orange, a dense texture and an earthy taste, as the surface has been washed with brine during ripening to give it a deeper flavour. Munster, Pont l'Evêque and Livarot are the best-known examples, and these are cheeses that should be served on a cheese board but never used for cooking.

Although technically known as ripened soft and soft rind-washed cheeses, cheeses in the above two categories can also be called semi-soft.

VEINED or BLUE CHEESES, on the other hand, can be used to great effect in soups (see page 62) and biscuits (see page 62), as well as just being served sliced on top of a piece of steak for added piquancy or simply

eaten with chunks of good bread or biscuits. All blue cheeses are cultured with a particular bacteria to give them their distinctive blue- or green-veined appearance and their creamy mellow sharp flavour: the best include cows' milk Stilton and ewes' milk Roquefort.

HARD or PRESSED CHEESES, which have been pressed before maturation, include such famous examples as Cheddar, Edam and Parmesan. With hard cheese in particular, it is fair to say that you get what you pay for, as a hand-made well-matured cheese will cost a lot more. Farmhouse Cheddar, made in the traditional way on the farm with its own milk, pressed in huge cheese presses into 56 lb/123 k wheels which are matured and turned regularly for a minimum of 14 months, is bound to taste better and more complex than blocks of cheese churned out of a highly industrialized and efficient creamery. What has been removed by industrialization is the craft element – the human contact of the expert who can tell so much by smell and feel that he is able to create a great cheese. Block and industrialized cheeses are fine for cooking, but for eating on their own I urge you to seek out a good farmhouse cheese which bears the stamp and flavour of its maker.

PRESSED AND COOKED CHEESES are made by the same process as hard cheeses except that the milk is heated to a high temperature and 'cooked' during the cutting stage. They are then generally matured for a comparatively shorter period. The result is a rubbery cheese such as Gruyère or Emmental, which form long elastic strands on being heated and so are delightful when tipped into a hot soup or in making fondue.

Possibly the most used BRINED CHEESE is Feta which originates from Greece, where it is made with ewes' milk. A good Feta should have a sharp tangy, slightly salty flavour with a crumbly texture, neither too wet nor too dry. It can be flaked into salads, beaten into a soufflé mixture for extra pungency, or eaten on its own with a mound of good olives.

When choosing either hard or soft cheese, if possible buy those cut straight from a whole cheese at a cutting counter rather than in pre-packed slices from the chilled cabinets of a supermarket. The chances are that the former will have been better matured, allowed to breathe and ripen more naturally and kept at a more 'cheese-friendly' temperature. (The legislation on temperature control in food storage which is about to be introduced in Britain is making most cheese-makers tear out their hair as it will simply not allow their cheese to ripen correctly.) What is important when you are buying pieces cut from a whole cheese is to look for how firm and fresh it is and whether or not it is dried out and sweating, curling up at the edges or showing signs of uneven ripeness. If in doubt, always ask to taste.

To store cheese, wrap it loosely in greaseproof paper or film and keep it in a cool place or in the warmest part of the refrigerator. If the latter, remember to take it out to let it breathe and come up to room temperature a good 30 minutes before you want to eat it.

Farmhouse cheeses

In this country there has recently been an incredible revival of small cheese-makers producing interesting cheeses on the farm, using the farm's own milk to give them specific and distinctive flavours.

Farmhouse Cheddar has already been mentioned, but have you ever tried Bonchester, a creamy full-fat Jersey milk cheese that is on a par with the best Camembert but is made in the Scottish borders? Or Cecilia, a pressed ewes' milk cheese matured in Kentish hops; Cornish Yarg with its downy rind covered in a coat of nettles; or Beenleigh Blue which will beat any Roquefort. These cheeses – and many others – are quite superb. Although there is a limited supply and they have limited distribution, it is well worth seeking them out.

Unpasteurized cheeses

Many of the finest cheeses are made with unpasteurized (raw) milk, as most aficionados agree that if the milk is subjected to the high temperatures involved in the pasteurization process it will kill off the inherent flavour and characteristics of that milk. The cheese is less likely to develop its full depth and complexity and the resulting flavour will probably be far more bland.

In spite of what some would have you believe, semi-soft and hard cheeses made with unpasteurized milk are not necessarily a health hazard; if the farmer is practising good husbandry they represent no threat at all.

Spinach, Curd Cheese and Raisin Tart

SERVES 4–6

55 g/2 oz raisins
1½ tbsp dry sherry or white wine
55 g/2 oz butter, plus extra for greasing
225 g/8 oz shortcrust pastry (see page 199)
450 g/1 lb spinach, trimmed
pinch of grated nutmeg
pinch of grated fresh root ginger
zest of 1 orange
15 g/½ oz caster sugar
170 g/6 oz medium-fat fresh curd cheese (see page 57)
55 g/2 oz pine nuts
2 eggs, beaten
sea salt and freshly ground black pepper

Soak the raisins in the sherry or wine for about 30 minutes, or until they plump up. Preheat the oven to 190C/375F/gas5.

Generously grease a 20 cm/8 in quiche or pastry tin with butter, roll out the pastry to a thickness of about 1 cm/½ in and use it to line the prepared tin. Leave it to rest in the refrigerator for about 15 minutes.

Then prick the bottom of the pastry case with a fork, cover it with a sheet of greaseproof paper weighted down with baking beans or rice and bake it blind in the preheated oven for 15 minutes. Leave to cool but keep the oven on.

Meanwhile wash the spinach, but do not drain it. Put it in a saucepan over a medium heat, cover and cook for about 2 minutes or until it is wilted. (Provided it is still quite wet, it should not be necessary to add any water to the pan.)

Strain and, using the hands, squeeze out all excess moisture, then chop the leaves roughly. Put them in a bowl, add the nutmeg, ginger, orange zest, salt and pepper. Stir together and spread the spinach mixture over the base of the pastry.

In a clean bowl, cream the butter and sugar until light and fluffy. Beat in the curd cheese and stir in the pine nuts and raisins in sherry. Stir the eggs into the mixture, then spread it over the spinach.

Cover with a sheet of greaseproof paper and bake in the hot oven for about 15 minutes, then remove the paper and bake for another 20 minutes, or until the filling has set and has turned golden brown.

Serve immediately.

SPINACH, CURD CHEESE AND
RAISIN TART opposite.

Stilton Soup

When buying Stilton make sure it is fresh and still creamy — the edges turn a deeper yellow — if it is not, ask for it well-matured.

SERVES 4

30 g/1 oz butter
1 onion, finely chopped
1 tbsp flour
zest of ½ lemon
900 ml/1½ pt chicken stock (see page 106)
115 g/4 oz Stilton
2 tbsp single cream (optional)
small bunch of chives, chopped
salt and freshly ground black pepper

In a large pan over a medium heat, melt the butter and cook the onion for about 5–7 minutes, until soft and golden. Sprinkle over the flour and cook for a minute or two, stirring frequently. Add the lemon zest and stock to the pan and bring to the boil.

Either chop the cheese or crumble it with the fingers. Stir it into the pan, turn down the heat and simmer for about 3 minutes until it is melted.

Remove the pan from the heat and, if you like your soup really smooth, put it into a food processor and whizz until smooth.

Season with plenty of black pepper but, depending on the cheese, go easy on the salt. Serve with a swirl of cream, if wished, and sprinkled with chives.

Blue Cheese Sablés

For this recipe you can choose any of the blue cheeses which may be crumbled. Roquefort gives the biscuits a particular bite.

MAKES ABOUT 32

115 g/4 oz butter, plus extra for greasing
55 g/2 oz blue cheese, crumbled
55 g/2 oz mature Cheddar, grated
115 g/4 oz self-raising flour
pinch of cayenne
pinch of salt
55 g/2 oz walnuts, crushed

Preheat the oven to 190C/375F/gas5 and lightly grease a baking tray with butter.

Put the 2 cheeses in a food processor with the butter, flour, cayenne and salt. Whizz until the mixture comes together to form a ball. (If you are mixing it by hand: put all the dry ingredients into a bowl, melt the butter and, using a wooden spoon, stir it into the mixture until it comes together to form a ball.)

Using a knife, cut the pastry in half and then break off equal quantities with your fingers and roll them into small balls about 2.5 cm/1 in in diameter in the palms of your hands.

Scatter the crushed walnuts on a lightly floured surface. Roll the balls on top of the nuts, pressing a few into the pastry to make sure each ball is well coated with the nuts. Press the balls on the prepared tray with a fork so they form a small thick biscuit.

Scatter any remaining nuts on top and bake in the preheated oven for about 15 minutes, or until they are golden brown. Serve with pre-dinner drinks, either straight from the oven or when cool.

Roquefort is salted before being taken to the caves where it matures left.
STILTON SOUP WITH BLUE CHEESE SABLÉS right.

Twice-baked Goats' Cheese Soufflés

Goats' cheese has a delightful earthy and gamey flavour. For this recipe you can use a soft, semi-soft or pressed cheese. The harder the cheese, the stronger its flavour will be.

SERVES 4

15 g/½ oz unsalted butter, plus extra for greasing
15 g/½ oz hazelnuts
15 g/½ oz fresh breadcrumbs
15 g/½ oz flour
5 tbsp milk
1 egg yolk
115 g/4 oz goats' cheese
4 egg whites
½ tsp lemon juice
salt and freshly ground white pepper

Preheat the oven to 190C/375F/gas5 and grease 4 ramekins generously with butter.

Scatter the hazelnuts on a baking tray, roast them in the preheated oven for 10–15 minutes, or until golden brown. While still warm, rub them in a dry cloth to remove the skins. Whizz in a food processor until finely ground then mix with the breadcrumbs. Turn the oven down to 180C/350F/gas4.

Spoon some of the nut and breadcrumb mixture into each of the ramekins. Swirl the ramekins around so the sides and base are thoroughly coated in the mixture, tip out any excess and reserve.

Melt the butter in a small saucepan over a low heat. Add the flour and, stirring constantly, cook for a couple of minutes. Gradually pour in the milk, stirring constantly to prevent any lumps forming. Turn up the heat, bring to the boil and simmer for 1 minute.

Remove from the heat and beat in the egg yolk.

Depending on whether you are using a hard or soft cheese, either grate or mash it with a fork and add 85 g/ 3 oz of cheese to the mixture. Season.

In a clean bowl, whisk the egg whites with a pinch of salt and the lemon juice until they form stiff peaks. Then, using a metal spoon, carefully fold them into the cheese mixture. Half fill the ramekins with the soufflé mixture, sprinkle the rest of the goats' cheese on top, then cover with the remaining mixture.

Using a spatula, smooth the surface. Then scatter any of the remaining crumb mixture on top and run your thumb around the inside edge of the ramekins to create a little groove which prevents the soufflés spilling over the edges as they rise.

Place the ramekins in a roasting tin, pour in enough boiling water to come about halfway up the ramekins and bake in the preheated oven for 10 minutes.

Remove the soufflés from the oven, leave them to cool for about 10 minutes, then turn them out on a lightly oiled baking tray.

For their second cooking, either return them to the oven for a further 5 minutes or place them under a hot grill for 3–4 minutes. Serve on a bed of salad leaves dressed with a hazelnut vinaigrette.

Circular cheese moulds, skimmers and a ladle hang ready for use above.
TWICE BAKED GOATS' CHEESE SOUFFLÉ right.

The Rivers and Seashore

*Rivers and lakes teem with countless freshwater fish,
delighting anglers and cooks alike; while from coastal waters
and deep-sea fishing grounds comes an even greater choice,
from huge halibut and cod to tiny cockles and shrimps.*

Freshwater Fish

Considering the number of rivers that flow through Britain and the thousands of anglers who patiently spend hour after hour on the banks with rod, line or net in hand, it is surprising how few freshwater fish we actually eat.

Salmon, trout and eel are all well known and easily available. Although not all freshwater fish are worth the trouble, because they are too bony or their flesh too soft or their flavour too coarse, there are several less well-known species which are worth seeking out.

The best include: CHAR, which is a speciality of Lake Windermere and similar in both taste and appearance to trout; CARP, which is popular in the cooking of the Chinese and the East Europeans and is a meaty fish which is superb baked and served with a sweet-and-sour sauce; PERCH, much favoured by the landlocked Swiss, is not unlike sole and is best cooked in butter; TENCH, particularly smaller fish, are excellent lightly fried in oil; BREAM, with its soft vapid flesh, can be delightful when served with a highly seasoned accompaniment to set it off; PIKE is a real treat baked in foil and served with a delicate beurre blanc sauce, or, if you cannot cope with the bones, turned into quenelles; ZANDER (pike-perch), less bony than pike and more robustly flavoured than perch,

Carp and eel are less commonly eaten freshwater fish.

needs no more elaborate preparation than a light coating of flour before being quickly sautéed in butter to bring out its flavour.

Freshwater fish are at their best if caught from clear, clean rivers. When they come from the brackish waters of slow-running rivers or deep stagnant ponds, there is a danger of their tasting a little dank and muddy. If this is potentially a problem, clean them thoroughly and soak them for several hours in either ice-cold water or water mixed with a dash of vinegar, changing it at least every couple of hours.

One basic problem is that these freshwater fish can be rather difficult to come by. A good answer is to cultivate a friendly angler who may be prepared to treat you to the vagaries of his catch.

Salmon

The salmon is a curious fish in that it spends half its life in fresh water and half in the sea, but it does count as a freshwater fish as it is in rivers and streams that it is usually caught.

The Atlantic salmon is rightly known as 'the king of fish'. It is far superior to, and should never be confused with, the Pacific and Coho salmon; they are of a different genus, generally much smaller and with a far less interesting flavour.

The finest specimens of the Atlantic salmon, recognizable by the silvery-blue streamlined body lightly marked with black spots, are thought to come from the cool clear waters of Scottish rivers. Salmon migrate to the sea to feed and then return to the same river, eventually to spawn when mature. Most fish caught weigh anything from 1.5 k/3½ lb to 4.5 k/10 lb, but older fish can be as heavy as 27.5 k/60 lb. A Miss Ballantine, fishing on the river Tay in October 1922, established the British rod-caught record for salmon. Her catch weighed an incredible 28 k/64 lb, and her record has still to be challenged.

As a mature salmon does not feed once it has come back to its river, it is at its best caught at the estuary or on a run upstream on its homeward journey. It is still plump and full of flavour from the rich feeding grounds at sea and has yet to exhaust itself by laying or fertilizing its eggs. The open salmon season (the period during which they may be fished legally) varies considerably from river to river; it can be as early as mid-January and as late as April, and is generally closed during September.

As with most fish, freshness is of prime importance. A whole salmon should be stiff, with a sheen to its skin and blood red gills. Both wild and farmed salmon are sold in a variety of cuts, including steaks, cutlets, escalopes or fillets, and tail pieces, either whole or filleted. It is more difficult to ensure that a cut is fresh, as you do not have the gills to act as a guide: the flesh should be firm and bright, and limpness and tiredness in any fish is a sure sign of old age.

Salmon may be cooked in any number of ways: poached, grilled on its own or with butter, steamed over a bed of vegetables, roasted or baked. Despite its high oil content, it dries out rather quickly and does not take kindly to over-cooking.

For a summer meal, a whole cold salmon is unbeatable and there is only one way to cook it to make certain it is done to perfection.

Poaching a whole salmon to serve cold
As salmon is quite a rich fish with compact meaty flesh, I generally allow a 2.3 k/5 lb fish for 8–10 people. Once the fish is cleaned and gutted, lay it flat in a fish kettle or a suitable pan with a lid. Pour over a mixture of three parts water to one part white wine, until the fish is completely submerged. Add the white parts only of a couple of leeks, two sliced carrots, a couple of slices of lemon, a large bunch of parsley stalks, a couple of peppercorns and a generous pinch of sea

salt. Then – and this is the real trick – very slowly bring it to the boil, just after the first bubbles have risen and broken on the surface, count slowly to three and turn off the heat. Cover the fish kettle or pan and leave the fish to cool in the liquid until stone cold. (This will take a good 4–5 hours.) When you lift the fish out you will find that, miraculously, it is cooked right through, while still remaining moist and succulent. Serve it with a Mousseline Hollandaise (see page 128) or a Green Sauce (see page 45).

Wild or farmed salmon?

Over the last 10 years there has been a tremendous growth in salmon farming. This means that there is a constant supply of fresh salmon all year round, and farmed salmon is far cheaper than wild salmon, although it is thought by many to be an inferior product. Bred in cages, the farmed salmon is flabbier and holds more fat due to the lack of exercise. Depending on what it is fed, it may have a more bland flavour and possibly may flake more easily in cooking.

Unfortunately, unless you are an expert, it is difficult to distinguish wild from farmed salmon just by looking at the fish. Because of the enormous difference in price, it must be a terrific temptation for an unscrupulous fishmonger to palm you off with the inferior fish while charging the higher price. One way of attempting to discriminate, which I admit is not foolproof, is to look for a head with a blunter shape and a tail which is more forked when buying a whole fish: the heads of farmed salmon have a more pronounced 'v' shape and the tails are less defined. When it comes to buying cuts, examine the flesh closely: that of farmed salmon looks more ribbed and has thicker rings of fatty deposits.

Tartare of Salmon with Cucumber Salad

This recipe is taken from Raymond Blanc's magical book Recipes from Le Manoir aux Quat' Saisons. *Although he stipulates wild salmon, I think that as it is marinated it is an extravagance probably better suited to a two-star restaurant than home cooking.*

As fillet of salmon is essential for this recipe and as it is also easier to make if you have a matching pair to lay one on top of the other, I suggest buying a whole tail and asking the fishmonger to fillet and skin it for you.

SERVES 8

450 g/1 lb farmed salmon tail piece, filleted and skinned

$1\frac{1}{2}$ tbsp chopped fresh dill

zest and juice of 1 lemon

1 tbsp caster sugar

$\frac{1}{2}$ tsp Dijon mustard

3 tbsp sour cream

½ cucumber, peeled
1 tsp white wine vinegar
2 tbsp safflower oil
8 sprigs of dill
sea salt and freshly ground white pepper

Remove any stray pin bones from the salmon with a pair of tweezers, then lay the fillets flat on a plate. Mix 1 tablespoon of the dill together with the lemon zest, sugar and about 1 tablespoon of salt and rub the mixture all over both sides of the salmon. Place one fillet on top of the other, cover with foil and leave to marinate in the refrigerator for 12 hours.

At the end of this time, unwrap the salmon and rinse it under cold running water to remove the salt. Drain it well, pat dry with a paper towel and cut it into thin strips about 2.5 cm/1 in long.

In a large bowl, mix the lemon juice with the mustard, 2 teaspoons of the sour cream, the remaining dill and a little pepper and stir in the salmon. Leave in a cool place for 1 hour.

Meanwhile, prepare the cucumber by cutting it in half lengthwise and scooping out the seeds with a teaspoon. Slice it finely, put it in a colander, sprinkle over about 1 teaspoon of salt and let it stand for 30 minutes. Then rinse under cold running water, drain and pat dry. Put the cucumber slices in a small bowl, add the vinegar, oil and a little pepper and mix thoroughly.

Raymond Blanc serves the salmon stunningly presented in individual moulds: very effective but surprisingly simple. Using a 5 cm/2 in pastry cutter as a mould, place it in the centre of a plate and fill it almost up to the top with the salmon, pressing down gently with the back of a teaspoon to pack the fish firmly. Spread 1 teaspoon of sour cream on the top, smoothing it with a spatula, then carefully lift off the pastry cutter. Arrange slices of cucumber around the base and decorate the top with a sprig of dill.

Serve with slices of toasted Brioche (see page 196).

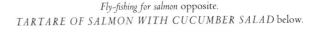

Fly-fishing for salmon opposite.
TARTARE OF SALMON WITH CUCUMBER SALAD below.

The Yellowstone river in Montana, known for its superb trout.

Eog Rhost, Roast Salmon or Sewin

Roasting salmon or 'sewin' was a favourite practice of the Welsh fisherwives living by the banks of the Teifi and Tywi rivers. Although some true salmon are netted in these rivers, the catch usually consists mostly of SEWIN, ie SEA or SALMON TROUT.

The fishermen still fish from coracles, which are light tub-like boats rowed with one oar. Traditionally made from horse- or ox-hide stretched over a framework of osiers, the coracle requires great skill just to keep it upright. Catching fish from one is even more difficult as two boats work together, rowing side by side with a net stretched between them.

Although they are two distinct species, sea trout is often confused with salmon. This is hardly surprising as, although salmon trout tastes like salmon, is a similar size, follows a similar life-cycle of migrating to the sea and returning to the river and can be cooked in exactly the same way, it is actually a trout.

SERVES 6–8

140 g/5 oz butter, plus extra for greasing
1 sea or salmon trout, weighing 1.8–2.3 k/4–5 lb,
cleaned and gutted
large pinch of grated nutmeg
large pinch of ground ginger
2 bay leaves
sprig of rosemary
2 cloves
2 tbsp dry white wine
grated zest of 1 orange
grated zest of 1 lemon
salt and freshly ground white pepper

Preheat the oven to 180C/350F/gas4 and grease a baking dish and a large piece of greaseproof paper with some butter.

Season the fish inside and out with salt and pepper. Melt 115 g/4 oz of the butter, stir in the nutmeg and ginger and, using a pastry brush, paint the fish all over with the mixture. Dip the bay leaves into the mixture and tuck them, along with the rosemary and cloves, inside the salmon.

Place the salmon in the dish and cover with the greased paper. Bake in the oven for 60–75 minutes, allowing 15 minutes per 450 g/1 lb, basting it occasionally with its juices. Transfer the cooked fish to a warmed serving dish and carefully peel off its skin.

Strain the cooking juices into a small saucepan and add the white wine and the orange and lemon zest. Bring to the boil and boil rapidly until the liquid reduces by about half. Turn down the heat, cut the remaining butter into small pieces and whisk it into the sauce, one piece at a time. Adjust the seasoning and pour the sauce over the salmon.

Trout

The BROWN TROUT and the SEA or SALMON TROUT (see opposite) are the only wild trout species native to Britain. The brown trout lives in rivers, streams and lakes and, like all freshwater fish, has pale creamy-grey flesh. Rarely seen on sale, it is delicately flavoured and responds best to simple cooking methods, such as grilling or light sautéing in butter.

The RAINBOW TROUT was introduced to our rivers from the USA in the late nineteenth century. Trout farming developed in this country about 15 years ago and, as the rainbow trout thrives in confinement, it was the choice for fish farming: it follows that all farmed trout on sale are rainbow trout.

Although the flesh of farmed rainbow trout is pink, do not be fooled into thinking that this is natural or that you are buying a sea trout. The colour is achieved merely by adding a supplement to its feed on the basis that the fish farmers think that we the consumers 'find it more attractive'. Available in a range of sizes from 225 g/8 oz to 3.5 k/8 lb, farmed rainbow trout has a coarser texture and a more robustly flavoured flesh than its wild cousins.

Honeyed Trout

SERVES 6

55 g/2 oz butter, plus extra for greasing
3 onions, thinly sliced
2 tsp ground cumin
2 tbsp honey
150 ml/¼ pt dry white wine
6 farmed trout, each weighing 225–285 g/8–10 oz,
cleaned and gutted
115 g/4 oz button mushrooms, thinly sliced
salt and freshly ground black pepper

Preheat the oven to 160C/325F/gas3 and generously grease an ovenproof dish with butter.

Melt half the butter in a saucepan over a medium heat and soften the onions in it. Stir in the cumin and season. Add the honey, 2 tablespoons of water and the wine and gently simmer for 2–3 minutes.

Arrange the onions in a layer on the bottom of the prepared dish. Season the trout and place them on top. Scatter over the mushrooms, tucking a few inside the fish, and dot with the remaining butter. Cover and bake for about 25 minutes, or until cooked.

Using a slotted spoon, transfer the fish and vegetables to a warmed serving dish, pour over the juices and serve immediately.

Eels

The COMMON or FRESHWATER EEL (*Anguilla anguilla*) is a wriggly wily snake-like fish, happy both in and out of water. It lives swimming on the bottom of muddy rivers.

The best time to eat eel is in the autumn when the fat mature silver eel is plump and juicy and its flesh is rich and succulent with plenty of texture. Eels are usually trapped in racks as they swim downstream, returning to the sea to make their mysterious and arduous journey back to the Sargasso Sea to spawn.

Check with the fishmonger where your freshwater eel has been caught as, unlike other freshwater fish, they are less able to discard any poisons from polluted rivers. If the source cannot be identified you may prefer farmed eel.

The dark-skinned seawater CONGER EEL also makes good eating, although its flesh is denser with a more pungent flavour.

Eels in a Green Sauce

Always buy live eels: good fishmongers often keep them in a tank. Insist that the fishmonger does the really hard work; ask him to kill, skin and fillet the eel.

SERVES 4

30 g/1 oz butter
1 tbsp olive oil
450 g/1 lb eel fillets
115 g/4 oz spinach
55 g/2 oz fresh sorrel, chopped
zest and juice of $\frac{1}{2}$ lemon
2 tsp finely chopped fresh parsley
1 tsp finely chopped fresh tarragon
175 ml/6 fl oz dry white wine
1 egg yolk
1 tbsp double cream
salt and freshly ground black pepper

Melt the butter with the oil in a sauté pan over a medium heat and sauté the eel fillets in it for about 3–4 minutes.

Add the spinach, sorrel and lemon zest and simmer until the vegetables have softened into a purée. Add the parsley and tarragon, pour in the white wine and lemon juice and simmer for a further 10 minutes.

In a bowl, beat the egg yolk with the cream and stir in a little of the hot sauce to stop it from curdling. Add this to the pan, season and stir gently over a very low heat until it starts to thicken. Adjust the seasoning. Carefully transfer the eel fillets to a warmed plate and serve covered with the sauce.

HONEYED TROUT opposite. Eels are usually sold alive and should be cooked as quickly as possible after killing left.

Seafish

I am lucky enough to have friends living in France – in Barfleur, a pretty fishing port with rows of weathered stone houses crowding around a horseshoe-shaped harbour. As it is only 20 minutes from Cherbourg, I can catch the overnight ferry from Portsmouth, unpack, have my croissant and *café crème* and still be ready for market by 9 o'clock in the morning.

Friday is market day at nearby Valognes and every time I go there I reel with amazement at the difference crossing the Channel makes. Valognes is a tiny town, but you can buy an amazing selection of fish and shellfish from at least six stalls. Even in the major fishing ports in Britain you never see the like; in fact you are lucky to find one fishmonger, and his range is bound to be limited. It makes me so sad and frustrated to think of what we might have, if only enough people were sufficiently interested.

What is also glorious about the fish in the markets of Northern France is their freshness. Laid out on beds of crushed ice, they look as if they have been plucked straight out of the sea. Brilliantly coloured

fish glisten with translucent slime, their eyes shine and protrude with clear black pupils, their gills are full of bright red oxygenated blood, they smell of airy sea breezes and they are still pert – or to use the correct technical term 'stiff alive' – held rigid by rigor mortis. These are the sure signs of fish in splendid condition.

Here in Britain, on the other hand, you rarely find fish so fresh. Even when sold as 'fresh', it has sometimes been frozen and then defrosted and may suffer from 'freezer burn', when it has dried during cold storage, or a slight discoloration or dark glassy look if it has been frozen too slowly.

The signs that fish are not at their peak include: a certain slackness or flabbiness; a dull colour; eyes sunken in their sockets; the blood in the gills a dark red; and a slight off smell which, at its most highly developed, will remind you of sour milk or stale cabbages. When buying fish, insist on examining them closely for the tell-tale signs; your fishmonger will not mind if he has nothing to hide.

I have divided seafish into three main groups: oily fish, in which the oil is dispersed throughout the flesh; white fish, in which the oil is concentrated in the liver (remember the cod liver oil capsules you were forced to take as a child?), and shellfish. Within these groups the fish are sometimes interchangeable for culinary purposes, and I give the substitutes when possible.

Oily fish

ANCHOVY, HERRING, MACKEREL, PILCHARD, SARDINE, SPRAT and TUNA are among the best-known oily fish. Because of their high oil content, these fish can be canned, salted, cured or smoked successfully, but they also make interesting eating when fresh.

Preparing the catch to take away left. Some fish are as attractive to look at as to eat – the bluey-black stripes of the mackerel, the orange spots of the plaice and the distinctive 'thumb-print' of the John Dory are particularly striking right.

Grilled Mackerel with Gooseberry Sauce

A firm-textured fish, mackerel is a northern member of the tuna family. In season all year round, it is excellent value, especially since it is free of tiresome small bones. Rich in vitamin A, its flesh is highly nutritious and has a meaty taste, slightly reminiscent of rare cold roast beef. Like all oily fish, mackerel is at its best plainly cooked by grilling or baking and served with a sharp sauce to cut its oiliness.

Use any fruit with a tart taste for the sauce, such as rhubarb, cranberries, Bramley cooking apples or, as here, gooseberries lightly sweetened with sweet cicely and a touch of pastis.

SERVES 4

4 mackerel, each weighing 170–225 g/6–8 oz, cleaned and gutted
450 g/1 lb cooking gooseberries, topped and tailed
1 tsp fennel seeds
sprig of sweet cicely
1 tbsp pastis
30 g/1 oz butter, diced
sea salt and freshly ground black pepper

Preheat the grill. With a sharp knife, slash the mackerel diagonally 3 times on each side so the heat can permeate the flesh. Season with pepper and grill under the hot grill for about 5 minutes on each side.

Meanwhile, make the sauce: put the gooseberries, fennel seeds and sweet cicely in a saucepan with enough water to cover. Bring to the boil over a medium heat and simmer for about 7–10 minutes, or until the fruit has softened to a pulp. Pass the fruit through a sieve, pressing hard to extract all the juices. Alternatively, if you do not mind the skin and pips, liquidize the whole fruit in a food processor until smooth.

Return the purée to the pan over a low heat, add the pastis and beat in the butter, a few pieces at a time. Season and serve with the grilled fish.

Herrings Stuffed with Apple

Although herrings are sold all year round, the best time to eat them is between May and December when they are at their most succulent. Fresh herrings, full of their natural oil, are certainly worth eating; frozen ones, however, are best avoided as they can be tough and dry with an unpleasant, slightly rancid taste.

In Holland, fresh herrings are a delicacy and the start of the season causes great excitement. For the first few weeks, when the herrings are still young, tender and sweet, they are eaten raw — and chased down with a measure of genever, the local Dutch gin. The fish start to fatten up in June, and as they then swim down both the East and West coasts of Britain, they are caught for curing and smoking as kippers.

SERVES 6

6 herrings, each weighing 170–225 g/6–8 oz, cleaned and gutted
55 g/2 oz butter
1 small onion, finely chopped
115 g/4 oz fresh breadcrumbs
1 cooking apple, peeled, cored and chopped
pinch of cinnamon
1 tsp sugar
1 egg, lightly beaten
salt and freshly ground black pepper
olive oil, for greasing

Preheat the oven to 190C/375F/gas5 and generously grease an ovenproof dish with some olive oil.

With a sharp knife, score the herrings diagonally twice on each side so the heat can permeate the flesh.

Melt the butter in a pan over a medium heat and cook the onion in it for 4–5 minutes until soft.

Meanwhile, mix the breadcrumbs, apple, cinnamon and sugar together in a bowl. Add the cooked onion, stir in the egg to bind the mixture and season.

Spoon this stuffing into the cleaned cavities of the fish. Place the herrings in the prepared dish on their sides. Brush them lightly with a little olive oil and bake for 20–30 minutes.

Serve with Mustard Butter (see page 55).

Deep-fried Fish

Most small oily fish, such as anchovies, pilchards, baby sardines, whitebait, the small fry of herrings and freshwater minnows or baby gudgeon, can be deep-fried and served with lemon slices as a first course.

My particular favourite are ELVERS, or baby eels, which actually look more like transparent Chinese noodles than fish. A spring delicacy, they are caught any time between March and May in several of the European tidal rivers flowing into the Atlantic Ocean. If you can find them, they are well worth the exorbitant price you may have to pay for them.

Apart from gudgeon, whatever fish you choose it will not be necessary to gut them provided they are quite small. For deep-frying such baby fish, I always use seasoned flour rather than a batter as a coating; the result is a far lighter and crisper finish.

SERVES 4

45 g/1½ oz flour
1 tsp finely chopped fresh parsley
225 g/8 oz small fish (see above), thoroughly rinsed and drained
sunflower oil, for deep-frying
sea salt and freshly ground black pepper

to serve:
1 lemon, quartered
slices of brown bread and butter

In a paper or plastic bag, mix the flour with the parsley, salt and pepper. Put the fish into the bag, a handful at a time, and give it a good shake so they are well coated with the seasoned flour.

Heat the oil until it gives off a haze. Test it by dropping in a small cube of dry bread; if it sizzles and starts to change colour almost immediately, the oil is at the right temperature. Deep-fry the fish in the oil in small batches, ensuring they have room enough to spread, for 2–3 minutes or until golden brown. Drain and turn out on paper towels. Keep warm and continue cooking the fish in batches, until they are all cooked.

Sprinkle with sea salt and serve with lemon quarters and brown bread and butter.

DEEP-FRIED FISH left.

White Fish

For the purposes of cooking, white fish are generally divided into two groups: round and flat. The round fish which we eat in the greatest quantities is the meaty COD. A demersal fish which lives on or near the sea bed, cod is fished in the North Atlantic all the way from Newfoundland to Norway. Most of what is on sale is deep-sea cod, caught in the trawl-nets of boats which spend several weeks at sea. They obviously have to preserve their haul, so they clean, gut and freeze the fish while still at sea.

It is a pity, as really fresh cod that has never glimpsed a freezer is unbeatable. Fishermen tell me that, aboard ship, they prefer to eat it 'rested', or a day old, when its succulent meaty flesh has firmed up slightly and its sweetness has intensified – we should be so lucky! Occasionally you will see inshore cod and codling (baby cod) for sale and these may have landed on the slab unfrozen. Buy them if they look fresh.

Once defrosted, as a large fish can weigh anything up to 35 k/80 lb, cod is usually sold in steaks cut across the bone, fillets, fillet portions, block fillets or cutlets, which are paired fillets joined down the back. Other members of the extensive cod family are COLEY, HADDOCK, HAKE, LING and WHITING. These vary widely in succulence and quality of flavour, but all are worth eating.

Other favourites among round fish include: SEA BASS, which is excellent steamed over a bed of seaweed; the JOHN DORY with its distinctive thumb-print mark which legend says was made by St Peter; and the firm-fleshed MONKFISH, the head of which is so ugly that it is always cut off prior to being put on display, but whose tail is rich and juicy and particularly fine roasted whole and then served with a pungent Green Sauce (see page 45).

RED MULLET, known as the 'woodcock of the sea' when the fashion was to serve it well-hung with its liver intact, is very tasty brushed with oil and baked wrapped in greaseproof paper parcels. GREY MULLET, actually no relation, is a much coarser fish and needs strong flavours, such as ginger or fennel, to set it off.

The WEEVER, a curious bony fish only found in the warmer waters around Cornwall, is far too fiddly to eat on its own but adds great depth to a fish soup. Also useful in soups are: GURNARD, which may be red, grey or yellow in colour; CONGER EEL for a deep richer soup; and the long thin GARFISH, provided you do not mind its curious green bones.

Flat fish should be treated with care as they break up easily, and are generally best cooked simply, for example by grilling, poaching or dipping them in flour and pan-frying them in butter. DOVER SOLE, especially the slip (baby fish), having such a distinct flavour needs nothing more elaborate to set it off. However, the distantly related LEMON SOLE and the rest of its family which includes the DAB, FLOUNDER, HALIBUT, PLAICE and WITCH (also known as the TORBAY SOLE) are all more coarsely textured and flavoured, and may be steamed, fried or stuffed and baked. The only acceptable way to cook SKATE is to pan-fry it, whereas TURBOT and BRILL, the latter often referred to as the 'poor man's turbot', are superb poached or baked and served with a delicate Herb Butter (see page 55).

Poached Cod with Capers

The secret to poaching cod, or indeed all fish, is to use a well-flavoured liquid, such as a court-bouillon (see below) or fish stock (see page 86). It is also important to simmer it over a very low heat so that the liquid hardly trembles, with only the odd bubble rising to the surface. Poaching is a gentle means of cooking fish: if the heat is too fierce, you will toughen its texture. For this recipe I like to use relatively chunky steaks, about 5 cm/2 in thick, otherwise they may fall apart while cooking.

SERVES 4

4 cod steaks, each weighing 170–225 g/6–8 oz (see above)
30 g/1 oz pine kernels
5 tbsp extra-virgin olive oil
1 garlic clove, chopped
30 g/1 oz capers, rinsed
2 anchovy fillets, rinsed and chopped
4 sun-dried tomatoes, chopped
bunch of flat-leaf parsley, chopped
sea salt and freshly ground black pepper

for the court-bouillon:
1 carrot, thinly sliced
1 small onion, thinly sliced
1 celery stalk, thinly sliced
sprig of parsley
sprig of thyme
150 ml/¼ pt dry white wine
2 black peppercorns

Make the court-bouillon by putting the carrot, onion, celery, parsley and thyme in a sauté pan large enough to hold all the cod steaks, along with the white wine and 575 ml/1 pt of water. Add about 1 teaspoon of salt and the peppercorns. Bring the liquid to the boil, cover,

POACHED COD WITH CAPERS

reduce the heat and simmer for 10 minutes to allow the vegetables to release their flavour.

Add the fish, turn down the heat very low and poach gently for about 5–7 minutes, until the fish flesh turns a translucent white right through to the centre, but is still quite firm. Using a slotted spoon, transfer the fish steaks to a serving dish. Strain the liquid, discarding the vegetables and return it to the pan. Bring it to the boil and boil rapidly to reduce it by about two-thirds.

Meanwhile, fry the pine kernels in 1 teaspoon of the olive oil until golden. Mix them in a bowl with the garlic, capers, anchovies, tomatoes and parsley. Stir in the rest of the oil and about 5 tablespoons of the poaching liquid. Season to taste and pour the sauce over the cod. Leave it to cool for at least 1 hour to allow the flavours to seep into the fish.

Fishcakes

There are endless recipes for the wonderful fishcake, one of the great treats of British cooking. As I think that the perfect fishcake should be soft, buttery and textured with shards of meaty fish, I use hake as it has a delightful creamy taste and performs well, especially if poached in one piece. This way you do not run the risk of drying out the fish, and it is particularly good value if cut from the tail end as fishmongers often sell these off cheap. You could use cod, haddock or salmon or any other succulent fleshy fish that flakes well without falling apart.

Never overcook the fish, or the fishcakes will be far too dry. More importantly, never let it anywhere near a food processor as the fish will, more likely than not, be reduced to a mass of crumbs, resulting in a dense texture more like a hamburger than a light fishcake.

SERVES 4

300 ml/½ pt milk
1 small onion, sliced
2 black peppercorns
350 g/12 oz piece of hake (see above)
225 g/8 oz Cara or Pentland Squire or other
floury potatoes, peeled
30 g/1 oz butter
1 tbsp chopped fresh parsley
1 egg, hard-boiled, shelled and chopped
grated zest of ½ lemon
pinch of cayenne
1 egg white, lightly beaten
1 tbsp flour
sunflower oil, for frying
salt and freshly ground black pepper
1 lemon, sliced, to serve

Put the milk in a saucepan with the onion and peppercorns and place over a medium heat until it is almost boiling. Turn the heat down, add the fish, cover and poach very gently for between 10–15 minutes,

until the flesh just begins to break apart. Strain, reserving the milk, and leave to cool.

Meanwhile, boil the potatoes until soft. Drain and mash them, adding the butter, parsley and about 1 tablespoon of the poaching milk. You may find you need a little more milk: how much you add depends on the flouriness of the potatoes. However, do be careful not to overdo it: if the mash is too wet and sloppy, the fishcakes will not hold together while cooking.

Once the fish is cool enough to handle, skin it and flake the flesh into a bowl with your fingers, taking care to remove all bones. Then mash it lightly with a fork and stir in the hard-boiled egg, lemon zest, cayenne and season to taste. Gently fold the fish into the potatoes, adding the beaten egg white to bind the mixture. Leave it to rest for about 30 minutes.

Divide the fish mixture into 8 equal portions and roll them each into a ball between the palms of the hands. Press them gently to flatten them. Sift the flour over a board and roll the fishcakes in it until they are lightly covered.

Fry the fishcakes in fairly hot oil for a couple of minutes on each side, or until they start to turn a golden brown. Serve immediately, with slices of lemon.

SALMON FISHCAKES right.

Whiting with Curd Cheese

With a reputation of being an insipid but highly digestible fish, whiting was dismissed as invalid food in Victorian times . If caught in the deep seas, however, and sold when still pearly fresh with a shiny bloom, it is light and delicate with a smooth flesh and is excellent value.

Whiting can weigh anything up to 1.8 k/4 lb. Although it is usually sold in fillets, if possible buy a smaller whole fish and ask to have it filleted, then you can see exactly how fresh it is. Like most of us, it grows tired and slack all too quickly; old whiting makes very dull eating indeed.

SERVES 4

4 whiting fillets, each weighing about 170–225 g/6–8 oz
juice of 1 lemon
255 g/9 oz medium-fat curd cheese
2 garlic cloves, finely chopped
small bunch of flat-leaf parsley, finely chopped
85 g/3 oz stale breadcrumbs
55 g/2 oz Parmesan, freshly grated
salt and freshly ground white pepper
butter, for greasing

Season the whiting fillets and put them in a shallow dish. Pour over the lemon juice and leave them to marinate in a cool place for between 1–2 hours, turning them over at least once.

Preheat the oven to 180C/350F/gas4 and generously grease a gratin dish with butter.

Mash the curd cheese with a fork until it is quite smooth, then beat in the garlic, parsley, breadcrumbs and season to taste. Strain the juices from the fish and stir them into the mixture.

Spread a little of the cheese mixture thinly over the inside of the fish, then fold the fillets over in half

lengthwise and arrange them in the gratin dish. Spread the remaining cheese mixture over and around the fillets, sprinkle over the Parmesan and bake for 30–40 minutes, or until lightly browned on top. Serve immediately.

Spiced Haddock

A smaller member of the cod family and easily recognizable by a distinctive thumb-print and a black line running down its body, the haddock has firm-textured white flesh and makes good eating.

In early spring in the North-East of England and Scotland, you can often find whole tiny haddock, or 'coble', named after the flat-floored inshore fishing boats from which they are caught. When fresh, these are amazingly sweet and are best simply fried or grilled with a little olive oil or butter. Most haddock on sale, however, weigh 1.8–3.5 k/4–8 lb and are sold either in single fillets or cutlets (paired fillets joined down the back). If haddock is unavailable, cod or hake may be used instead.

SERVES 6–8

4 tbsp olive oil
2 onions, finely chopped
1 tsp peeled and finely grated fresh ginger
1 tsp sugar
2 tsp ground cumin
2 tbsp ground coriander
pinch of garam masala
large pinch of cayenne
450 ml/$\frac{3}{4}$ pt Greek-style cows'-milk yoghurt
2 tbsp lemon juice
1 k/2$\frac{1}{4}$ lb haddock fillets, cut into 7.5 cm/3 in pieces
salt and freshly ground black pepper
butter, for greasing

Preheat the oven to 190C/375F/gas5 and generously grease a shallow ovenproof dish with butter.

Heat I tablespoon of the olive oil in a heavy-based frying pan over a medium heat and sauté the onions in it for 2–3 minutes.

Add the ginger, sugar, cumin, coriander, garam masala and cayenne and stir for a few minutes until the onions are soft. Beat the yoghurt in a bowl with the lemon juice and remaining oil. Season with about $1\frac{1}{2}$ teaspoons of salt and black pepper and then tip the onions into this mixture and give it a final whisk.

Spread a little of this sauce on the bottom of the prepared dish. Arrange the pieces of haddock on top in a single layer, then spread the rest of the sauce in a thick layer so it completely covers the fish. Cover the dish with foil and bake for about 20 minutes, or until the fish is cooked. Serve immediately.

Fish Pie

A good fish pie depends on the mix, texture and quality of the fish. Cod, hake, haddock, huss and ling are all good round white fish to use. If you are feeling a little extravagant, you could splash out on monkfish or John Dory. Flat fish tend to be rather expensive and are too delicately flavoured or totally unsuited to baking in a pie. Oily fish are best avoided as their flavours are too overpowering.

SERVES 4–6

675g/1½ lb mixed white fish (see above)
4 sprigs of parsley
bay leaf
2 black peppercorns
3 tbsp Noilly Prat
115 g/4 oz butter, plus extra for greasing
30 g/1 oz flour
pinch of saffron threads
300 ml/½ pt milk
900 g/2 lb Cara or Pentland Squire potatoes, peeled and quartered

115 g/4 oz peeled cooked prawns
1 onion, finely chopped
2 hard-boiled eggs, shelled and sliced
salt and freshly ground black pepper

Put the fish in a large pan with 2 sprigs of parsley, the bay leaf, peppercorns, a large pinch of salt and 2 tablespoons of Noilly Prat. Add just enough water to cover and poach gently over a low heat for about 15 minutes. Drain the fish, reserving the cooking liquor.

Preheat the oven to 200C/400F/gas6 and generously grease a pie-dish with butter.

To make a white sauce: melt 30 g/1 oz of the butter in a saucepan over a low heat, stir in the flour and saffron and cook gently for 1 minute. Measure 150 ml/¼ pt of the cooking liquor, mix it with the same volume of the milk and pour this into the pan, a little at a time, stirring continuously and vigorously. Once all this liquid has been added, simmer for about 5 minutes, stirring occasionally, until the sauce thickens. Season.

Meanwhile, boil the potatoes until soft. Drain and mash them, adding the remaining butter and milk. Season to taste.

Once the fish is cool enough to handle, skin and flake it coarsely with the fingers, taking care to remove all bones. Put the fish in the prepared pie dish. Scatter over the prawns, onions, hard-boiled eggs and remaining parsley, chopped, and sprinkle over the rest of the Noilly Prat. Pour over the white sauce, then cover with the mashed potatoes.

Bake in a preheated oven for about 30 minutes, or until the top is a golden brown.

Fish Soup

A good fish soup depends on two things: a good stock and a wide variety of fish.

Never make fish stock with a cube, it just does not taste right. Unless you can buy fresh stock, there is nothing for it but to make your own. It is actually incredibly easy and, as you are going to buy various fish, your fishmonger will certainly oblige you with a selection of trimmings.

As for the fish, choose firm fish which do not break apart and which have gutsy flavours. The most appropriate include hake, monkfish, red mullet, cod, grey or red gurnard and weever. I usually buy a mixture of whatever is available. There is no need to go for prime white flat fish: they work out far too expensive. Equally, avoid oily fish, such as herring, mackerel, sardines or tuna, as they upset the balance of the soup.

SERVES 8–10

675 g/1½ lb fish (see above), cut into 1 cm/½ in cubes
3 tbsp olive oil
2 carrots, sliced
1 leek, sliced
2 onions, sliced
1 fennel bulb, trimmed of its feathery tops and sliced
2 garlic cloves, crushed
1.5 l/2½ pt fish stock (see above)

250 ml/8 fl oz dry white wine
bay leaf
2 sprigs of thyme
2 sprigs of parsley
2 sprigs of lemon balm
450 g/1 lb ripe tomatoes, skinned, de-seeded and chopped
pinch of sugar
1 tbsp pastis
salt and freshly ground black pepper

for the stock:
900g/2 lb fish trimmings, such as bones, skin, head etc
1 onion, sliced
1 carrot, sliced
1 leek, sliced
bay leaf
piece of lemon peel
blade of mace
8 black peppercorns
150 ml/¼ pt dry white wine

To make the stock: put all the ingredients into a large pot, along with the trimmings from the fennel, and cover with 1.75 l/3 pt of water. Bring to the boil, skim and simmer gently for about 15 minutes. (Never overcook a fish stock as it will end up with the taste and texture of glue.) Strain the stock through a fine sieve.

In another large pan, heat the oil over a medium heat. Add the carrot, leek, onion, fennel and garlic and soften gently for about 5 minutes.

Add the stock, wine, the herbs tied together in a bundle, salt and pepper. Cover and simmer for 10 minutes. Add the prepared fish and simmer for a further 5 minutes. Then add the tomatoes and sugar and simmer for 5 minutes more. Stir in the pastis, adjust the seasoning and serve immediately.

Skate with Onions and Raisins

Usually you only see the 'wings' of the large skate or ray on sale. They are best kept until they are about 3 days old: any earlier and they are tough and tasteless. Look for a very faint smell of ammonia, which is strong when the fish is too fresh.

The best size of wings to buy weigh 450 g–1.35 k/1–3 lb and are sold skinned: sometimes on one side, sometimes on both. When larger, they tend to become a little coarse. Although you can find smaller wings, they are not really worth the trouble; they are a bit skimpy or meanly fleshed and lack the fullness and gelatinous qualities that make eating skate such a pleasure.

SERVES 4

24 pickling onions, peeled
bay leaf
8–10 black peppercorns, crushed
300 ml/½ pt dry cider
2 skate wings, each weighing about 675 g/1½ lb, cut into 2 pieces
170 g/6 oz butter
1 small onion, sliced
30 g/1 oz raisins, soaked in water until plump
1 tsp sugar
2 tbsp white wine vinegar
sea salt and freshly ground black pepper

Put the pickling onions, bay leaf, crushed peppercorns, cider and 300 ml/½ pt water in a sauté pan over a high heat and bring to the boil. Cover and boil for a further 5 minutes.

Reduce the heat, add the skate wings to the pan and simmer gently for about 7–10 minutes. With skate you can easily tell when the fish is cooked as the flesh starts to detach itself from the bone in shards. Using a slotted spoon, transfer the fish to a warmed serving dish and remove the pickling onions and reserve.

Melt the butter in a frying pan over a high heat until it just begins to turn brown. Add the sliced onion, the reserved pickling onions, raisins and sugar and stir together. Then pour in the vinegar, season, turn up the heat and stir and scrape the pan until the sauce begins to foam. Pour over the skate and serve immediately.

Making a gill net, which traps fish as they swim into its mesh.

Turbot in Rock Salt

Distinctively diamond-shaped with knobbly sludge-brown spotted skin, turbot is the most delicious and delicate of flat fish. Unfortunately it is also the most expensive.

Mainly fished from the Baltic Sea, the English Channel and the Atlantic waters off France and Northern Spain, it is not unusual to land huge turbots weighing 18 k/40 lb. A 'chicken' turbot is a far more manageable proposition: it has all the qualities of the larger fish, but only hits the scales at 1–2.3 k/2¼–5 lb.

The traditional way of preparing turbot is to poach it then serve it with a Hollandaise Sauce (see page 128). By way of a change, I have followed a method common in the North of Spain, whereby a whole fish is baked buried in salt. The salt does not overpower the fish: it hardens into a thick crust and, when you break this, the turbot emerges superbly tender.

PREPARING TURBOT IN ROCK SALT

SERVES 4–6

2 tbsp milk
2 black peppercorns
bay leaf
1 chicken turbot, weighing 1–1.5 k/2¼–3½ lb
(see above)
1 k/2¼ lb rock salt
grated zest and juice of 1 lime
300 ml/½ pt double cream
1½ tsp grated fresh horseradish or 1 tsp prepared
cream of horseradish
pinch of sugar
salt and freshly ground white pepper
butter, for greasing

Preheat the oven to 190C/375F/gas5 and generously butter an ovenproof dish which is just large enough to fit the turbot.

Put the milk in a small saucepan with the peppercorns and bay leaf. Bring to just below the boil over a low heat and simmer for 5 minutes to infuse the milk. Leave it to cool.

Brush the fish all over with the cooled milk and place it in the dish. Dampen the salt slightly and pack the dish tightly with it, tucking it in around the edges of the fish so that the turbot is completely enclosed. Bake in the preheated oven for about 20 minutes. Remove and leave to cool for 30 minutes.

Meanwhile, prepare the sauce: put the lime zest in the cream and bring it to the boil over a medium heat. Stir in the horseradish, sugar and lime juice, lower the heat and simmer for a couple of minutes. Season.

Break open the salt crust by crushing it with a rolling pin. The skin sticks to the salt, so lift off the pieces of salt peeling away the skin as you go. Serve the turbot cut into fillets, with the sauce served separately.

Terrine of Lemon Sole with Prawns

This recipe comes from Richard Stein's English Seafood Cookery *which is based on his many years of experience running one of this country's best seafood restaurants in Padstow, Cornwall. He suggests that you use lemon sole, which is actually not a sole but a member of the dab family, and that you first chill the ingredients for a light, airy terrine. He also warns that this terrine 'hovers on the edge of being difficult to handle'.*

SERVES 8–10

225 g/8 oz uncooked prawns in their shell
1 tsp tomato paste
1 small celery stalk, trimmed and finely chopped
2 small shallots, finely chopped
225 g/8 oz lemon sole fillet, skinned and chilled
1 egg, chilled
2 tsp lemon juice
6 sprigs of flat-leaf parsley
6 sprigs of chervil
small bunch of chives
300 ml/$\frac{1}{2}$ pt double cream, chilled
pinch of cayenne
sea salt and freshly ground white pepper
butter, for greasing

Peel the prawns and chill in the refrigerator, reserving the shells and heads.

Start making the sauce: put the prawn trimmings in a saucepan with the tomato paste, celery and half of the shallots. Add just enough water to cover, bring to the boil then reduce the heat and simmer for 25 minutes.

Preheat the oven to 180C/350F/gas4 and butter an 850 ml/I$\frac{1}{2}$ pt terrine or mould and a piece of foil to cover it.

Put the lemon sole, egg, remaining shallot, half the lemon juice and a large pinch of salt into a food processor and reduce to a smooth purée. Add the parsley, chervil and chives and, with the machine still running, slowly pour in 250 ml/8 fl oz of cream. Season and chill the mixture for about 15 minutes.

Fold the peeled prawns into the chilled mixture and carefully spoon into the mould. Cover loosely with the buttered foil, put it in a roasting pan and half fill it with hot water. Transfer to the preheated oven and bake for about 40 minutes. To test whether it is cooked, pierce it to the centre with a skewer or thin knife; if it comes away cleanly, the terrine is ready. Remove it from the oven and leave to stand for about 10 minutes before carefully turning it out.

To finish the sauce: liquidize the prawn stock and strain it into a small saucepan. Add the rest of the cream, bring it to the boil and boil the sauce to reduce it until it is thick enough to coat the back of a spoon. Stir in the remaining lemon juice and cayenne.

Serve the terrine in slices on a bed of the sauce.

Shellfish

The British coast is rich in shellfish, much of which is exported to France.

LOBSTERS from the clear cold waters of the Minch off the Scottish coast are amongst the best in the world and should be simply grilled or poached and served with hot melted butter. The CRAWFISH with its firm creamy white meat is superb eaten cold with mayonnaise. Although it looks rather like a lobster, you can easily distinguish it by its lack of large front claws.

There are numerous SHRIMP, both brown and pink, and PRAWNS swimming around our shores. Apart from the DUBLIN BAY PRAWN, also known sometimes as SCAMPI or NORWAY LOBSTER because of its lobster-like front claws, no large prawns inhabit our

colder northern seas. However, we do have Cornish or Cromer brown CRABS which are full of buttery rich flesh and are at their best in summer, and SCALLOPS and MUSSELS which are meatier and with fuller flavours during the winter. Scallops are graded in size: king scallops are the largest, up to 17.5 cm/7 in across; 'queenies', or queen scallops, measure about 7.5 cm/3 in; and 'princess' or baby scallops, which have recently started to be grown in Scotland, are about the size of a large mussel. Mussels either grow wild in beds in coastal shallows or attached to rocks, or they are artificially bred and grown on ropes and stakes or 'sown' in beds and then transplanted into deeper waters to fatten up.

We also have WHELKS, WINKLES and sweet fat Penclawdd COCKLES from Wales, which are still raked and sieved by hand and are a speciality of Swansea market.

Probably the best of all our native shellfish are our OYSTERS. The round crinkly-shelled Native oyster can only be eaten when there is an 'r' in the month. However, with its silky grey flesh and slightly salty juice, it is well worth waiting for. The most famous oysters come from Colchester, Whitstable and Helford, but many of these are seriously under threat from disease.

Throughout Britain, and particularly in Scotland, Portuguese and Pacific oysters are farmed throughout the year. The former, as you might expect, came originally from Portugal and is longer, thinner and less delicate than the native, with a succulent flesh tinged with purple. The Pacific oyster is larger and more dome-shaped, with a richer taste which can almost be overpowering. Although it is safe to eat these all year round, they are best avoided when seeding during the summer months as they go a little milky.

Making a lobster pot left. Cooked and uncooked shellfish right.

An oyster farm uses an old-fashioned means of transport to bring oysters in from the beds.

Oysters should really never be cooked as they taste so good as they are that it seems a travesty to heat them or drown them in some sauce or other. Simply dress them with lemon juice or a dash of tabasco and eat them with slices of brown bread lightly spread with a good unsalted butter.

Shrimp Bisque

The fish trade seems to differentiate rather haphazardly between shrimp and prawns: shrimp are generally smaller than prawns, but even this rule is not consistent.

However, for this recipe there can be no confusion. Fresh tiny brown or Morecambe Bay shrimp are the best ones to use. They have a light sweet taste and, when simmered in their shells, impart a richness of flavour that gives great body to the soup.

There is no need to peel the shrimp at any stage as their shells are broken by the food processor and the pieces removed by sieving.

SERVES 8

1.5 l/2½ pt fish stock (see page 86)
3 tbsp olive oil
2 leeks, trimmed and chopped
2 onions, chopped
675 g/1½ lb shrimp in their shells (see above)
675 g/1½ lb ripe tomatoes
small bunch of curly parsley
sprig of lemon thyme
few strands of saffron
200 ml/7 fl oz dry white wine
300 ml/½ pt double cream
2 tbsp brandy
salt and freshly ground white pepper

Make the fish stock using a mixture of fish and as many shellfish trimmings as your fishmonger will give you.

Heat the olive oil in a large pan over a moderate heat, add the leeks and onions and sauté for 5 minutes until soft. Stir in the shrimp (reserving a few for garnish, if wished), tomatoes, parsley, lemon thyme, saffron, wine and fish stock. Cover and simmer for about 30 minutes over a medium heat.

Whizz the mixture in a food processor until it is reduced to a purée. Pass this through a fine sieve, pressing down hard to extract all the juices and return the strained soup to the pan. Pour in the cream and brandy and bring to just below the boil over a low heat. Adjust the seasoning and serve the bisque hot with croutons and perhaps garnished with a few whole shelled shrimp.

Crab and Saffron Tart

For the freshest possible crab meat, buy a live crab and cook it yourself. Everyone has their own way of killing crab and lobsters in the kindest way: mine is to put them in a large pot of boiled water which has been allowed to cool and then bring it back to the boil. As the boiled and cooled water has been deoxygenated, the crab or lobster swiftly 'drowns'.

A medium crab will probably need about 15 minutes simmering, by which time it should have turned bright pink, then it should be drained and left to cool. Once it is cool enough to handle, twist off the legs and claws and crack them open to extract the meat. Turn the crab over and, with the thumbs, force the shell and body apart. Scoop the flesh out of the shell with a spoon and throw away the gills or 'dead men's fingers' attached to the body, then cut it in half and extract the meat. Keep the white and dark meat separate.

SERVES 4

170 g/6 oz shortcrust pastry (see page 199)
175 g/6$\frac{1}{2}$ oz crab meat from 1 live crab
150 ml/$\frac{1}{4}$ pt double cream
1 egg + 2 egg yolks
small bunch of chives
few strands of saffron
juice of $\frac{1}{2}$ lemon
2 tbsp dry sherry
pinch of cayenne
salt and freshly ground white pepper

Preheat the oven to 190C/375F/gas5.

Roll out the pastry to a thickness of about 1 cm/$\frac{1}{2}$ in and line a 20 cm/8 in open tart or quiche tin with it. Leave to rest in the refrigerator for about 15 minutes, then line, weight and bake it blind (see page 242) for 15 minutes and leave to cool in its pan.

Cook the crab and prepare the crab meat (see above), keeping the white and dark meat separate. Spread the white meat in an even layer on the bottom of the pastry case and chill. Put the dark meat in a food processor with the cream, egg and egg yolks, chives, saffron, lemon juice and sherry and whizz until smooth. Season to taste with the cayenne and salt and pepper, then pour the mixture on top of the layer of white meat in the pastry case.

Bake the tart uncovered in the preheated oven for about 25–30 minutes, until it turns a golden brown and is just set.

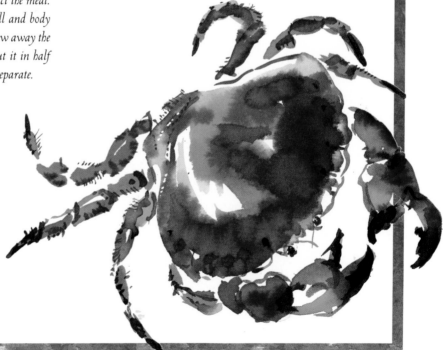

Mussels with Garlic, White Wine and Bacon

The edible or blue mussel is native to our shores and, because of the modern farming methods, it can be eaten all year round, although it is at its plumpest and tastiest during the cold winter months.

Another advantage of farmed mussels is that they are sold in packs, scrubbed, scraped and de-bearded which saves you a lot of work. Once you get them home, put them to soak in cold water and throw away any that float to the top or remain open, even after you have given the shell a quick firm tap.

SERVES 4

1 tablespoon olive oil
30g g/1 oz butter
115 g/4 oz smoked bacon, finely chopped
115 g/4 oz shallots, finely chopped
2 garlic cloves, finely chopped
450 g/1 lb tomatoes, skinned and chopped
3 sprigs of oregano
pinch of sugar
200 ml/7 fl oz white wine
2.25 l/2 qt fresh mussels
1 tbsp finely chopped flat-leaf parsley
salt and freshly ground black pepper

MUSSELS WITH GARLIC, WHITE WINE AND BACON

In a large deep pan with a tight-fitting lid, heat the olive oil with the butter over a medium heat. Sauté the bacon, shallots and garlic for about 5 minutes or until soft. Add the tomatoes, oregano, sugar and white wine and bring to the boil.

Put the mussels in the pan, cover and cook for 5–7 minutes, or until they have opened. Using a slotted spoon, lift the mussels out of the pan and remove most of them from their shells, leaving just a few in their shells for effect, and keep warm.

Turn up the heat and bring the sauce to the boil. Boil rapidly for 2–3 minutes to reduce the quantity of liquid by about half.

Stir in the parsley, adjust the seasoning and pour the sauce over the mussels. Serve either on its own or with freshly cooked pasta.

Steamed Scallops with Leeks and Orange Butter

Always buy scallops in the shell and ask the fishmonger to open them for you. All you then have to do is lift them out of the shell and separate the muscle (the white meaty chunk) and the coral (the bright orange crescent) from the frilly 'skirt' which is only useful for a stock. Never be tempted to buy unshelled scallops loose as, more often than not, they will have been frozen and will therefore have the texture of a new school rubber.

SERVES 4

225 g/8 oz butter
4 leeks, trimmed and cut into fine shreds
zest and juice of 3 large oranges
150 ml/$\frac{1}{4}$ pt dry white wine
12 fresh scallops, prepared and cleaned (see above)
6–8 sprigs of chervil
salt and freshly ground white pepper

In a wide-bottomed sauté pan with a tight-fitting lid, melt 55 g/2 oz of the butter over a medium heat and sweat the leeks and orange zest for about 2–3 minutes until soft. Stir in the orange juice and white wine and slowly bring almost to the boil.

Season the scallops lightly, place the muscles and corals in a single layer on top of the leeks. Cover and steam-boil for 3–4 minutes. With a slotted spoon, transfer the scallops and leeks to a warm serving dish and arrange the scallops on a bed of the leeks.

Turn up the heat and reduce the liquid by about one-third. Reduce the heat and cut the remaining butter into small cubes. Whisk them, one at a time, into the sauce without letting it become more than hand-hot, otherwise the sauce will curdle. At the last minute when all the butter has been added, stir in the chervil and pour the sauce over the scallops.

Mixed Poached Seafood with Samphire

In Britain we tend to ignore our seaweed, although several varieties, especially dulse, purple laver, carragheen, sea lettuce and bladderlocks, make fine eating indeed.

Samphire, or glasswort, is my favourite although strictly speaking it is a sea plant which grows wild on the 'saltings' or mudflats around the coast of Britain. Traditionally said to be ready for eating on the longest day in the year, its season is short, from July to August, and you can either pick it yourself or buy it from a good fishmonger. Samphire does not keep very well, so make sure you wash it thoroughly and eat it within a couple of days. With its salty flavour and crunchy texture, it is particularly good in a mixed fish stew.

MIXED POACHED SEAFOOD WITH SAMPHIRE overleaf

SERVES 4–6

18–20 mussels, cleaned and scrubbed
150 ml/¼ pt fish stock (see page 86)
170 g/6 oz monkfish tail, cut into 2.5 cm/1 in slices
170 g/6 oz red mullet fillet, cut into 5 cm/2 in slices
10 Dublin Bay prawns, shelled
4–6 scallops, cleaned
30 g/1 oz unsalted butter
white of 1 leek, thinly sliced
1 shallot, thinly sliced
1 small carrot, thinly sliced
150 ml/¼ pt dry white wine
1 parsley stalk
300 ml/½ pt whipping cream
55 g/2 oz samphire, washed and drained
salt and freshly ground white pepper

Put the mussels with the fish stock in a heavy-based sauté pan over a medium heat. Cover and simmer for 5–7 minutes, or until the mussels have opened. Transfer to a warm dish, discarding any closed shells.

Put the monkfish into the same pan and poach gently for 2–3 minutes. Add the red mullet and prawns and cook for a further minute. Slice the scallops in two horizontally and, leaving the corals, add them to the pan. Poach for 1 more minute. Transfer the fish, prawns and scallops to the dish with the mussels, reserving the cooking liquor.

Meanwhile, in a separate saucepan, melt the butter over a medium heat and soften the leek, shallot and carrot. Add the wine and parsley and boil to reduce by half. Pour in 5 tablespoons of the reserved cooking liquor and again reduce the quantity by half. Stir in the cream and simmer for 5 minutes.

Pass the sauce through a fine sieve into a clean pan. Add the samphire and poach it in the sauce for a couple of minutes. Put in the mussels, still in their shells, and carefully add the rest of the seafood. Re-heat for about 1 minute. Adjust the seasoning and serve.

Smoked Fish

Long before refrigeration was even thought of, food was usually preserved by smoking, drying, salting, brining or pickling. Now smoking is merely a means of adding flavour and, unfortunately in these times of 'added value' or processed food, a misguided fashion exists for smoking just about anything that stays still long enough. From eggs, nuts, cheese and chicken to prawns, nothing escapes, and the processors would be best to leave well alone. Most of the time they are ruining perfectly good raw ingredients, drowning their inherent taste in smoke.

Smoking is a subtle craft and only certain ingredients, principally some fish and meat, are suitable. Salmon, eel, mackerel, cod, herring and haddock are obvious candidates as they have a robust flavour that is in no danger of being overpowered. Moreover, as their flesh is firm-textured and succulent with a reasonably high oil content, there is no risk of it drying out.

Before smoking the fish must first be cured. This may either be done in a dry salt cure or in brine. Other flavouring ingredients, such as whisky, sugar or herbs, are sometimes added to the cure. Once cured the fish may either be hot-smoked at a fairly high temperature for a relatively short burst of time to 'cook' it; or cold-smoked, a longer, more gentle process.

If you are buying Scottish SMOKED SALMON, the best quality is sold with the Scottish Salmon Smokers Association golden label on the pack; this guarantees that the smoked salmon within is from a fresh Scottish salmon as opposed to a frozen foreign import which is then just smoked in Scotland.

The fishing fleet in Stornoway harbour, on the Isle of Lewis in Scotland left.
Sides of freshly smoked salmon right.

The richest SMOKED EEL is made from mature freshwater silver eel. These fat eels take anything up to 12 years to mature and are caught during the autumn when they are at their plumpest, on their descent downstream to the sea. Hot-smoked over beech mixed with a little applewood for sweetness, they are a great delicacy of the South-West of England.

Cornish SMOKED MACKEREL are the juiciest and, to get the most out of their flavour, should be bought as a whole fish, sliced and served with Cream of Horseradish Sauce (see overleaf). Fillets, I find, are a pale imitation of the real thing and are not improved

when dressed in peppercorn coatings. SMOKED COD ROE is sensational when served thinly sliced with lemon juice, a few drops of virgin olive oil and a little ground black pepper; or you can easily make your own *taramasalata* by whizzing it in a food processor with some bread soaked in milk, lemon juice, garlic and olive oil.

The versatile herring is left whole and ungutted, lightly salted and cold-smoked to make BLOATERS; red herrings are beheaded, gutted and hot-smoked as BUCKLING or split down the middle, gutted, salted and smoked as KIPPERS. The best kippers come from Loch Fyne or Craster in Northumberland, made from the fat summer herring, and can be grilled or 'jugged' (simply stood in a jug of hot water for a few minutes) and eaten with melted butter.

Arbroath smokies and Finnan (or Findon) haddock are both types of SMOKED HADDOCK. The former are gutted, beheaded, dry-salted, tied by the tails into pairs and briefly hot-smoked; the latter are gutted, cleaned, beheaded and split open. They are then lightly brined, hung on 'speats' (metal rods) and cold-smoked for around 4 hours.

It goes without saying that the best smoked fish are never coloured. Some smokers add dark brown to kippers or bright yellow (usually annatto based) to their haddock and then have the temerity to call it a 'naturally coloured fish' on the grounds that annatto is a natural colouring.

Cream of Horseradish Sauce

The best and simplest way of eating smoked eel and mackerel is to fillet them and eat them with slices of a good country bread (see page 191) and a creamy, but cutting, sauce.

SERVES 4–6

1 shallot, finely chopped
2 tsp cream of horseradish
1 tbsp finely chopped fresh dill
5 tbsp sour cream
1 tsp lemon juice
salt and freshly ground black pepper

Mix all the ingredients together, except the lemon juice. Season to taste but remember to be sparing with the salt, depending on the saltiness of the fish.

Leave to stand for 30 minutes, to allow the flavours to infuse. Taste and, if you do not think the sauce is sharp enough, add the lemon juice.

Kedgeree

Arbroath smokies are hot-smoked over oak or beech for up to two hours.

Kedgeree is only worth making with a quality smoked haddock. Those brash yellow fillets just will not do. Choose cold-smoked Finnan haddock with its mild, slightly nutty flavour, pale honey colour and springy texture. Once poached it flakes easily into satisfying chunks and holds together well when mixed into the rice.

SERVES 6–8

225 g/8 oz Finnan haddock
1 small onion, sliced
3 black peppercorns
bay leaf
300 ml/¼ pt milk
225 g/8 oz rice
115 g/4 oz butter, melted
3 tbsp double cream
3 hard-boiled eggs, chopped
3 tbsp finely chopped curly parsley
cayenne
salt and freshly ground black pepper

Put the haddock in a saucepan along with the onion, peppercorns, bay leaf and milk. Place over a medium heat and bring almost to the boil. Turn down the heat and simmer gently for about 5–7 minutes, until the fish is cooked. Drain the fish, discarding the onion, bay leaf and peppercorns. Reserve the milk and leave the fish to cool. Meanwhile, boil the rice in salted water and drain thoroughly.

When the fish is cool enough to handle, remove the skin and any bones and flake it gently into sizable chunks with the hands; do not be too rough or break the fish down into too small pieces as it will disintegrate when you stir it into the rice.

In a clean pan, melt the butter over a medium heat, add the cream, a couple of tablespoons of the reserved milk and the rice and stir until it is thoroughly coated with the mixture. Carefully fold in the flaked fish, the hard-boiled eggs and parsley and cook over a low heat for 1 minute. Adjust the seasoning and serve sprinkled with cayenne.

The Farmyard

The farmyard has always been home to chickens and turkeys, ducks and geese, often as valued for their eggs as for their meat. Quail and guinea fowl, originally game birds, are now more frequently found alongside them.

Poultry

In the sixteenth century Henri IV of France wrote that he wanted no peasant in his kingdom to be so poor that he could not have a chicken in his pot every Sunday. His ambition was never realized for, although most farms did keep poultry, the birds were usually fattened for market rather than for the farmer's own table.

Poultry, domestic fowl or birds kept for eggs or meat, including chicken, turkey, goose, duck, guinea fowl and occasionally quail, were until recently generally the domain of the farmer's wife. It was she who would feed and tend them and collect their eggs. During the day the birds would waddle contentedly around the farmyard, scratching for food and only being locked up at night. This, however, was for their own safety and to keep them away from foxes or any other greedy predator rather than for purely commercial considerations.

Times have changed, and the rearing of poultry has become an intensive and lucrative industry in which few birds ever see the light of day. The result is that their flavour, texture and health have been compromised.

Chicken

The price of chicken may nowadays be remarkably low but, ironically, this has been achieved at great cost, as the eating quality and the health and welfare of the birds have been sacrificed. Chickens reared intensively in battery farms, in particular, are prone to various diseases. So much so that nowadays we are advised to cook chicken thoroughly, preferably without stuffing, to kill off any bacteria lurking in their cavities.

The alternative to buying a battery bird is to opt for FREE-RANGE or extensively reared chickens. Unlike

Traditionally most country women kept fowl, deriving extra income from their eggs.

intensively reared chickens, they are produced under more humane conditions. They are not subjected to constant light and consequently grow at a slower rate. They also have space to move around and access to the open air.

There is no doubt that a free-range chicken actually does taste better. Several factors affect eating quality: breed, feed, housing, age and method of slaughtering. If a bird is fed with a cheaper feed compound bulked up with fish meal, its flesh will be tainted; or if it has been forced to grow too fast without any exercise, the flesh will be vapid and probably covered with an excess of fat.

There are also CORN-FED birds, fed on maize rather than wheat. Their distinctively yellow-hued flesh has a particularly fine creamy taste and they can be reared to any of the normal standards.

Obviously the more stringent the specifications for a bird, the more it costs to rear and the more we, the customers, will have to pay for these better grades. However, when you try them I think you will agree that a fully flavoured chicken really is worth the expense.

Grades apart, what size or types of chickens are there? BABY CHICKEN or POUSSIN usually weighs about 900 g/2 lb and will serve two. They are very tender, but are too young to have developed much flavour. BOILING FOWL are tough old laying birds which are just the ticket for soups, stocks or poaching. However, never even think of trying to roast one, as its flesh will be far too stringy and dry. CAPONS, castrated cock birds, are illegal in this country but you can occasionally find a young cockerel, or a large hen, which will be sold as a 'capon-style bird'. These may be roasted, braised or poached to develop their full dense taste. ROASTERS or BROILERS, the latter description only used of battery chickens, are those most commonly found on the supermarket shelves.

A high proportion of poultry is sold frozen, or may be frozen at some stage in its progress to the customer. I find such birds a waste of money: not only do they take hours to thaw thoroughly, but the processing robs them of much of their flavour and succulence.

When choosing a fresh bird, look for a plump breast, a smooth dry unbroken skin (wet skin is a sign that the bird may well have been frozen) which is free of blotches. As a rough guide, allow about 350 g/12 oz of chicken on the bone per person: so a 1.5 k/3½ lb bird should feed 4 people.

What is free-range?

Until recently no legal definitions existed in this country for free-range chickens. However, the EC has recently introduced standards and the situation should, at last, be clearer. In order to sell free-range birds the producers must comply with these new conditions. Three categories of free-range bird have been defined: 'free-range', 'traditional free-range' and 'free-range total freedom'.

Birds in all three categories must have continuous daytime access to open-air runs, and their feed must contain at least 70% cereals (although rather alarmingly there is no banning of the addition of antibiotics to their feed). 'Free-range' chickens can be of any breed and are slaughtered at the comparatively young age of 56 days; whereas for the other two categories, only slow-growing strains are allowed and these cannot be slaughtered before 81 days, thus allowing a fuller flavour to develop. 'Traditional free-range' birds have more space to run around in (about 2 square metres per chicken) and 'free-range total freedom' must have open-air runs of unlimited area. The latter should be particularly well textured.

Despite all this, however, perhaps the best birds of all are those raised to organic standards (see page 134). The flavour and texture of such birds surpasses those of even 'free-range total freedom'.

To roast a chicken

Roast the bird in an oven preheated to 220C/425F/ gas7 for about 15 minutes. Then turn the oven down to 180C/350F/gas4 and allow about a further 15 minutes per 450 g/1 lb. Do not forget to baste the chicken every so often. The one certain way of being sure that the bird is thoroughly cooked is to prick the thickest part of the thigh with a skewer; the juices that ooze out must be clear, without any trace of pink. If you are worried about the breast drying out, cook the bird breast down for the first 30 minutes.

Another interesting way of adding flavour to a bird, which also has the added benefit of keeping the breast really moist, is to loosen the skin over the breast and stuff it with a flavoured butter (see page 54). Finish by rubbing the skin all over with a little more of the butter and sprinkling over a pinch of sea salt.

Because of the current risk of cross-contamination, it is probably best not to stuff chickens with the traditional forcemeats. Instead, pop into the cavity a knob of butter, a whole unpeeled lemon, a couple of cloves of garlic or even a handful of fresh herbs, such as tarragon or rosemary.

To make chicken stock

The recipe for chicken soup which follows is also a master recipe for a chicken stock, or indeed stock for any poultry. You can make stock with a whole bird; with a raw carcass stripped of its meat; a roasted carcass after carving; or even just the giblets, ie the heart, liver, gizzard and neck. You will only need to simmer any of these for about 1 hour.

To remove the fat from the stock, strain and leave it to chill until the fat rises to the surface and forms a thick layer on the top. This can then be removed with a spoon or metal skimmer or by using some paper towel rather like blotting paper, patting it over the surface so that it soaks up the fat. This fat may then be clarified by heating it gently and passing it through a sieve lined

with a damp cloth. Clarified fat may then be potted and will keep for several weeks in the refrigerator. It is very useful for cooking.

To turn any poultry stock into a sparklingly clear consommé, it must also be clarified after skimming. The stock is heated gently and a couple of lightly beaten egg whites are then whisked in along with their crushed shells. The liquid is whisked until it comes to the boil and the heat is then turned down to allow it to simmer gently for about 10 minutes. The stock is then carefully strained through a sieve lined with a damp cloth or muslin.

A solitary chicken rules the roost.

Jewish Chicken Soup with Matzo Balls

For this deep and richly flavoured soup, use a boiling or 'over-age' hen and simmer it for hours. Although a roasting bird would cook in half the time, it would only have half the flavour. Some people might say it is rather extravagant to use a whole bird just for a soup, but once you have tasted it . . .

Not for nothing is this soup called 'Jewish Penicillin': it is so wholesome that it cures all ills. Traditionally a Jewish-style chicken soup is never skimmed or clarified and so comes streaked with fat.

SERVES 6–8

1 bowling fowl, including neck and gizzard
1 large onion
2 carrots
2 celery stalks
2 leeks
large bunch of parsley
6 peppercorns
salt and freshly ground black pepper

for the matzo balls:
1 egg
1 tbsp clarified chicken fat, melted (see opposite) or vegetable oil
2 tbsp chicken soup or water
large pinch of ground ginger
1 tbsp ground almonds
75 g/2½ oz matzo meal
salt and freshly ground white pepper

Put the chicken in a large pot with the vegetables, parsley, peppercorns, some salt and about 2.25 l/4 pt water. Slowly bring it to the boil over a medium heat, occasionally skimming off the scum as it rises to the surface using a metal skimmer.

Simmer gently for about 2 hours or until the chicken is tender and actually starts to fall away from the bones.

Lift the bird out of the pot, draining carefully, and allow to cool slightly. Strip the flesh off the bones and set it aside. Although the flesh will not have much taste, you can chop and dress it in Green Sauce (see page 45) and use it in sandwiches or salads. Put the bones back into the pot and simmer for a further hour.

Meanwhile make the matzo balls: in a large bowl, lightly beat the egg with the chicken fat or vegetable oil, the 2 tablespoons of chicken soup or water, the ginger and ground almonds. Season with a generous pinch of salt and some pepper and stir in the matzo meal to make a soft, almost runny mixture. The meal will absorb plenty of liquid, so if you think it is still too dry add a little more soup or water. Cover and leave to rest in a cool place for about 1 hour.

When the soup has simmered for the hour, strain it to remove the vegetables and bones. Return it to a clean pan and bring to the boil again over a medium heat.

Wet the hands with cold water, take a small amount of the matzo mixture about the size of a walnut and roll it into a round ball between the palms. Do this until all the mixture has been used up. When the soup has reached a good rolling boil, drop in the balls, cover and cook for about 5 minutes. Adjust the seasoning and serve immediately with the soup.

As the matzo balls soak up a fair amount of the soup while cooking, you may prefer to cook them in a pan of lightly salted boiling water rather than in the chicken soup.

Liver Parfait with a Basil and Tomato Sauce

Chicken livers are a wonderfully economical buy. Usually sold frozen in pots, they can be used in pasta sauces, pâtés and mousses. Once they are defrosted, any discoloured bits tainted with the bile should be cut away. Rinse and drain the livers thoroughly to get rid of the bloody liquid, the taste of which can overpower the delicate flavour of the meat, and trim away any connective tissue.

SERVES 4

115 g/4 oz chicken livers, trimmed
$\frac{1}{2}$ garlic clove
1 egg
50 ml/2 fl oz port
150 ml/$\frac{1}{4}$ pt double cream
4 large chard leaves
salt and freshly ground white pepper
butter for greasing

for the sauce:
150 ml/$\frac{1}{4}$ pt dry white wine
55 g/2 oz unsalted butter, cut into dice
2 tomatoes, skinned, deseeded and diced
12–14 fresh basil leaves, finely chopped

Preheat the oven to 190C/375F/gas5.

Put the chicken livers and garlic in a food processor and season generously. Whizz until smooth, then add the egg and port and, with the machine running, slowly pour in the cream. Pass the mixture through a fine sieve and leave it in the refrigerator for at least 15 minutes.

Meanwhile, tear off and discard the stalks from the chard leaves and blanch the whole leaves for a few seconds in boiling water. Refresh them immediately in iced water and then pat dry.

Have ready 4 lightly buttered round or oval 100 ml/ $3\frac{1}{2}$ fl oz moulds, such as ramekins, and 4 matching circles of buttered greaseproof paper. Line each

LIVER PARFAIT WITH A BASIL AND TOMATO SAUCE

mould with one chard leaf, pressing it down so it takes on the shape of the mould, but leaving it to hang over the edges. Spoon the liver mixture into the moulds and fold the overhanging leaf over to enclose the top. Cover with the circles of greaseproof paper.

Place the moulds in a roasting pan and fill the pan with boiling water until it comes to about halfway up the moulds. Bake in the oven for 15 minutes.

Meanwhile, make the sauce: in a saucepan bring the white wine to the boil over a medium heat and boil rapidly until it has reduced by half. Turn down the heat to low and whisk in the butter, a piece at a time, until the sauce is creamy. Stir in the tomatoes and the basil and remove from the heat.

To unmould the parfaits, peel off the circles of greaseproof paper. Place a warmed plate on top of each mould, turn them over together, give the mould a quick sharp shake and then carefully lift it off. Serve with a little sauce spooned over the parfait.

Chicken Breasts with Orange

Boned and skinned chicken breasts, sometimes called 'escalopes' or 'côtelettes' even by British retailers, are sold pre-packed in supermarkets and are very useful. My butcher also sells chicken 'suprêmes', a French cut consisting of the breast complete with the upper wing, trimmed of its tip, left attached. Both are ideal for this recipe as the delicate flavour marries well with that of the fruit.

SERVES 4

zest and juice of 2 oranges
3 celery stalks with their leaves, chopped
4 spring onions, chopped
4 chicken breasts, skinned and boned
45 g/1½ oz unsalted butter
zest and juice of 1 lemon
100 ml/3½ fl oz double cream
salt and freshly ground white pepper

Make the marinade: mix the juice of one of the oranges with a few of the chopped celery leaves, the chopped green tops of the spring onions and a pinch of salt and pepper.

Put the chicken breasts in a glass or stainless steel dish suitable for marinading, pour over the marinade and leave for at least one hour in a cool place, turning the breasts over once or twice.

In a sauté pan over a low heat, melt the butter and soften the celery and remaining spring onions in it for a couple of minutes. Turn down the heat to very low, cover the pan and cook for 10 minutes, stirring occasionally. As the vegetables should not colour, add a couple of tablespoons of vegetable stock or water to the pan if they start to brown. Equally if the lid is not very tight-fitting and allows some of the moisture to escape, cover the vegetables with a sheet of buttered greaseproof paper.

Lift the chicken pieces out of the marinade and scrape off the pieces of vegetable. Place the chicken in the sauté pan on top of the vegetables and cook them for about 2 minutes on each side. Strain the marinade, pour it over the chicken and cook for a further 5 minutes or until the chicken is cooked through. Using a slotted spoon, transfer the chicken breasts and vegetables to a warmed dish and keep warm.

Add the orange and lemon zest and the remaining fruit juices to the pan. Turn up the heat and simmer for 1 minute. Pour in the cream and mix together thoroughly. Simmer for a minute or two.

Return the chicken and vegetables to the pan with any juices and simmer for a couple of minutes to allow the flavours to blend. Adjust the seasoning and arrange the chicken pieces on a warmed serving dish with the sauce spooned over them.

Grilled Chicken Joints with Red Pepper Sauce

One of the major growth areas in the chicken industry is the sale of fresh and frozen chicken portions, such as breasts, drumsticks, wings or thighs — and very convenient they are too! However, my aversion to frozen chicken extends to such portions, as these seem to lack both flavour and texture. Moreover, no matter how carefully they are defrosted, the skin is always flabby. Freshly prepared pieces, especially after a spell in a judicious marinade, are much more acceptable. Trimmed drumsticks or thighs are best grilled and served with a robust sauce. Depending on their size and thickness, they can be cooked in a remarkably short time.

SERVES 4–6

8 chicken drumsticks or thigh portions

for the marinade:
5 tbsp olive oil
juice of 1 lemon
1 tsp harissa paste
1 garlic clove, crushed
salt and freshly ground black pepper

for the sauce:
2 red peppers
2 garlic cloves, unpeeled
5 tbsp virgin olive oil
salt and freshly ground black pepper

Using a sharp knife, slash the skin of the drumsticks or thighs diagonally a couple of times on each side and put them in a glass or stainless steel dish suitable for marinating.

Mix all the marinade ingredients together and pour this over the chicken. Leave for at least an hour in a cool place, turning the chicken over once or twice.

Make the sauce: preheat the grill and brush the red peppers and garlic with a little of the oil. Put them under the hot grill and cook, turning them occasionally, for about 12–15 minutes, or until the peppers are slightly charred and have softened. Transfer them, with the garlic, to a plate.

To make them easy to peel, cover them with film and leave them for about 10 minutes to cool slightly. Then peel off their skins. Using a spoon, scoop out and discard the seeds and fleshy centres.

Slit the skin of the garlic cloves with a knife and then press the cloves gently to extract the cooked pulp. Put this into a food processor with the pepper flesh and whizz until smooth. With the machine still running, slowly add the oil to make a smooth pillar-box-red sauce.

Preheat the grill again. Take the pieces of chicken out of the marinade and grill them for about 12–15 minutes, or until they are a deep brown and cooked right through. Turn them and baste them occasionally with the marinade during cooking.

Serve the chicken pieces with the sauce on the side, or to dip into, and with a large green salad.

GRILLED CHICKEN JOINTS WITH RED PEPPER SAUCE

Poulet Sorges

For a really authentic flavour, you should use a capon for this dish. However, as these are not available in this country, a large fat hen or cockerel can be used instead.

SERVES 8

2 slices of smoked bacon, rinds removed
2 garlic cloves
2 shallots
3 spring onions, trimmed
140 g/5 oz fresh breadcrumbs
small bunch of parsley
½ tsp freshly grated nutmeg
285 g/10 oz chicken livers, trimmed and finely chopped
1 egg yolk
3.5 k/8 lb capon-style bird (see above)
30 g/1 oz clarified chicken or goose fat (see page 106)
3 carrots, cut into 5 cm/2 in pieces
2 turnips, cut into quarters
3 leeks, trimmed and cut into 5 cm/2 in pieces
3 celery stalks, trimmed and cut into 5 cm/2 in pieces
1 large onion
1 clove
450 g/1 lb Swiss chard, tied in a bunch
salt and freshly ground black pepper

for the sauce:
1 tsp smooth French mustard
150 ml/¼ pt extra-virgin olive oil
2 tbsp white wine vinegar
small bunch of parsley, chopped
2 spring onions, chopped
1 shallot, finely chopped
2 eggs

Put the bacon in a food processor with the garlic, shallots, spring onions, breadcrumbs, parsley and nutmeg. Whizz until the ingredients are well chopped.

Add the chicken livers and egg yolk and process to mix together. Season and spoon the mixture into both the neck and vent of the chicken, securing the skin flaps tightly so the stuffing cannot escape.

In a large heavy-based casserole, melt the chicken or goose fat over a medium heat and brown the chicken all over. Pour over enough boiling water to submerge the bird completely. Add the carrots, turnips, leeks, celery, onion stuck with the clove and the chard along with a generous teaspoon of sea salt and plenty of pepper. Cover and simmer gently for about 1½ hours.

Make the sauce towards the end of that cooking time: beat the mustard with the olive oil and vinegar and stir in the parsley, spring onions and shallot. Soft-boil the eggs for 3 minutes, lift them out of the pan with a slotted spoon and put them under cold running water. When they are cool enough to handle, carefully crack the shells, spoon out the yolks and whisk them into the vinaigrette.

Pour 3–4 tablespoons of the stock from the chicken into a clean saucepan and bring it to the boil. Carefully shell the egg whites, add them to the pan and cook for about 3 minutes or until the whites are quite firm. If the whites are still very runny, you can always cook them first and remove the shell afterwards. Strain off the liquid, chop the whites finely and stir them into the sauce. Season.

When the chicken is cooked, lift it out of the pan and then serve surrounded by the vegetables, with some of the chicken stock as a gravy and the sauce served separately.

Chicken in a Loaf

You really must use a free-range chicken for this recipe as you need a meaty full-flavoured bird to complement the richness of the sauce.

The idea of presenting chicken inside a whole loaf of bread like this comes from Southern Italy, where it is served cut in thick slices. In those distant days long before anyone dreamed of the food processor, the nuts and bread were pounded painstakingly by hand to obtain a smooth texture.

SERVES 6–8

5 tbsp virgin olive oil
1.35 k/3 lb chicken, cut into pieces
500 ml/16 fl oz chicken stock (see page 106)
1 round crusty white loaf of bread
30 g/1 oz shelled almonds, toasted
30 g/1 oz shelled pistachios
2 eggs
juice of 1 lemon
45 g/1½ oz capers, drained
bunch of flat-leaf parsley, chopped
salt and freshly ground black pepper

Using a heavy-based pan which has a tight-fitting lid, heat 3 tablespoons of the oil over a medium heat and brown the chicken pieces all over in it.

Pour in 250 ml/8 fl oz of the stock. Season, cover and simmer for 15–20 minutes, or until the chicken is tender, adding more stock if the pan looks in danger of drying out. Drain the chicken and leave it to cool, reserving the stock.

Preheat the oven to 180C/350F/gas4.

Prepare the bread 'dish' and 'lid' by cutting the loaf in two horizontally, about one-third down from the top. Hollow it out carefully so as not to tear the crust, keeping the soft dough from the centre. Brush the crust all over, both inside and out, with the remaining olive oil.

Put the almonds and pistachios together in a food processor along with the dough from inside the loaf and whizz until reduced to the texture of fine crumbs. With the machine still running, slowly add the rest of the stock, followed by the eggs and lemon juice. As the mixture should be quite runny, be prepared to add an extra tablespoon or two of stock if necessary.

When the chicken is cool enough to handle, skin it and remove the flesh from the bones. Cut the meat into small pieces and stir in the capers and parsley, followed by the sauce. Season and spoon this mixture into the prepared bread crust. Cover with the lid and bake in the oven for about 20 minutes or until golden. Serve either hot or cold.

Although it is traditional festive fare, turkey makes good eating all year round.

Turkey

Like chicken, the best-tasting turkey is always fresh and never frozen, and will have been fed on an additive-free diet, primarily of vegetables. It should be grown and matured at a natural rate and given enough space to move around in. Killed at about 18 weeks, it should be dry-plucked, ie using wax rather than being immersed in hot water, to ensure no flavour loss. It should then be hung uneviscerated, ie complete with its innards, for at least 4 days for a more gamey flavour.

Taste also varies according to breed. Most of the turkeys in the shops are White Turkeys, a commer-cially developed variety which may have the advantage of a buxom breast with plenty of meat but their flavour is insipid. The old-fashioned breeds, such as the Cambridge Bronze and the Norfolk Black, have a far richer gamey taste. Despite their superior flavour, they are all too often passed over because of their keel-bone breasts, which yield comparatively little meat, and their stubbly skin. Some customers actually will not buy them because of their five o' clock shadow, as they prefer a pale smooth skin.

One word of warning! When you are choosing a turkey do not be taken in by claims such as 'free-range' or 'additive-free' unless they can be backed up. As until recently with chicken, there is no legal definition for a 'free-range' turkey and 'additive-free' feed means different things to different people. If in doubt, ask your butcher or poulterer.

A turkey from the Traditional Farm Fresh Turkey Association is a good buy and conforms to high standards. Their birds, sold with a distinctive golden triangle logo, are extensively reared, fed no antibiotics or growth promoters, unless specified by a vet on grounds of welfare, and only given vegetable protein after 6 weeks. They are fresh, well-hung and really meaty, with a moist, well-textured flesh. Buy one either straight from a farm or from a good butcher.

However, the Association does not stipulate any particular breeds, unlike the French turkeys sold under the Label Rouge scheme. These are always the Black Footed breed, a succulent and richly flavoured bird. However, these may not necessarily be the best buy, as some of the advantages of the birds' inherent flavour are lost as they are wet-plucked, ie immersed in water, gutted and sold oven-ready with no hanging time to allow the flavour to develop.

For the best of all birds, buy a traditional breed that has been well reared and hung. It will probably cost quite a lot more, but its incomparable taste and texture will be well worth it.

To roast a turkey

The simplest and most effective way to cook a whole bird is to put it breast down in the hot oven (see below), turning it right side up for the last hour only. This gives a crisp golden finish without any danger of dried-up breast meat.

If your bird will not balance on its breast, leave it breast side up and protect it by covering it with a J-cloth soaked in melted butter. This will baste it continuously but still allow it to crispen.

It is probably safest to cook meat stuffings separately (see page 150 for sausage meat recipe). Just fill the cavities with any, or a mixture, of the following: fresh sage, cored Orléans Reinette or Cox's eating apples, onions studded with cloves, chopped potatoes and garlic, whole unpeeled oranges, raisins or prunes soaked in brandy, walnuts or chestnuts moistened in white wine.

Roasting times for an unstuffed turkey:

Slow roasting (for larger birds) 160C/325F/gas3	Weight	Fast roasting (for smaller birds) 190C/375F/gas5
$3\frac{1}{2}$–$3\frac{3}{4}$ hrs	3.5–4.5 k/8–10 lb	$2\frac{1}{2}$–$2\frac{3}{4}$ hrs
$3\frac{3}{4}$–4 hrs	5–6 k/11–13 lb	$2\frac{3}{4}$–3 hrs
$4\frac{1}{4}$–5 hrs	6.5–8 k/14–17 lb	3–$3\frac{3}{4}$ hrs

To test if the bird is thoroughly cooked, insert a skewer in the thickest part of the thigh near the body: the juices should run clear without a trace of pink.

To make a gravy, boil up the giblets with an onion, carrot and plenty of fresh parsley. When the turkey is cooked, remove it from the roasting pan and leave it to one side, covered, to rest. Drain the pan to remove most of the fat and then set it over a high heat. Stir and scrape up all the delicious sticky bits on the bottom of the pan, pour in the stock from the giblets and a generous glass of dry white wine and simmer to make a rich gravy.

Escalope of Turkey with Ginger and Sherry

Domestic or imported French turkey breasts are now generally on sale in the supermarkets. These usually weigh about 115–170 g/ 4–6 oz and can be an economical and worthwhile buy. As they can be a little bland, they are best cooked with a spicy sauce.

I think they cook better if first flattened: simply place each turkey breast between two sheets of film and then roll them out using plenty of pressure.

SERVES 4

2 tbsp sunflower oil
4 turkey breasts, each weighing 115–170 g/4–6 oz
3 spring onions, finely chopped
2 garlic cloves, finely chopped
30 g/1 oz fresh lemon grass, finely chopped
15 g/$\frac{1}{2}$ oz fresh root ginger, peeled and finely chopped
5 tbsp medium sherry
100 ml/$3\frac{1}{2}$ fl oz chicken stock (see page 106)
45 g/$1\frac{1}{2}$ oz cold unsalted butter, diced
salt and freshly ground white pepper

In a heavy-based sauté pan, heat the oil over a medium heat. Season the turkey breasts and sauté them for about 5 minutes on each side. (Although if they are quite thin they will probably cook a lot more quickly.) Using a slotted spoon, transfer them to a warmed serving dish and keep warm.

In the same pan, sauté the spring onions, garlic, lemon grass and ginger for about 5 minutes or until soft. Add the sherry and stock, turn up the heat to bring to the boil. Boil rapidly until the liquid has reduced by one-third. Turn the heat right down and beat in the butter, one piece at a time, until it is all incorporated and the sauce has a rich shiny texture. Pour it over the turkey breasts and serve.

Goose

In season from September to December, geese were once very popular in Britain. All over the country, farmers would drive their geese to market to sell them at Goose Fairs. A green goose, the young tender bird fed on grass or 'stubbings' from the recently harvested fields, was traditionally eaten at Michaelmas on September 29th; whereas older, larger and considerably fatter birds were the usual fare on Christmas Day.

Most geese nowadays are bred from the Legarth variety, with a good meat-to-bone ratio. However, you can still find some Toulouse or Embden Cross birds which, although less plump, are juicier and more gamey. In spite of a recent revival of interest in geese, only about half a million birds are produced annually in Britain by about one thousand producers, ranging from the farmer's wife who might rear a few dozen birds for local trade to larger concerns supplying up to 50,000 birds.

Again a fresh, rather than frozen, goose is a far better buy. Look for a plump breast, with firm meat that is resilient to the touch, and for legs that are soft, still pliable and which have had their sinews removed, otherwise they will be far too tough.

As a general rule, allow over 450 g/1 lb per person, so a 4.5 k/10 lb goose should feed 8 people. The best birds are usually in the weight range from 3.2 k/7 lb to about 6.5 k/14½ lb; when heavier they are usually too fatty or tough for roasting.

The products of the goose, particularly its fat, are not only useful in cooking below. Formerly goose fat was also used as a medicinal ointment and goose feathers as down for bedding. ROAST GOOSE STUFFED WITH APPLES right.

20 minutes extra, or fast-roast it at 200C/400F/gas6 for 15 minutes per 450 g/1 lb plus 15 minutes extra. Turn it breast side up for the last 90 minutes of cooking to allow the skin to crispen.

To cut the fattiness of the bird, serve it with Onion Marmalade (see page 23), Spiced Crab Apples (see page 224) or a tart apple sauce made with peeled, cored and quartered apples simmered in cider flavoured with orange and lemon zest and generous pinches of cloves and sugar and salt. As with turkey, I prefer to bake the stuffing separately and either prepare a traditional sage, breadcrumb and onion stuffing enriched with the goose liver, or make a more unusual mixture of chopped fennel mixed with brandy-soaked prunes, slices of lemon and breadcrumbs.

To roast a goose

Goose is a rich meat with a very high fat content and is therefore best roasted standing on a trivet or roasting rack in a baking tray so the fat can drain off. Never throw the fat away as, once it has been clarified (see page 106), it will keep for months and can be used for cooking potatoes (see page 21) or browning poultry (see Poulet Sorges, page 112).

First rub the breast with salt and, if you wish, prick the skin all over to let the fat run free. Then stuff it with peeled and quartered apples and onions soaked in cider or calvados and sprinkled with ground cinnamon, salt and pepper. Stand the bird, breast down, on a trivet and either slow-roast in an oven preheated to 180C/350F/gas4, allowing 20 minutes per 450 g/1 lb plus

Duck

Farmyard ducks are milder flavoured, far fattier and a good deal larger than mallards, their wild cousins.

A good duck should neither be too fatty nor too bony. The breeds with the best eating qualities are the Rouen, which is smothered rather than bled so that its blood remains in the muscle to give it fine-flavoured red-tinged flesh; the large, fat Aylesbury with its buttery flesh; the similarly sized but more delicately flavoured Pekin; the Nantes, a small strongly flavoured bird with a good layer of fat; and the Barbary or Muscovy with a full breast, meaty legs and dark lean flesh with a slightly musky, almost smoky, flavour.

In Britain, two new hybrids have recently been developed, both offering plenty of meat. The Gressingham, bred from the mallard, has a good meat-to-bone ratio and a gamey flavour; the larger Lunesdale, a Gressingham and Pekin cross, has a far milder flavour.

Depending on the breed and its fat content, a 1.8 k/ 4 lb duck will usually serve about 4 people. As you can now also buy duck breasts or leg portions rather than whole birds, duck has become a more convenient buy. The only disadvantage is that you no longer have a whole carcass to boil up for a stock or soup, or the liver to transform into a pâté or forcemeat.

To roast a duck

First stuff the bird with a couple of cored apples soaked in brandy, or peeled and quartered Seville oranges or a traditional sage and onion stuffing. Rub the skin all over with salt. If it is very fatty, prick it with a fork. Roast it on a rack in a roasting pan in an oven preheated to 200C/400F/gas6, allowing about 10 minutes per 450 g/1 lb plus an extra 10 minutes. If the legs are still bloody you may need to detach them and return them to the oven for an extra 10 minutes.

Quail, guinea fowl, duck right. *Ducks enjoy a ride home from market* opposite.

Duck Legs Braised with Onions and Cabbage

In traditional French country cooking, succulent duck legs were sometimes turned into confit, *one of the oldest ways of preserving meat. They were salted, slowly cooked in their own fat, then sealed and stored in the same fat.*

This recipe, taken from Chez Panisse Cooking *by Paul Bertolli with Alice Waters, is based on this old-fashioned method. However, as you might expect from these Californian cooks, it has been cunningly adapted so that although the meat is still meltingly soft, it has a lighter cleaner flavour and none of the cloying quality which can result from too much duck fat.*

SERVES 4

1 tbsp finely chopped fresh thyme
1 tbsp freshly ground black pepper
25 g/¾ oz sea salt
4 duck legs, each weighing about 140 g/5 oz
3 large red onions, sliced
350 g/12 oz Savoy or Primo cabbage, cut in thick slices
3 tbsp balsamic vinegar
500 ml/16 fl oz poultry stock (see page 106)
350 g/12 oz ripe tomatoes, skinned, quartered and deseeded
large pinch of caster sugar
sea salt and freshly ground black pepper
4 sprigs of thyme, to garnish

Make a dry marinade by mixing together the thyme and the measured amounts of black pepper and sea salt. For this recipe you really must use sea or rock salt, otherwise the taste is far too harsh.

Using a sharp knife, slash the duck skins to make a couple of thin cuts about 3.5 cm/1½ in long, rub the mixture into the duck legs all over and leave to marinate at room temperature for 1½ hours, by which time the duck will have absorbed a fair amount of the salt.

Preheat the oven to 180C/350F/gas4.

Using a damp cloth, wipe the duck legs free of the dry marinade and place them, skin side down, in a heavy-based ovenproof casserole over a low heat and cook them very slowly for 20 minutes, or until golden brown. If the heat is low enough, you do not need any oil or butter as the legs give off so much fat there is no risk of them burning. Sometimes they give off so much fat that you should remove some of it with a spoon during the course of cooking and reserve. Transfer the duck legs to a warm plate and keep warm.

Rinse the casserole, warm 3 tablespoons of the duck fat over a medium heat, add the onions and cook gently for 5–7 minutes or until soft. Stir in the cabbage and balsamic vinegar, season and simmer for about 3 minutes, or until the cabbage is wilted.

Arrange the duck legs on top of the cabbage and pour over the stock. Sprinkle the tomatoes with the sugar and scatter them over the duck legs. Cover the casserole and bake in the oven for 1½ hours, or until the legs are tender. Using a slotted spoon, transfer them to a serving dish with the vegetables and keep warm.

Make a simple sauce by straining the liquid into a pan and boiling it vigorously to reduce it until only about 250 ml/8 fl oz remains. Season and serve the duck legs on a bed of vegetables, garnished with a sprig of thyme. Serve the sauce separately.

Duck Breast with Pears

A couple of years ago magret de canard, *ie boned duck breast*, was all the rage with top chefs, and there was no end to the sweet, sharp or sour sauces dreamt up to serve with it. As a result, duck breasts are now on sale in most supermarkets for the home cook.

Magret is traditionally from the French Barbary duck and comes with its skin and underlying layer of fat intact. It is sold either in portions weighing around 170 g/6 oz from the female duck, which has been killed at about 7 weeks, or around 325 g/11 oz from the male duck which has been allowed to grow to about 12 weeks and killed after its second feathering. One large magret will easily feed two people, so cut it diagonally across in half before cooking to divide it into two portions.

English duck breasts, or fillets or suprêmes as they are sometimes called, are mostly from the Gressingham duck. These are usually slightly smaller than the Barbary and, unlike the French, both sexes are almost always killed at 7 weeks, resulting in a milder flavoured duck with a breast weighing around 170 g/6 oz – a good size for one person.

SERVES 6

6 duck breasts, each weighing about 170 g/6 oz or 3 large magrets,
each weighing about 325 g/11 oz, cut in half diagonally
(see above)
6 firm Comice pears, peeled, cored and quartered
1 cinnamon stick
30 g/1 oz butter
1 tbsp olive oil
1 tbsp clear honey
2 onions, sliced
1 tbsp five-spice powder
2 ripe tomatoes, peeled and chopped
pinch of sugar
2 tbsp sherry vinegar
100 ml/3½ fl oz dry sherry
300 ml/½ pt chicken or duck stock (see page 106)
salt and freshly ground black pepper

Preheat the oven to 220C/425F/gas7. Season the duck breasts with salt and pepper.

In a saucepan over a medium heat put the pears, cinnamon stick and enough water to cover. Bring to just below the boil and simmer for 8–10 minutes, or until the pears are just tender. Strain the pears, reserving the cooking liquid.

Meanwhile melt the butter with the oil in a heavy-based ovenproof pan over a medium heat. Fry the duck breasts skin side down for 6–8 minutes. This not only seals them but also allows the fat to infuse the meat. Drain off the fat, keeping it for later, turn the breasts over, brush the skins with the honey and bake them in the oven for 15 minutes, or a little longer if you do not like the meat pink.

Meanwhile heat 3 tablespoons of the duck fat in a clean heavy-based pan over a medium heat and fry the pears until just golden. Using a slotted spoon, transfer them to a plate and keep warm. Sprinkle the onions with the five-spice powder and sauté them in the same fat along with the tomatoes and sugar for about 10 minutes, or until soft. Pour in the sherry vinegar and sauté for another 5 minutes.

Remove the duck from the oven and keep warm. Tip the fat from the dish into the onions. Turn up the heat, add the sherry, stock and about 300 ml/½ pt of the strained cooking liquid from the pears, bring to the boil and cook rapidly, uncovered, for about 10 minutes so that it reduces by about two-thirds.

Transfer the contents of the pan to a food processor and whizz until smooth. Return the sauce to the pan, stir in any juices from the cooked breasts and adjust the seasoning. Arrange the duck breasts with the pears on top of that and heat for a couple of minutes. Serve immediately.

DUCK BREAST WITH PEARS

Quail

As there are virtually no wild quail left in this country, all the quail we eat are farmed from a Japanese variety.

Farmed quail usually weigh between 115–140 g/ 4–5 oz and tend to have less flavour than those reared in the wild. They may be braised or casseroled whole, or spatchcocked (see page 168) and then grilled or roasted.

It is also a good idea to stuff the birds for roasting, in which case you could buy them ready boned. Sometimes quails are sold with their livers; chop these up, sauté them gently in oil or butter for a couple of minutes and then add them to the stuffing.

The breast can readily dry out when roasting. To prevent this, cover with a slice of unsmoked streaky bacon or, as in the following recipe, with vine leaves.

Quails with Lemon and Coriander

If you grow a vine, you can use the leaves for wrapping the quail provided you blanch them for a few seconds in boiling water; otherwise buy leaves in brine and rinse and dry them thoroughly.

SERVES 6

170 g/6 oz long-grain rice
115 g/4 oz pine nuts, toasted
zest and juice of 2 lemons
6 tbsp finely chopped fresh parsley
6 tbsp finely chopped fresh coriander leaves
12 fresh quail, whole or boned (see above)
1 tbsp olive oil, plus extra for brushing
12 vine leaves (see above)
150 ml/¼ pt extra-virgin olive oil
3 shallots, finely chopped
300 ml/½ pt dry white wine
salt and freshly ground black pepper

Preheat the oven to 200C/400F/gas6 and generously grease a baking dish with some oil.

Cook the rice in a pan of salted water until soft, according to the instructions on the packet. Drain it thoroughly and put it into a large mixing bowl. Stir in the pine nuts, with the lemon zest and half the juice, half each of the parsley and coriander and season.

While the rice is cooking, wipe the quails all over with a damp cloth, both inside and out. Remove the livers from their cavities and chop them finely. Heat the 1 tablespoon of olive oil in a sauté pan over a medium heat and sauté the livers for a couple of minutes until they have changed colour. Tip the contents of the pan into the rice and stir it in.

Spoon the stuffing into the cleaned cavities of the quail, packing it in quite tightly but not too firmly otherwise the birds will burst when cooking. Secure the opening with a wooden toothpick, so the stuffing cannot fall out, and pat them into an even shape. Using a pastry brush, paint the birds with some olive oil, place a vine leaf over each breast, tucking it into the wings, and brush that again with some more olive oil.

Place the quail in the prepared baking dish and bake in the oven for about 25 minutes.

Meanwhile, in a clean sauté pan heat 2 tablespoons of the extra-virgin olive oil over a medium heat. Add the shallots and sauté them until soft. Pour in the white wine and boil uncovered for about 5–7 minutes, or until the wine has reduced by half.

When the quails are cooked, transfer them to a warmed serving dish and keep warm. Strain any juices from the baking dish into the saucepan and simmer for a minute. Turn down the heat and stir in the remaining parsley, coriander and lemon juice and slowly trickle in the remaining extra-virgin olive oil, stirring constantly. Season and serve immediately.

QUAILS WITH LEMON AND CORIANDER opposite.

Guinea Fowl

The French rave about the guinea fowl, deeming it a superior alternative to chicken, although I am not completely convinced. Originally a game bird, guinea fowl is now farmed like chicken. Unfortunately, however, it is never hung. So, although its mild gamey taste reveals its wild origins, its flesh is slightly fibrous with a tendency to dryness unless it is cooked very carefully.

For this reason, I prefer to buy a whole bird and use its leg meat in a pâté, its carcass for stock (see page 106) and fillet the breasts into suprêmes with the upper wings attached. I then pan-fry the suprêmes separately, as in the following recipe, ensuring that they remain moist and succulent.

Breast of Guinea Fowl with Lentils

I am indebted for this recipe to the excellent chef Ian McAndrew, whose book On Poultry and Game *remains one of my favourites.*

SERVES 4

15 g/½ oz unsalted butter

2 tsp olive oil

4 guinea fowl suprêmes (see above)

55 g/2 oz smoked bacon, diced

1 onion, chopped

1 carrot, thinly sliced

100 ml/3½ fl oz dry white wine

350 ml/12 fl oz poultry stock (see page 106)

55 g/2 oz split brown lentils, rinsed and drained

1 tomato, skinned, deseeded and diced

1 tbsp chopped fresh thyme leaves

salt and freshly ground black pepper

Melt the butter with the oil in a sauté pan over a medium heat. Season the breasts and pan-fry them skin side down for about 5 minutes, or until they are golden brown. Turn them over and cook the other side in the same way. Using a slotted spoon, transfer them to a warmed serving dish and keep warm.

Strain off all but 1 teaspoon of the fat from the pan. Heat this over a medium heat and sauté the bacon in it for 2–3 minutes. Stir in the onion and carrot and cook for 4–5 minutes, or until golden brown.

Pour in the white wine, turn up the heat and leave to simmer until it has reduced by half. Then add the poultry stock, bring to the boil and stir in the lentils. Reduce the heat, cover and simmer for 15 minutes or until tender, adding the tomato and thyme leaves after 10 minutes. Adjust the seasoning.

Serve the guinea fowl on a bed of the lentils.

Eggs

Not only are eggs nutritious, as they contain 11% of our recommended daily protein requirement, vitamins A, B and D and minerals such as iron, calcium and iodine, but they are also incredibly versatile as you can boil, poach, bake, scramble or fry them.

CHICKEN EGGS are the most commonly used and they are invaluable in cooking, in areas as diverse as making sauces (see Hollandaise Sauce, page 128) and setting and enriching terrines (see Terrine of Lemon Sole with Prawns, page 89). Whipped egg whites are also the most common means of aerating and lightening mixtures (see Soufflé Omelette, page 131).

All commercial eggs must be sold in packs showing their size, class, packing station, packing date and sell-by date. This is actually not as much help as it should be as it does not tell the buyer exactly how old (or fresh) the eggs really are, the method by which they have been produced and, of equal importance, on what the hens have been fed.

The diet of laying hens leaves a lot to be desired; they are usually fed animal protein — sometimes even ground-up chicken waste — along with artificial colourings to ensure that the yolks of their eggs are a sunshine yellow. However, contrary to what you may think, there is absolutely no inherent difference in the flavour of a brown- or white-shelled egg: it is just a question of breed; some hens are born to lay white eggs, others brown.

It is possible to buy 'real' farm or organic eggs directly from a farm or a good health food shop. These will be from hens which are reared extensively and humanely, which are free to scratch around on grass and are fed on a vegetable and cereal diet without antibiotics. If fresh, these should be superb. You may also find the small intensely flavoured PULLET EGGS from sexually immature hens. Instead of buying eggs from modern hybrids which have been developed primarily for their laying efficiency, you might be lucky enough to find eggs from such old-fashioned breeds as the Silky, Maran, Aracuna or Wellsummer hens. These really do taste better.

Of course, chicken's eggs are not the only eggs we eat. During the spring and early summer months you can buy enormous rich and creamy GOOSE EGGS for baking. In recipes one goose egg is the equivalent of about two size-2 hen's eggs. Another late spring treat are GULL EGGS, with their light fishy flavour. Hard-boil them by lowering them into a pan of cold water, bringing them to the boil and then cooking for 3 minutes. Serve with salt spiced with cayenne. DUCK EGGS make excellent omelettes, although as some people are wary of their safety, they must always be thoroughly cooked. TURKEY EGGS are very delicately flavoured and take 15 minutes to hard-boil; whereas tiny speckled QUAIL EGGS cook in a matter of minutes and are superb soft-boiled and tossed into a salad.

... the chicken or the egg?

BATTERY EGGS are from hens with cropped beaks, kept 4–7 in a cage the size of a small portable television set; DEEP-LITTER EGGS are from hens kept at 7 per square metre; BARN or PERCHERY EGGS are from hens kept at 25 per square metre; FREE-RANGE EGGS are from hens kept at 1,000 per hectare/395 per acre with continuous day-time access to runs which are mainly covered with vegetation. In spite of what people believe, there is actually very little to choose between all these different types of egg in terms of quality and taste, so buying free-range eggs is really more a matter of conscience and animal welfare.

Chicken's eggs are graded according to weight in grams: size $1 = 70$ g and over; size $2 =$ between 65 g and 70 g; size $3 =$ between 60 g and 65 g; size $4 =$ between 55 g and 60 g; size $5 =$ between 50 g and 55 g; size $6 =$ between 45 g and 50 g; Size $7 =$ under 45 g. Size 3 is that most commonly used and most recipes employ eggs of this size.

Under EC regulations there are also three quality grades. Only Class A, the highest grade, is available in the shops and these are naturally clean eggs, internally perfect with the shells intact and, as a measure of their freshness, with an air sac not exceeding 6 mm/$\frac{1}{4}$ in deep (the less air an egg contains, the fresher it is). Classes B and C are used principally in the food industry.

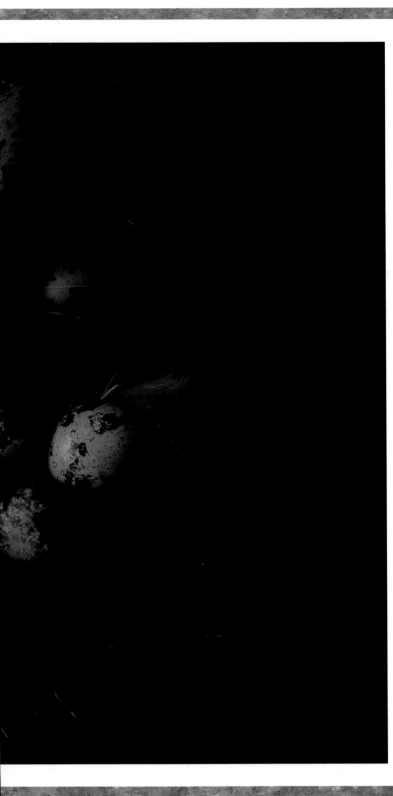

Mirror Eggs

An excellent starter which can also be made with duck eggs, this dish is William Verrall's version of the French classic. Master of the White Hart Inn in Lewes in the first half of the eighteenth century, Verrall had served his apprenticeship under St Clouet, the Duke of Northumberland's renowned French chef.

SERVES 4–6

30 g/1 oz butter
10–12 spring onions, finely chopped
3 tbsp finely chopped fresh parsley
1 tbsp finely chopped fresh tarragon
zest of 1 and juice of 3 oranges
6 eggs
300 ml/½ pt double cream
juice of 2 lemons
salt and freshly ground white pepper

Preheat the oven to 190C/375F/gas5 and generously grease a shallow ovenproof dish with the butter.

Sprinkle the onions, parsley, tarragon and orange zest into the buttered dish and then carefully break the eggs on top.

Mix the cream with the orange and lemon juice, season and pour over the eggs. Bake for about 20 minutes, or until the eggs are just set. Serve immediately.

Eggs range in size and colour
from the huge creamy white goose egg to tiny brown-
speckled quail eggs. Eggs from traditional breeds, such as the speckled dark brown egg
of the Wellsummer hen, look much more interesting
than those of modern hybrid hens.

Basic Hollandaise Sauce

MAKES ABOUT 300 ML/½ PT

6–8 black peppercorns, coarsely crushed
150 ml/¼ pt white wine
100 ml/3½ fl oz white wine vinegar
4 egg yolks
225 g/8 oz unsalted butter, diced
salt and freshly ground black pepper

Put the peppercorns with the wine and vinegar in a saucepan over a moderate heat and bring to the boil. Boil rapidly to reduce the liquid until only about I tablespoon remains.

Meanwhile slowly heat some water in the bottom of a double boiler. If you don't have one, balance a copper, stainless steel or glass bowl over a saucepan half filled with water so it just touches the bottom of the bowl.

Strain the reduction into the bowl to get rid of the peppercorns and whisk in the egg yolks until they are thick and warm, taking care not to let them over-heat or they will start to scramble.

Slowly beat in the butter, one piece at a time, to make a thick smooth sauce. If it should curdle, put a teaspoon of vinegar in a clean bowl and start all over again, beating the curdled mixture into the bowl a drop at a time.

When all the butter has been added, season the sauce lightly. If the taste is a little too sharp add a little more butter. Keep warm in the double boiler, or in the bowl over the saucepan of water, until required.

Variations

1 To make a Maltaise Sauce, add the zest and juice of ½ an orange once all the butter is added.
2 To make a Lemon Hollandaise, add the zest and juice of ½ a lemon once all the butter is added.

3 To make a Mousseline Hollandaise, fold in 4 tablespoons of lightly beaten whipping cream once all the butter is added.
4 To make a Béarnaise Sauce, add I chopped shallot and a couple of sprigs of tarragon to the vinegar while it is being boiled and reduced. Then stir I tablespoon each of chopped tarragon and chervil into the finished sauce.

Basic Sabayon Sauce

Serve this on its own or with fresh fruit, or as a dip with slices of sweet cake.

SERVES 4–6

4 egg yolks
55 g/2 oz caster sugar
200 ml/7 fl oz white wine

In a copper, stainless steel or glass bowl, whisk together the egg yolks and sugar until thick and creamy. Add the wine and carry on whisking until the mixture is light, airy and very frothy.

Balance the bowl over a saucepan half filled with boiling water so it just touches the bottom of the bowl. Whisk the mixture continuously until the sauce thickens to the texture of lightly whipped cream. Serve immediately.

Variations

1 Replace the white wine with Champagne.
2 Replace the white wine with Marsala to make the Italian Zabaglione.

ROULADE WITH ASPARAGUS right.

Roulade with Asparagus

A roulade only works if the eggs are very fresh, otherwise the whites cannot be properly aerated, ie beaten into stiff peaks, and will collapse quickly producing an unfortunate flat roll with a heavy texture, rather than the light fluffiness of a proper roulade.

SERVES 4

4 size-1 eggs, separated
15 g/½ oz butter, melted, plus a little more for greasing
450 g/1 lb fresh asparagus, trimmed
300 ml/½ pt Maltaise Sauce (see opposite)
salt and freshly ground black pepper

Preheat the oven to 200C/400F/gas6.

Whisk the egg yolks until thick, pour in the melted butter and season. Whisk the egg whites in a separate bowl until they form stiff peaks. Then using a metal spoon, carefully fold them into the yolks. Season.

Have ready a Swiss roll pan lined with a piece of baking parchment which has been lightly greased with butter. Spread the mixture into the prepared pan and cook for about 10 minutes, or until just set.

Meanwhile tie the asparagus into a bundle and cook in a pan of lightly salted boiling water, with the tips standing up out of the water, or in a steamer for about 10 minutes, until just tender. Drain and cut the asparagus into 5 cm/2 in pieces and keep these warm.

Make the Maltaise sauce and keep warm.

Remove the roulade from the oven and turn it out on a warm serving plate covered with a damp tea towel. Carefully peel off the parchment and spread the roulade evenly with the Maltaise. Arrange the asparagus in rows running across on top and cover with the remaining sauce. Gently pull up on the corners of one end of the tea towel to start rolling up the roulade so that it conveniently turns over on itself on the serving plate. Serve immediately.

Soufflé Omelette with Sorrel and Crème Fraîche

One of the tips I learned when working in the kitchens of Oswald Mair, the tyrannical chef of the London Hilton, was to beat egg whites in a copper bowl and fold them into a mixture with a metal spoon to ensure that they are light and keep in the air — it does work!

SERVES 2

4 size-1 eggs, separated
30 g/1 oz butter
225 g/8 oz fresh sorrel, trimmed and chopped
small bunch of flat-leaf parsley, finely chopped
small bunch of chervil, finely chopped
2 tbsp crème fraîche
salt and freshly ground black pepper

Preheat the oven to 200C/400F/gas6.

In a bowl, whisk 3 of the egg yolks along with the whites of 2 of the eggs until light and frothy and season. In a separate bowl, whisk the remaining egg whites until they form stiff peaks. Using a metal spoon, carefully fold them into the yolk mixture.

Melt half of the butter and pour it into a shallow ovenproof dish. Swirl it around to coat the bottom, pour in the omelette mixture and bake it for about 10 minutes, or until it is just set.

Meanwhile, melt the remaining butter over a low heat, add the sorrel, parsley and chervil and cook for about 5 minutes, or until soft, stirring occasionally. Remove the pan from the heat, add the crème fraîche and stir in the remaining egg yolk. Season, return the pan to the low heat and cook, stirring constantly, until the mixture thickens. Take care not to let the mixture get too hot or it will scramble.

When the omelette is ready, spread this filling over one half of it and then gently fold over the other half. Serve immediately.

Scrambled Eggs

Scrambled eggs are the ultimate in nursery food. Warm, soft and comforting, they are what I long for whenever I am feeling old, sad or tired. Proper scrambled eggs are meltingly creamy and slowly cooked, although I cannot help thinking that Molly Keane, in her Nursery Cooking, *slightly overdid it when the eggs were 'sighed over for twenty minutes in a bain-marie'.*

SERVES 2

55 g/2 oz unsalted butter
5 eggs
1 tbsp double cream
salt and freshly ground black pepper
2 slices of granary toast, cut into triangles, to serve

In a heavy-based saucepan over a low heat, melt half the butter. Beat the eggs until light and frothy. Cut up the remaining butter into small pieces and stir them into the eggs.

Whisk the mixture into the saucepan and remove from the heat. Carry on whisking while counting slowly to 10, then return the pan to the low heat and, using a wooden spoon, stir the eggs gently until they start to scramble.

The eggs will carry on cooking even when they are no longer in contact with the heat. So, when they look just done, remove them from the heat, immediately stir in the cream and season. This will lower their temperature and stop the cooking. Spoon the eggs over the toast and serve immediately.

SOUFFLÉ OMELETTE WITH SORREL AND CRÈME FRAÎCHE opposite.

The Pastures

According to geography and climate, meat-eating habits vary considerably from country to country. Lush pastures are suited to rearing beef cattle; sheep thrive in harsher conditions; while that invaluable domestic animal, the pig, is to be found in countless areas.

Fresh meat

British meat, beef and lamb in particular, was once renowned throughout the world for its quality and flavour. After the Second World War the government of the day decided that Britain had to be self-sufficient in food and, as a result, food production was heavily subsidized in order to achieve this aim. Consequently, there have been several changes in the methods of rearing and producing meat and, it is fair to say, not all of them have been to the good.

The production of quality produce depends on many factors, such as breed, feed, age, housing conditions, medication, slaughtering, hanging and butchering, and they all affect the eating quality of meat. However, in the switch to intensive farming, when efficiency rather than taste is the motivating factor, the farmers' energies were directed to producing meat at as low a price as possible. Short-cuts have been taken and, as a result, eating quality has been thrown out of the window.

Breeds are selected to mature faster and the animals are fed on concentrates and kept indoors so they do not waste valuable energy by exercising; they are regularly given antibiotics as a preventative, rather than simply curative, means; they are slaughtered as young as 10 months, in stressful conditions; and the carcasses are then hung for a few days only to ensure as little weight loss as possible. It is no wonder that most of today's meat lacks flavour and texture.

However, all is not lost! In response to both the taste and welfare issues, 'alternative' methods of production have recently gained support with the discerning public, producing 'organic' and 'conservation' grade meat. However, as these extensive methods of farming are less cost-effective, it also follows that you may have to pay more for the meat.

There is obviously a demand for this better kind of meat as even the high-street chains of supermarkets and butchers' shops have started to introduce 'greener' or 'kinder' meat. Two or three supermarket chains even sell 'Soil Association Organic' or 'Conservation Grade' meats, which are backed by meaningful standards. The rest have decided to set their own terms of reference, resulting in a proliferation of descriptions, from 'Real' and 'Naturally Produced' to 'Traditionally Reared', which – although appealing to the public – are viewed by many as mere marketing ploys or attempts to climb on the 'green' bandwagon.

What is 'organic' meat?

Organic meat is reared using traditional husbandry techniques at all times, to reflect proper care and concern for animal welfare, and all feedstuffs conform to organic standards: in other words an organic diet to produce an organic animal.

The animals are reared with no restriction on their movement, allowed to develop at a natural pace, only given medication when absolutely necessary and are slaughtered as humanely as possible. Some people do remain sceptical as to whether the meat actually does taste better. However, any animal reared slowly on a cereal and grass diet will develop a fuller flavour; if it is allowed to exercise it must have a better texture, and if slaughtered humanely it will show fewer of the signs of stress that affect the texture of its meat. If the other factors of breed, feed, hanging and butchering are all the same, it follows that the meat will be superior. 'Conservation Grade' follows the same principles except the animals are not fed on an organic diet.

Various breeds, including a creamy beige Charolais, graze on Scottish pastures.

While I do not want to appear to be disparaging about any improvements, I cannot help thinking that better explanations are needed, so that people know exactly what they are being sold. More often than not, butchers will focus on one area, for instance the conditions in which the animal was reared, while totally disregarding what it was fed. There is a good deal of confusion, and until some overall regulations are introduced (possibly by the government), we must all ask very carefully exactly what it is that our extra money is buying.

Beef

For the finest tasting beef, nothing beats pure-bred grass-fed Aberdeen Angus, with Hereford coming a close second. Because of the trend for larger leaner carcasses, however, most of our beef now comes from Continental breeds, such as Charolais, Simmental and Limousin, which are cross-bred with our smaller indigenous cattle.

As with all meat, there are many factors affecting the eating quality of beef. It is particularly important that beef be well hung, as hanging improves the tenderness and allows the flavour to develop and mature. Most retailers are reluctant to hang, because of the inevitable weight loss and the tying up of valuable space and capital. You should, however, insist that your beef has been properly hung for up to about 10 days. It is particularly essential for those highly priced cuts which are cooked by dry heat, such as roasting, grilling or frying; the difference is less marked in cheaper cuts for stewing, boiling or braising.

Although most people think the colour of the flesh should be that of fresh blood, it is not necessarily a sign of good quality. Some of the best beef I have ever bought has been of a much darker hue, a sign that it has been well-hung. Look instead for a firm, slightly moist piece of flesh with a clean aroma and a layer of glossy fat, the colour of which, depending on the breed, can vary from a milky white to a buttery yellow.

For a roast, choose a joint from the rib, fillet or sirloin. Although top side, cut from the inside top of the back leg, is often sold for roasting, I find it is a little dry and is usually better pot-roasted or braised. Shin, from the foreleg, or leg, from the hind leg, are also excellent for braising and stewing, as are the thick and thin flank.

Shop-made mince comes from I know not where, so I generally prefer to buy a piece of lean chuck (usually sold as stewing steak) or steak off-cuts and mince them myself in the food processor.

Steak is still a great favourite; with rump, sirloin, T-bone (from the sirloin), minute (extra thinly cut fillet), or entrecôte (meaning literally 'between the ribs') as the most usual cuts, they can be either grilled or pan-fried and then served with a flavoured butter (see page 54).

To roast beef

Allow 20 minutes per 450 g/I lb plus 20 minutes extra at 200C/400F/gas6, if it is on the bone; or 25 minutes per 450 g/I lb plus 25 minutes extra at the same temperature, if it is off the bone. For rare meat allow 5 minutes less per 450 g/I lb.

For extra flavour you can smear the fat with mustard or roast the beef on a bed of sliced onion and garlic cloves.

Daube of Beef

For this glorious robustly flavoured and slowly cooked dish, it really is a waste of money buying an expensive cut. Shin is a good example of the type of cut which has a great deal of connective tissue running through the meat; this breaks down during long slow cooking to give a rich gelatinous quality. Buy a whole piece, trim away some of the excess fat and cut it into cubes.

Two ideas for adding extra flavour are to place a piece of pork skin, skin side down, on top of the daube while it cooks (which also prevents evaporation), and to stir in a gremolada (traditionally an accompaniment to risotto) at the last moment for extra piquancy.

SERVES 6

5 tbsp olive oil
1.35 k/3 lb shin of beef, cut into 2.5 cm/1 in cubes
225 g/8 oz salt pork or belly of bacon, cubed
2 large onions, sliced
10 garlic cloves, chopped

700 ml/1¼ pt red wine
675 g/1½ lb ripe tomatoes, peeled and chopped
8 g/¼ oz allspice
1 tbsp chopped fresh parsley
1 tbsp chopped fresh thyme
1 tbsp chopped fresh marjoram
large piece of pork skin
115 g/4 oz stoned black olives, halved
salt and freshly ground black pepper

for the gremolada:
3 garlic cloves, finely chopped
grated zest of 2 large oranges
bunch of parsley, finely chopped

In a large flameproof casserole with a tight-fitting lid, heat the oil over a medium heat and lightly brown the beef. If the pan is not large enough to hold the meat in a single layer, brown it in batches. Remove the browned meat from the pan.

In the same casserole, sauté the salt pork or belly of bacon for a couple of minutes, then add the onions and garlic and cook for a further 2–3 minutes. Add the wine, tomatoes, allspice, parsley, thyme and marjoram. Turn up the heat until it just starts to boil.

Turn the heat down to low, return the meat to the casserole, and season. Place the piece of pork skin on top, fat side up. (If you cannot obtain one, a piece of greaseproof paper will do to prevent any evaporation, although it will obviously not give the same rich flavour.) Cover with the lid and simmer very gently for about 2½ hours. Remove the pork skin, stir in the olives and simmer for a further 30 minutes, or until the meat is meltingly tender.

To make the gremolada, mix the garlic with the orange zest and parsley. Just before serving, sprinkle it over the top of the daube.

DAUBE OF BEEF

Boiled Fillet of Beef

Although this may seem an extravagance, boiling a piece of fillet results in a subtle dish that is quite superb. For this recipe, buy a whole piece cut from the long fillet and ask to have it trimmed and tied into a neat joint. Sometimes the butcher will sell you a tail piece cheaply; this is more than acceptable for our purposes.

SERVES 2

1 tbsp olive oil
285 g/10 oz fillet steak (see above)
250 ml/8 fl oz chicken stock (see page 106)
1 carrot, sliced
1 celery stalk, sliced
1 leek, sliced
2 spring onions
6–8 small new potatoes
2–3 black peppercorns
1 tbsp grated fresh horseradish
5 tbsp double cream
salt and freshly ground black pepper

In a sauté pan which has a tight-fitting lid, heat the olive oil over a high heat. Season the meat and seal it in the oil for a couple of minutes.

Pour in the chicken stock and add the carrot, celery, leek, spring onions, potatoes, peppercorns and a small pinch of salt. Turn down the heat, cover the pan and simmer for about 10–12 minutes, or until the meat is tender. Using a slotted spoon, transfer the meat and vegetables to a serving dish and keep warm.

To make the sauce, strain 100 ml/3½ fl oz of the stock into a separate pan and bring it to the boil. Boil it rapidly to reduce it by half. Stir in the horseradish and cream, turn down the heat and simmer for 2–3 minutes. Adjust the seasoning.

Serve the beef, cut into thin slices, surrounded by the vegetables, with the sauce poured over the top.

Oxtail with Grapes

This is one of my favourite Elizabeth David recipes. It is one she found cooked by the wine growers in France when the grapes are ripe during the vendange. I particularly love to cook it in October, when the rich sweet juicy muscat grapes are in season, as they give the sauce great body.

A meaty oxtail will serve 3 or 4 people, and can either be bought ready-trimmed or whole, in which case ask your butcher to cut it into slices. The ideal thickness for these slices is about 5 cm/2 in, as you can then simmer them slowly for ages to extract all the flavour without worrying about the meat becoming tough or dry.

SERVES 6–8

115 g/4 oz salt pork or unsmoked bacon, cubed
2 large onions, chopped
4 large carrots, diced
2 garlic cloves, crushed
2 oxtails, each weighing 1.35–1.8 k/3–4 lb, cut into
5 cm/2 in pieces
2 bay leaves
sprig of parsley
sprig of thyme
pinch of mace
900 g/2 lb white grapes
sea salt and freshly ground black pepper

Preheat the oven to 150C/300F/gas2.

Put the pork or bacon, onions, carrots and garlic in a large flameproof casserole which has a tight-fitting lid. Cook very gently over a low heat, without adding any oil, for about 10 minutes, or until the fat starts to run. Season the meat, add it to the casserole with the herbs, tied together in a bunch, and the mace. Cover and simmer for 20 minutes.

Pick the grapes off their stalks, lightly crush them in a bowl and add them to the casserole along with any of their juice. Line the lid of the casserole with a sheet of greaseproof paper and bake in the preheated oven for a minimum of 3½ hours, or until the meat is so soft and tender that it is falling off the bones.

Using a slotted spoon, transfer the oxtail and some of the bacon to a serving dish and keep warm. Whizz the sauce in a food processor until smooth, then pass it through a sieve to get rid of the grape pips. Season and pour the sauce over the oxtail.

If you prefer a lighter sauce, leave the oxtail to cool in the gravy overnight, skim off the fat, then whizz the grape sauce and thoroughly reheat the whole dish before serving.

Grilled Calves' Liver Kebabs with Lettuce Sauce

One advantage of buying a piece of the more expensive calves' liver is that it is easier to see exactly how fresh it is. It should be firm and a deep reddish-brown in colour, with a slight sheen and an unmottled surface. When cutting the slices, use a very sharp knife and cut against the grain to make sure it will not shrink during cooking.

SERVES 4

675 g/1½ lb piece of calves' liver
small bunch of marjoram, finely chopped
1 garlic clove, finely chopped
juice of ½ lemon
225 g/8 oz slices of smoked back bacon, rinds removed
4 tbsp olive oil
55 g/2 oz unsalted butter
small bunch of spring onions, chopped
1 small Cos lettuce, chopped
2 tbsp crème fraîche
sea salt and freshly ground black pepper

Preheat the grill.

Trim the calves' liver to remove any sinew or connective tissue and, using a sharp knife, cut it into pieces about 2.5 cm/1 in wide and 6 mm/¼ in thick. Mix the liver in a bowl with the marjoram, garlic and lemon juice, season and leave to stand for about 10 minutes, turning it over occasionally.

Meanwhile, cut the bacon into pieces the same size as the liver. Have ready 8 metal skewers and thread the liver and bacon alternately on the skewers. Pour the oil into a flat dish and roll the skewers in it.

Grill the kebabs for about 5 minutes, longer if you do not like liver pink, turning them over once and brushing them lightly with the oil during cooking.

Meanwhile, melt the butter in a sauté pan over a low heat and sweat the spring onions in it for 2–3 minutes. Add the lettuce and stir until coated in the butter, cover the pan and simmer for a further 5–7 minutes, or until the lettuce has softened.

Transfer the kebabs to a warm serving dish and tip the cooking juices from the bottom of the grill pan into the lettuce. Put this into a food processor and whizz until smooth. With the machine still running, pour in the crème fraîche. Season and serve with the kebabs.

Lamb

Strictly speaking, the description lamb should only be used if the animal was born on or after January 1st of any given year; if it has survived a winter it should be called HOGGET.

It does not follow that hogget is inferior; with its firm flesh and well-developed full flavour, it can be a joy to eat. However, its eating qualities are quite different from the soft, milky subtle flavour of new-season lamb, and I get annoyed when anyone tries to palm me of with hogget when I really want lamb.

Age, feed and breed all make a difference to the taste of lamb. MILK-FED LAMBS, taken from the ewe while still suckling, have pale-coloured soft and buttery flesh with a gentle flavour not unlike a creamy rice pudding. They are rarely sold this young in Britain (apparently such a small animal does not qualify for any subsidy), but in France and Spain they are rightly considered a treat. MUTTON, on the other hand, is about two years old and has dark dense flesh with a strong, almost cloying, flavour which can be so rich that it needs a sharp vinegar- or wine-based sauce to set it off.

Most of our British lamb is fed on grass, which gives it a well-rounded flavour. Sometimes, however, you can buy Shetland lamb which has a diet consisting predominantly of heather, or Romney Marsh lamb which graze on fields occasionally flooded by the sea, giving them a more pronounced taste. My favourite lamb of all is the *pré-salé*, or salt-marsh lamb of Normandy and Brittany. These animals graze right down to the sea and eat copious amounts of seaweed, resulting in a gently iodized meat.

Hardy breeds of sheep can survive harsh winter conditions.

At one time each region had its own breed of sheep specifically adapted to its local environment. The best-known included the earthy-flavoured Portland lamb, which grazed on the rich chalk- and clay-based soil of Dorset, and the goat-like Soay of isolated Scottish island communities, which had a gamey flavour. These breeds were never 'improved' during the agricultural revolution of the mid-eighteenth century, and have remained lean, but with a good covering of internal fat to protect them during the harsh winter months, and with their own individual flavours. Unlike our modern cross-breeds, they are smaller and slower to fatten. This was no doubt the reason they were dropped by most farmers, as they are not a commercial proposition, although a small speciality market for them is beginning to develop.

All lamb is naturally and extensively farmed. However, certain standards have been set, namely 'organic' and 'conservation grade', which prohibit or control the application of pesticides and fertilizers on the pastures and medical treatment for the animals. These grades of lamb may cost more, but the argument in their favour is that you are buying a purer product.

British lamb has become leaner over the years and the most popular cuts should have a thin layer of clean whitish fat. The colour of the meat can range from a pearly pink to a deeper red as the season progresses. The texture, however, should be fine-grained, with a good sharp finish. Whether or not lamb should be hung for any significant length of time is a subject of much opinionated debate. Julia Child, in her useful and explicit *Mastering the Art of French Cooking*, recommends that you wrap a leg of lamb in brown paper and keep it in the refrigerator for about 3–4 days to age it. On following her instructions, I found I had a robustly flavoured but meltingly tender piece of meat. On reflection it might perhaps have been a good idea to have asked the butcher first how long he had allowed the meat to mature.

Almost every cut of lamb can be roasted: the leg, saddle, rack and crown are the prime cuts, but a shoulder or even the fattier breast are fine.

For braising and stewing, use a boned shoulder, middle neck, scrag or shank, cut from the shoulder. Noisettes prepared from the saddle or best end are superb pan-fried, whereas the various types of chops, chump, best or middle end of neck, loin or chine, may be grilled as well as pan-fried.

To roast lamb

If you prefer lamb cooked right through, allow 25 minutes per 450 g/I lb in an oven preheated to 180C/350F/gas4, plus an extra 20 minutes. If you prefer the meat still *very* pink, allow 15 minutes per 450 g/I lb at the same temperature and then allow it to rest out of the oven for about 15 minutes before carving.

A good way of cooking a large leg is to put it in a very hot oven (220C/425F/gas7) for the first 10 minutes to sear the meat, then turn down the oven to 180C/350F/gas4 and allow 12 minutes per 450 g/I lb; the meat will then be crisp on the outside, but still succulent and pink inside.

For extra flavour, insert slivers of garlic into the meat or sprinkle it with rosemary.

Lamb Shanks with Flageolets and Garlic

Although most butchers ignore the cut, if pressed they will cut you a whole shank, the lower section of the foreleg, as a small joint trimmed on the bone, and it is excellent for slow braising. Depending on the size of the lamb, a shank can be really small and can weigh anything from 225 g/8 oz to 450 g/1 lb, enough to feed 2 generously; any larger than that and the meat may be a little stringy.

A baby shank is just right for one person and is the size I like to buy as it looks so good on the plate. If your butcher will not oblige, try this recipe with a lean boned and rolled shoulder instead, but allow about 20 minutes per 450 g/1 lb cooking time.

SERVES 4

2 tbsp olive oil
4 small lamb shanks, each weighing about 225 g/8 oz
4 garlic cloves, thinly sliced
1 onion, finely chopped
350 g/12 oz flageolet beans, soaked for 6–8 hours in water
400 g/14 oz canned Italian plum tomatoes
pinch of sugar
1 tbsp tomato paste
150 ml/¼ pint red wine
bunch of parsley, chopped
salt and freshly ground black pepper

In a large flameproof casserole with a tight-fitting lid, heat the olive oil over a medium heat. Using a sharp knife, cut about 3 or 4 thin slits in each shank and stuff them with a slice of garlic. Then season the shanks and brown them in the oil to seal them. Remove them from the casserole.

Add the onion and remaining garlic to the casserole and sauté for about 5 minutes, or until soft. Drain the beans, add them to the casserole and stir until they are coated with the oil. Add the canned tomatoes along with their juice, breaking them down with a wooden spoon. Stir in the sugar, tomato paste and red wine. Return the shanks to the pan, cover and simmer for about anything from 1 to 2 hours, or until the meat and beans are tender.

Stir in the parsley at the last moment, and serve with a Béarnaise Sauce (see page 128).

Grazing on rich grass gives lamb a well-rounded flavour left.
LAMB SHANKS WITH FLAGEOLETS AND GARLIC right.

Lambs' Kidneys with Mustard Sauce

For the freshest possible kidneys, buy them still in the suet, their protective coat of fat, rather than loose. A simple, if rather rich, way of cooking these is to split them in half, open them up and roast them still in their suet in an oven preheated to 190C/375F/gas 5 for about 25 minutes.

Lambs' kidneys have a good rounded flavour, neither too strong nor too insipid, and fresh ones are a rich brown colour, faintly tinged with red, quite soft to the touch and with a mild smell. All you need do to prepare them is to cut through the suet, peel it off, peel off the membrane from the kidneys, cut them in half and trim away their central core.

SERVES 4

100 g/3½ oz butter
8 lambs' kidneys, each weighing about 85 g/3 oz, halved and
trimmed (see above)
2 shallots, finely chopped
150 ml/¼ pt medium or dry white wine
2 tbsp grainy mustard
1 tsp lemon juice
3 tbsp finely chopped fresh parsley
salt and freshly ground black pepper

Preheat the oven to 160C/325F/gas3.

In a heavy-based ovenproof dish, melt 55 g/2 oz of the butter over a medium heat and sauté the kidneys in it gently for about 2 minutes on either side.

Put the pan in the preheated oven and roast for a further 5 minutes and then remove from the oven. Using a slotted spoon, transfer the kidneys to a warm dish and keep warm.

LAMBS' KIDNEYS WITH MUSTARD SAUCE

Sauté the shallots in the same pan over a medium heat for about 3–5 minutes, or until just soft. Pour in the wine, scraping the bottom of the pan to loosen the sediment, and turn up the heat. Boil rapidly to reduce the liquid by about two-thirds.

Meanwhile, mix the mustard in a bowl with the remaining butter and lemon juice. Remove the pan from the heat and whisk in this mixture, a little at a time, to make a creamy sauce. Stir in the parsley, season and pour the sauce over the kidneys.

Navarin of Lamb

One of the joys of spring is a navarin, *the sophisticated French version of our hot-pot. It must be made with new-season lamb, using any lean and trimmed cut from the shoulder, neck or loin — although I find small boned chump chops look very attractive. The spring vegetables should also be small, tender and sweet, assuring a succulent lamb stew which will remind you that all the good things of summer are just around the corner.*

SERVES 4–6

2 tbsp olive oil
900 g/2 lb boned lamb chump chops
1 onion, sliced
pinch of sugar
45 g/1½ oz flour
575 ml/1 pt vegetable stock (see page 12)
225 g/8 oz canned chopped tomatoes
2 garlic cloves, chopped
bay leaf
sprig of rosemary
225 g/8 oz baby new potatoes
225 g/8 oz pickling onions
225 g/8 oz baby turnips
225 g/8 oz baby carrots

225 g/8 oz shelled fresh green peas
225 g/8 oz shelled fresh young broad beans
small bunch of curly parsley, chopped
sea salt and freshly ground black pepper

In a large heavy-based flameproof casserole with a tight-fitting lid, heat the olive oil over a medium heat. Brown the chops in it for about 3–4 minutes on each side to seal them. Remove them from the casserole.

Add the onion to the pan and sauté it for about 6–8 minutes, or until soft. Stir in the sugar and flour and cook for a further minute or two, just to brown the flour slightly.

Pour in the stock and stir until smooth. Return the meat to the pan, season and add the tomatoes, garlic, bay leaf and rosemary. Cover with the lid lined with a sheet of greaseproof paper, turn down the heat to low and simmer for about 20 minutes. Add the potatoes, onions and turnips, cover and simmer for another 20 minutes. Add the carrots and cook for a further 10 minutes. Finally add the peas and broad beans and cook for about 5–7 minutes, or until these are tender.

If the sauce looks a little thin, turn up the heat to medium and leave the lid off the pan for the last few minutes. Adjust the seasoning and serve sprinkled with the parsley.

Pork

The pig is the most efficient of our domesticated animals, as not one jot of it goes to waste – even its bristles are used for brushes. Traditionally pigs were reared on farms where cheese was made, as they were fed on whey, a by-product of cheesemaking, resulting in a meat with a creamy, pearly finish. The breeds were the good old-fashioned ones (now incidentally classified as 'Rare Breeds'), such as Gloucester Old Spot, Saddleback or Tamworth Red, which have long since been dropped as they were not deemed commercial propositions, being too slow-growing and with too much fat for our modern appetites.

Most of the pork we eat nowadays comes from the modern Landrace, Large White or Duroc pure breeds or cross breeds. These have been developed for maximum growth with minimum fat in the shortest possible time, and are well suited to intensive rearing in pig units. Slaughtered while still young, between 4–5 months, their flesh is a pale pink, firm and smooth, and their thin layer of fat is a creamy white.

However, this meat lacks any distinctive flavour. Partly as a result of this bland taste and partly because of the consumers' interest in animal welfare, the supermarkets have taken the plunge and launched

various grades which are marketed under such labels as 'Traditionally Reared', 'Free-Range', 'Outdoor Housed' or 'Range Reared'. In other words, they are reverting to the old-fashioned methods, and even experimenting with cross breeding with some of the rare breeds, or even wild boars, for a rich, strongly flavoured meat.

There is no denying that this pork makes better eating, as the conditions under which the pigs live – their habitat, stress quotient and diet – are much improved. Their diet is more varied and they are allowed to develop at a slower rate, so their meat has a more complex, fuller flavour. Also, as they are loose-housed or kept outdoors in arks, they are able to exercise and rummage and this means that their meat also has a firmer texture.

However, it must be pointed out that these specifications are not always clearly defined, with the result that not everything in the farmyard is as rosy as it might at first seem. The terms used can be a little misleading, for instance once the pigs are weaned under the improved conditions, they are sometimes put back into indoor stalls for fattening. It is a good idea to check how the pork has been reared and how it has been fed. It is, for instance, still also legal to feed them antibiotics as a means of preventative medication and as a growth promoter.

When shopping, look for meat which is finely grained, pale in colour without any blemishes and neither too dry nor too wet. Never keep pork too long, as even under refrigeration it can go rancid.

The cut you choose will depend on how you want to cook the meat. For roasting, if you are expecting large numbers a whole leg weighing more than 4.5 k/10 lb should serve your purposes; usually it is cut into two smaller joints, the fillet and knuckle ends. Incidentally, the fillet end, from the top of the leg, is also sold cut into steaks, and these are excellent fried, grilled or braised. The loin also roasts well, either on or off the bone, but always ask the butcher to saw the chine (half backbone) for easier carving.

The leanest chops are from the fore or hind loin, often sold with the kidney, or chump chops from between the leg and loin. Spare rib chops from the neck end of the shoulder, although more heavily marbled with fat, are also a good buy. For pan-frying, médaillons cut from the tenderloin or escalopes from leg or chump are best. The shoulder and hand and spring are excellent cuts for slow braising, the belly is added to pâtés or turned into sausages and the bones are sold as Chinese spare ribs.

However you cook pork, do not use too fierce a heat as this makes it tough and fibrous. Remember always to cook pork right through as rare pork, unlike underdone lamb or beef, is rather unpleasant.

To roast pork

Roast pork in an oven preheated to 180C/350F/gas4, allowing 30 minutes per 450 g/1 lb, plus an extra 30 minutes. For crackling, score the skin with a knife, rub it with salt and then roast at 200C/400F/gas6 for the first 20 minutes of the cooking time.

Try cooking pork joints over a layer of sliced potatoes interleaved with sprigs of fresh thyme.

Braised Pork with Wild Mushrooms and Juniper Berries

Although some butchers do sell 'stewing pork' for slow braises or stews, I prefer to buy a whole piece and then cut it. Use one of the cheaper cuts from the forequarter, such as shoulder, blade or hand and spring. This way I know exactly what I am buying and how fresh the meat is. I can also trim off some of the excess fat when I am cutting the meat into cubes.

Surprisingly, you can often pick up a packet of dried wild mushrooms reasonably cheaply from a delicatessen. Porcini (see page 178) are a good buy as they hold together well in a stew and infuse the gravy with their rich flavour. Remember to soak them first.

SERVES 4

30 g/1 oz dried wild mushrooms
5 tbsp olive oil
1 small onion, chopped
675 g/1½ lb shoulder of pork, cut into 2.5 cm/1 in cubes
100 ml/3½ fl oz dry white wine
2 tbsp white wine vinegar
3 anchovy fillets, drained and chopped
1 tsp finely chopped fresh marjoram
bay leaf
20 juniper berries, crushed
salt and freshly ground black pepper

Soak the mushrooms for 30 minutes in 350 ml/12 fl oz of lukewarm water. Using a slotted spoon, lift them out of the water. As they can sometimes be full of grit, rinse them thoroughly under cold running water, drain and roughly chop them. Leave the soaking water to settle, so any grit sinks to the bottom, then strain it through a lined sieve and reserve.

In a flameproof casserole with a tight-fitting lid, heat the olive oil over a medium heat and soften the onion in it. Add the pork, turn up the heat slightly and brown the meat to seal it. Pour in the wine and vinegar and raise the heat again slightly. Cook for a minute or two, stirring constantly. Stir in the mushrooms, the water in which they have been soaked, the anchovies, marjoram, bay leaf and crushed juniper berries. Season with plenty of black pepper, but go easy with the salt as the anchovies are quite salty.

Turn the heat down to low, cover the pan with the lid lined with a sheet of greaseproof paper and simmer for 1½ to 2 hours, or until the meat is tender.

Roast Loin of Pork Studded with Ham

This Spanish recipe uses ham from Serrano in the Sierra Nevada mountains, a mild dry-cured and air-dried ham. You can also use the similarly flavoured Italian Parma ham instead.

Choose a lean loin, either middle or long loin from the rear, and ask the butcher to bone, skin and trim the fat. Keep the bones, as they make a useful rack for setting the meat on during cooking.

SERVES 6

1 k/2¼ lb boned and skinned loin of pork, bones reserved
55 g/2 oz raw cured ham, cut into thin strips
24 baby onions
200 ml/7 fl oz dry sherry
3 tbsp chicken stock (see page 106)
150 ml/¼ pt double cream
salt and freshly ground black pepper

Preheat the oven to 190C/375F/gas5.

Lay the loin of pork out flat, fat side downwards. Using a larding needle, lard the meat with the strips of ham until it is studded with them. Rub in a little ground pepper, roll up the meat so the fat faces outwards and tie it securely with string.

Arrange the bones in a roasting pan so they form a rack, place the pork on top, scatter the onions around it and season. Pour over 150 ml/¼ pt of the sherry and all the stock. Roast in the preheated oven, basting occasionally, for about 1 hour. Then raise the oven temperature to 200C/400F/gas6 and cook for a further 15 minutes to allow the onions to caramelize.

Using a slotted spoon, transfer the meat and onions to a warm serving dish and leave it to rest. Discard the bones from the pan and most of the fat, reserving about 1 tablespoon. Heat the pan over a medium heat, scrape up the sediment from the bottom with a wooden spoon, taking care that the juices do not burn.

Pour in the remaining sherry, turn up the heat and stir to deglaze the pan. Add the cream, simmer for a few minutes, then strain through a sieve and season. Serve the meat, carved in thin slices, with the onions and serve the sauce separately.

A Gloucester Old Spot pig in a traditional pen below.
ROAST LOIN OF PORK STUDDED WITH HAM right.

Sausages

Unlike the rest of Europe, with its cured sausages like salami, *chorizo* and *rohwurst*, the British sausage is made with fresh meat, primarily pork but sometimes beef or lamb or a mixture of all three.

There is no excuse for the standard of our average sausages: they are bland and boring; plumped up with gristle, binding (a euphemism for cereal or rusks), any number of allowed colourings, preservatives, emulsifiers and flavourings; and stuffed, more often than not, into plastic casings. Even the meat content of most sausages is suspect. British regulations state that a sausage must be made from at least 50% meat. However, somewhat bizarrely, over half of this can be fat, leaving a mere 22.5% for lean meat. As if this was not bad enough, 'lean meat' does not necessarily mean what you or I would imagine – it can include heart, kidney, tongue, tail or head meat.

Some good butchers do make their own sausages which are free of preservatives and have a good high meat content and these are well worth seeking out.

If you neither like nor trust shop-bought sausages and want to eat sausages without too much fat, the alternative is to make your own. This really is remarkably easy, provided you do not bother with the fiddly and hard part of stuffing them into skins or searching out caul fat in which to wrap them. How, you are probably wondering, do they hold together? Very simply, the meat is chopped in a food processor, kneaded lightly with the hands and rolled into sausage shapes which are wrapped in kitchen foil and lightly poached before being grilled or fried.

Homemade Sausages

Sausages are traditionally made from the cheaper cuts, and I use either shoulder or lean thin end of belly of pork. The proportions I work to are 4 to 1: so for every 115 g/4 oz of lean meat, I add 30 g/1 oz of flair, or hard-back fat, which is available from better butchers. This gives a good juicy mixture and allows for some of the fat to boil away whilst the sausages are simmering. (This is inevitable, as no matter how tightly you wrap the sausages some of the water will seep in.) If you think the mixture is still too fatty, just cut down on the amount of added fat.

MAKES 6 SAUSAGES

450 g/1 lb lean belly or shoulder of pork
115 g/4 oz hard-back fat
1 garlic clove
bunch of flat-leaf parsley
large pinch of sea salt
small pinch of ground cloves
small pinch of ground ginger
small pinch of ground nutmeg
30 g/1 oz fresh breadcrumbs
freshly ground black pepper

Roughly cut the pork and fat into pieces of a size that the food processor can handle. Put them in the food processor with the garlic, parsley, sea salt, cloves, ginger, nutmeg, breadcrumbs and a generous amount of black pepper. Whizz until all the ingredients are mixed together and reduced to the texture of reasonably coarse breadcrumbs. You do not want to over-process the meat or this will make the sausages far too dense; on the other hand, if you do not process them enough, they will not hold together.

Tip the meat out into a bowl and divide it into 6 portions, each weighing 85–115 g/3–4 oz. Using the fingers, knead the mixture lightly to make sure it sticks together, then roll it out between the palms into a sausage shape about 10 cm/4 in long. Wrap each sausage in a piece of foil and secure each end by twisting the foil tightly and tying it with string.

Have ready a large saucepan filled with gently simmering water, drop in the sausages and simmer

them for about 10 minutes. Using a slotted spoon, lift them out and put them in a colander. As soon as they are cool enough to handle, unwrap them and leave them to drain.

Finish by browning them: either by brushing them lightly with olive oil and grilling them under a preheated grill, or by frying them in a little olive oil or butter over a moderate heat. Serve with Onion Marmalade (see page 23).

HOMEMADE SAUSAGES, WITH COARSE-GRAIN MUSTARD (SEE PAGE 159) AND ONION MARMALADE (SEE PAGE 23).

Variations

1 Add a shallot and a teaspoon of tomato paste to the mixture in the food processor.

2 Replace the cloves and ginger with one teaspoon of fennel seeds.

3 Replace the parsley, nutmeg and cloves with 30 g/ 1 oz of shelled pistachio nuts.

Gammon, Ham and Bacon

As a result of the butchery trade itself employing various names for the same cuts, a fair amount of confusion exists about the definitions and differences between gammon, ham and bacon.

The first thing to remember is that they are all cured pork meat, either smoked or left green (unsmoked). Originally gammon meant the cured foreleg, although it has also come to include the cut sliced from the top of the ham. Ham is the cured hind leg and bacon comes from the bits left in between, ie the back, sides and belly of the pig.

Ham

A good ham is one of the great British delicacies: subtle and glorious, well balanced with a yielding texture but a biting edge. Producing a quality ham demands great skill as there are many stages and factors involved, all of which will affect its final taste and texture.

First you must start with a well-reared, firm-textured pig with well-developed hind legs. Two styles of curing are used: dry-salting and brining. The former is the old-fashioned way of rubbing salt mixed with saltpetre and dry flavourings into a ham and curing it for weeks, sometimes even months. Brining is a more modern method in which the ham is immersed

in (but not injected with, as with some sorts of bacon) a wet cure, usually a salt solution, resulting in a milder ham. To confuse the issue, however, some hams are even cured using a mixture of both techniques: dry-cured for a few days and then wet-cured or pickled for a longer period.

There are several traditional cured hams and the better-known ones include: Bradenham ham and Suffolk ham, both cured in molasses; dry-salted York ham; Wiltshire ham which is cured in sweet pickle; Devonshire ham which is cured in treacle, often with added vinegar; and Cumbrian ham, which is briefly dry-salted and then cured in an ale-flavoured pickle.

Hams may also be smoked, and this greatly affects both their taste and texture. Sometimes smoking does no more than set and deepen the cure; it may, however, add a completely new dimension of taste, a mustiness of mellow meat tinged with a rich woody haze.

Finally, the maturation or ageing process for hams can last anything from days to years. Maturing hams is like ripening cheese, an expert can tell by touch and smell when they are ready. Italian Parma hams or Spanish Serrano hams are left unsmoked and then air-dried. Our damp climate explains why we have so few air-dried hams; most British hams are smoked then hung, preferably in a dry atmosphere, or buried in sawdust. They usually require cooking before eating.

When choosing a whole ham, look for a well-rounded shape with plenty of meat and an even, but not too thick, layer of fat. The colour of the flesh will depend on the cure, and can vary from a dusky rose-pink to a deep burnt brown. If buying cooked ham in slices, avoid those nasty packets of slimy, rubbery meat; you will probably get a better deal buying it sliced from a whole ham on the bone, even if you may have to pay more.

Air-drying Parma hams left. *Slices of British and Continental cured hams* right.

To boil a ham

Depending on its cure, you may first need to soak the ham overnight to remove some of the saltiness; check first with your supplier.

To cook it, simply place the ham in a ham kettle or large preserving pan and cover it with enough water so that it is well and truly submerged. Add an onion studded with a couple of cloves, a couple of carrots, a handful of parsley stalks, a bay leaf and a few peppercorns and slowly bring it to the boil. Once it has started bubbling, leave it to simmer gently for about 1 hour, then turn off the heat and leave it in the pan until the liquid is quite cold. As it continues cooking in its own liquid as it cools, no matter the size of the ham, provided it is well covered with water, it will be cooked through while remaining moist and succulent. All you then need to do is to skin it with a sharp knife, trim the fat to an even layer, and then glaze and finish it as described in Ham in a Huff (see overleaf).

Jambon Persillé

For this recipe, either buy the knuckle end of the gammon or prime hock or gammon slipper. If you buy it on the bone, allow extra for the weight of the bone and make sure you skin it before cooking.

As jambon persillé should have quite a meaty — but not too overpowering — flavour, it is a good idea to start off by boiling the joint, throwing away the water and starting again. This way you are certain of getting rid of some of the saltiness.

If you do not have a terrine or pie dish, you can always make this in a bowl. The only disadvantage to this is that you will not be able to cut it into neat rectangular slices for serving. I dare say, if it tastes as good as it should, no one will mind.

JAMBON PERSILLÉ left.

SERVES 8

675 g/1½ lb gammon (see above)
11 black peppercorns
2 bay leaves
1 calf's foot
1 small knuckle of veal
few sprigs of chervil
few sprigs of tarragon
few sprigs of thyme
few sprigs of parsley
450 ml/¾ pt dry white wine
2 tsp white wine vinegar
large bunch of curly parsley, finely chopped

Put the gammon in a deep saucepan, add just enough water to cover and bring to the boil over a medium heat. Just as the water starts to bubble, remove the pan from the heat, pour off the water and start again. This time add 3 peppercorns and one of the bay leaves and leave the ham to simmer gently for 25 minutes.

Lift the gammon out of the water and, when it is cool enough to handle, trim away the fat and cut the meat into sizable chunks.

Meanwhile, in a clean saucepan, put the calf's foot, knuckle of veal, the herbs tied together in a bunch and the remaining bay leaf and peppercorns along with about 1.1 1/2 pt of water. Bring to the boil over a low heat, skimming off the fat as it rises. Cover and simmer gently for about 1½ hours, then pour in the wine, add the gammon meat and simmer for a further 30 minutes, or until the meat is very soft.

Using a slotted spoon, transfer the gammon to a terrine, pie dish or large bowl and flake it with a fork. Strain the liquid into a bowl through a strainer lined with muslin. Add the vinegar and leave it to set slightly, then stir in the parsley and pour it over the ham. Leave it overnight in a cold place to set and serve turned out on a serving dish and cut into slices.

Ham in a Huff

The most satisfactory way of baking a ham is first to wrap it up in a huff, or flour and water paste, as this seals in all the juices and stops the ham from drying out.

SERVES 20

1.35 k/3 lb plain flour
5.5–6.5 k/12–14 lb ham
about 30 cloves

for the glaze:
1 tbsp runny honey
zest and juice of 2 lemons
5 tbsp fine-cut marmalade
1 tbsp whisky
1 tsp smooth mustard

Preheat the oven 180C/350F/gas4.

Mix the flour in a bowl with about 850 ml/1½ pt water to make a stiff paste, turn it out on a flat surface and roll it into a rectangle large enough to enclose the ham. Wrap it around the ham, pinching the edges together tightly and sealing them with a little water.

Bake the ham in the preheated oven, allowing about 25 minutes per 450 g/1 lb. Remove the ham from the oven and leave it to cool for about 15 minutes, otherwise you may be scalded by the steam when you break the huff. Break the huff with a sharp knife, lift out the ham and leave to cool for a further 15 minutes.

Peel off the skin (it will usually just pull away easily while it is still warm). Trim the fat to a layer about 1 cm/½ in thick. Using a sharp knife, score the fat across into a diamond lattice pattern and stud the centre of each diamond with a clove.

Turn up the oven to 190C/375F/gas5.

To make the glaze, heat the honey with the lemon zest in a saucepan over a medium heat. Stir in the marmalade, lemon juice and whisky, then beat in the mustard and leave it to cook for about 2–3 minutes until it just starts to bubble.

Remove the saucepan from the heat and, using a pastry brush, paint the ham all over with the glaze. Roast for 30 minutes to set the glaze. If there is any glaze left over, brush the ham with it occasionally while it is roasting.

If you are serving the ham hot, leave it to rest for about 15 minutes before carving; otherwise leave it standing on a wire rack to cool.

Bacon

Finding good bacon is not always easy. Like a ham, it can either be dry-cured or brined; but regrettably some of the cheaper bacon, rather than being immersed in brine, is injected or pumped with curing solution to speed up the process. Although this may result in an exceptionally light cure which some people actually prefer, it does cause the bacon to absorb more water ('bulk up' is the technical term). You may, therefore, actually be getting less for your money. When you cook this sort of bacon it splutters and shrinks, leaving a most unattractive tide-mark of scum in the bottom of the pan.

Depending on your taste and on the requirements of the recipe, you can choose between a mild or sweet-cure and smoked and green (unsmoked) bacon. The rashers may be cut from the belly or streak for streaky bacon, which is useful for lining pâté tins, grilling or buying in a whole piece and cutting into lardons (see page 184); leaner back or long back rashers, cut from the back after the streak has been removed, are best for grilling and frying; middle or collar rashers are also useful for grilling, frying or adding flavour to soups and stews.

Ouillade

To make this hearty soup, based on a French recipe, I use a small piece of unsmoked hock and then finish the soup by crumbling in a chunk of Roquefort. Watch out, however, as French bacon tends to be far less salty, so adding a salty cheese to a soup made with British bacon may make it unpalatable. Taste the soup first and leave out the cheese if you are in any doubt.

SERVES 8

1 small hock of unsmoked bacon, weighing about 900 g/2 lb
450 g/1 lb white haricot beans, soaked overnight in water
2 tbsp olive oil
1 large onion, chopped
1 small white cabbage, finely sliced
3 Wilja or other boiling potatoes, sliced
1 turnip, sliced

to finish:
3 garlic cloves, finely chopped
2 tbsp finely chopped fresh parsley
1 small onion, finely chopped
55 g/2 oz Roquefort, or other blue cheese (optional), crumbled
freshly ground black pepper

Put the bacon in a deep saucepan, add about 1.1 1/2 pt water or just enough to cover and bring to the boil over a medium heat. Cover and simmer for about 45 minutes, then remove from the heat and leave the bacon to stand in its liquor.

Meanwhile, drain the beans and put them in a saucepan. Add about 575 ml/1 pt of water and bring to the boil over a medium heat. Cover, simmer for about 35 minutes, or until the beans are tender. Drain, reserving about 5 tablespoons of their liquor.

In another pan, heat the oil over medium heat and sauté the onion and cabbage until soft. Strain about 1.1 1/2 pt of the bacon liquor into the pan, add the potatoes and turnip and simmer for about 15 minutes, or until the vegetables are cooked.

Meanwhile, skin the hock, trim off the fat and chop the bacon into bite-sized chunks. Add these to the soup once the vegetables are cooked, along with the beans and their liquor. Simmer for a further 5 minutes to reheat the beans and meat.

To finish, mix the garlic, parsley and onion together in a bowl and add this to the soup off the heat. Add plenty of black pepper and, if you think it can take it, stir in the cheese, a little at a time just to be on the safe side. Serve immediately.

Fields of mustard plants turn golden in June.

Mustards

COARSE-GRAIN MUSTARD has been made for centuries in Britain by milling or lightly crushing a mixture of white and black mustard seeds and mixing them with vinegar, water, wine or cider and any number of spices and flavourings. Its strength depends on the quantity of white seeds, how finely they are ground (the finer you grind the seeds the stronger the bite), the quality of the vinegar and the blend of spices.

Colman's mustard, synonymous with ENGLISH MUSTARD, is made by a technique supposed to have been invented in 1720 by a Mrs Clements of Durham. She pounded a mixture of white and black seeds very firmly and then sifted the powder to remove the husks.

Her mustard flour became all the rage, because of its smooth texture and fierce flavour. Today Colman's still make their mustard along similar lines.

French mustard is also divided into two similar types. The grainy L'ANCIENNE type of mustard, of which *Moutarde de Meaux* is probably the best known, differs from English coarse-grain mustard in that it is made from a mixture of brown and black mustard seeds and the seeds are soaked first either in verjuice or wine vinegar before being gently crushed. This mixture gives the mustard a more tranquil nose, and the pre-soaking ensures a far creamier texture. DIJON MUSTARD, first produced in the eighteenth century, is a velvety textured, creamy condiment with a subtle aroma and deep beige-brown colour. It is made from a blend of pre-soaked brown and black seeds which are wet-ground, then spun in a drum so as to separate out the husks which are then discarded.

Your choice of mustard will obviously depend on your particular palate and the food with which it is being served. However, a good mustard will always be made with good ingredients. As William Tullberg, English mustard maker extraordinary of Wiltshire Tracklements, says 'it should never up and hit you on the fore-front of your palate; rather it should create a mild sensation that increases in warmth and strength as it goes'.

Making homemade mustards is really very simple. Mustard seed can be bought from health food shops or Chinese and Indian supermarkets. (Never buy seeds sold for sowing, as they have usually been treated with chemicals.) When first made, a mustard tastes rather harsh and needs to be stored in an airtight container for a minimum of two weeks to allow the flavours to mellow.

As well as being condiments, mustards may be used to flavour butters (see page 55), in glazing hams (see page 156) or simply spread over a piece of lamb or beef prior to roasting to give it a pungent crust.

Coarse-grain Mustard

30 g/1 oz white mustard seeds
55 g/2 oz black mustard seeds
1 shallot, finely chopped
100 ml/3½ fl oz white wine vinegar
1 tbsp sea salt

In a glass bowl, cover the mustard seeds with lukewarm water and leave them to soak overnight.

Drain them and crush them lightly in a mortar, then stir in the shallot, wine vinegar, about 4 tablespoons of water and the salt. Mix the ingredients thoroughly and then pot the mixture in an airtight jar. Leave for at least 14 days before use.

Tarragon Mustard

85 g/3oz black mustard seeds
30 g/1 oz yellow mustard seeds
small bunch of tarragon, chopped
100 ml/3½ fl oz dry white wine
1 tbsp white wine vinegar
1 tbsp sea salt

Grind the mustard seeds in a coffee grinder; but remember that the finer you grind them, the fiercer the mustard will be.

Tip the ground seeds into a bowl, stir in 3 tablespoons of water and leave them to stand for about 10 minutes.

Stir in the tarragon, white wine, vinegar and salt, cover the bowl and leave them to stand overnight. The following morning, pot the mixture in an airtight jar. Leave for at least 14 days before use.

Variations

1 For a garlic mustard, replace the tarragon with 1 chopped garlic clove.
2 Replace the white wine with 3 tablespoons of cider vinegar and 3 tablespoons of runny honey.

The Woods and Fields

The woods and fields have long been a source of free bounty for country dwellers. Prized game may have been restricted to a privileged few, but rabbit, hare and pigeon, densely flavoured wild mushrooms, delicious nuts and delicate wild plants have always been free to all.

Game

A hen pheasant in the snow.

All wild animals hunted for sport or food are described as game. It is classified into two types: furred, like venison, rabbit and hare; and feathered, like grouse, pheasant and wild duck.

Most game, with the exception of rabbit, hare and pigeon, is protected by law and can only be shot or culled between certain dates, the rest of the year being close season. In this country, shooting starts as early as

'The Glorious 12th' (August), when those privileged to own – or to have access to – a moor can 'pot' grouse or common snipe.

Often described as the finest of all game birds, the red or Scottish GROUSE lives on the moors of Scotland and the North of England. It feeds on heather and wild berries, which no doubt accounts for its subtle flavour. The larger capercaillie, the Ptarmigan and Black grouse are all members of the same family but their flavour is not quite as fine.

Like all game birds, grouse should be hung: exactly how long is purely a question of taste and how high you like the meat. So when buying, always ask how long it has already been hung. As with all game birds, older specimens should be stewed and casseroled whereas young grouse are best roasted. Allow about 35 minutes at 190C/375F/gas5 for an average-sized bird, and serve with the traditional trimmings of game chips, bread sauce and gravy made from the pan juices.

Britain is particularly rich in game birds; as well as pheasant and partridge there are wild ducks, such as mallard, teal and widgeon, and snipe and woodcock. Until quite recently in our cities, game was the preserve of the rich few and was sold only by licensed game dealers, hanging in serried rows in braces in feather – an unplucked pair of cock and hen birds. This made it easier to tell their sex by their plumage and to judge their age and condition. Nowadays game has become increasingly popular and is stocked oven-ready – plucked and drawn – by several of the supermarket chains as well as by the game dealers. Some birds however, notably snipe and woodcock, are still rarely sold and the only chance you will ever have of eating them is if you know someone who shoots.

With their relatively low fat content, both furred and feathered game make healthy alternatives to farmed meat. The disadvantage is that, for the same reason, they have to be cooked carefully to prevent the flesh from drying out.

Pheasant

The pheasant is the most common of our game birds. Every year countless numbers are bred in captivity and then released into the wild to be shot as game during the season from October 1st to February 1st.

Although the cock bird is far more attractive, with his showy colours and flowing tail feathers, it is the dumpy dull-brown hen bird that makes better eating, with its tender, fine-textured, delicately flavoured flesh. Smaller than a male, it makes between two to three portions, as against three to four from the male. However, how many people you can actually feed from the bird depends on how you divide up the breast and leg meat.

Pheasants must be hung in order to tenderize the flesh and to allow a good flavour to develop. How long you hang them depends both on how high you like the meat and how cold it is, so anything from three to ten days is acceptable. If sold unplucked, it is easier to tell both their sex and age, as young birds have soft pliable beaks and smooth soft legs; as they grow older the males develop longer and more pointed spurs. However, as supermarkets and game dealers now sell both fresh and frozen game plucked and drawn, it is becoming increasingly difficult to know exactly what you are buying. So, if in doubt, try to seek advice from the butcher or poulterer.

At the beginning of the season, when the birds are still tender, pheasants are ideal roasted. An average-sized pheasant needs about 45–60 minutes at 190C/375F/gas4. Remember that like all game birds, they have a tendency to dryness; so either roast them breast down or bard the breast with a couple of rashers of unsmoked bacon. It is also a good idea to pop a knob of butter into their cavity and to baste them regularly during roasting. As the season progresses, the birds get tougher, so they need longer slower cooking and are best braised or casseroled.

Pheasant with Celery

Casseroling is the ideal way of dealing with frozen pheasants or older tougher birds shot later in the season. As winter sets in, pheasants acquire more fat and their sauce can be quite greasy. The way to cope with this is to leave it to stand for a few minutes until the fat rises to the surface, then you can skim the fat off with a spoon. If you then clarify this fat by reheating it gently and straining it through a muslin-lined sieve, you can use it instead of oil or butter for cooking.

To make pheasant stock, or indeed a game stock of any kind, simply follow the recipe for chicken stock (see page 106), using the carcasses or bones of the game in question in place of the chicken.

SERVES 6–8

30 g/1 oz butter
450 g/1 lb unsmoked streaky bacon, chopped
2 pheasants
2 heads of celery, trimmed and sliced
small pinch of celery seeds
300 ml/½ pt port
575 ml/1 pt game or chicken stock (see page 106)
salt and freshly ground pepper

Preheat the oven to 160C/325F/gas3.

In a large heavy-based casserole which has a tight-fitting lid, melt the butter over a medium heat. Add the chopped bacon and sauté until it is golden brown. Using a slotted spoon, remove the bacon from the pan and reserve.

Season the pheasants with salt and pepper and brown them all over in the bacon fat in the same pan.

Meanwhile put the celery in a bowl, pour over enough hot water to cover and leave to stand for about 1 minute to blanch. Using a sieve, strain the celery and refresh it under cold running water.

PHEASANT WITH CELERY

Add the celery to the casserole, along with the bacon and celery seeds. Pour over the port and stock. Cover the pan and cook in the preheated oven for about 1 hour, or until the pheasants are tender.

Using a slotted spoon, transfer the pheasants to a suitable carving board, carve into quarters and keep warm. Strain the contents of the casserole through a sieve into a saucepan, adding any juices from the carved pheasant. Leave the casserole juices to stand for about 5 minutes to allow the fat to separate and rise to the surface, then spoon it off.

Meanwhile, whizz the strained ingredients in the food processor until smooth, adding a little of the juices if necessary. Return this purée to the pan along with the juices and stir together over a low heat to reheat the sauce.

Pour the sauce over the pheasant and serve.

Partridge

With its paler meat, the grey or English partridge is far more highly prized than the coarser fleshed red-legged or French partridge, although sadly it is a much rarer bird. Partridge are in season from September 1st to February 1st, and the best time to eat them is early in the season – up to November. The younger birds should only be hung for a couple of days, otherwise their delicate flavour is lost; older birds benefit from being left several days and then cooked slowly.

Allow one partridge per person and, like pheasant, the young birds are best roasted. An average-sized bird needs between 20–30 minutes at 200C/400F/gas6. Serve with the classic accompaniments of game chips, bread sauce, watercress and a gravy made from its cooking juices. If they come with their livers, use them in a stuffing or rich sauce. Alternatively, lightly fry the livers, spread them on a piece of toast and serve the partridge sitting on top of this.

Salmis of Partridge

A classic salmis is a rather complicated affair: game, usually partridge, woodcock, pheasant or wild duck, is two-thirds roasted and then cooking is finished in a saucepan with truffles. It is finally coated with a demi-glace sauce – a rich brown sauce that is simmered and skimmed for hours – made with the carcass.

This recipe is a version simplified to bring it within the realms of possibility for every competent cook. As partridges are nowadays often sold without their livers, chicken livers are used instead.

SERVES 2

2 young partridges, plus their livers or 85 g/3 oz chicken livers,
trimmed and chopped
45 g/1½ oz unsalted butter
3 tbsp olive oil
2 carrots, finely chopped
2 onions, finely chopped
2 shallots, finely chopped
sprig of thyme
bay leaf
15 g/½ oz flour
300 ml/½ pt game or chicken stock (see page 106)
300 ml/½ pt dry white wine
2 tbsp brandy or Cognac
salt and freshly ground black pepper

Preheat the oven to 200C/400F/gas6.

Using a damp cloth, wipe the partridges all over. Then pat them dry and season with salt and pepper. Melt one-third of the butter and, using a pastry brush, paint the birds all over with it. Put them in a roasting dish and roast in the preheated oven, basting occasionally, for 20–25 minutes or until tender.

Meanwhile, melt the remaining butter with the oil in a sauté pan over a medium to low heat. Add the carrots, onions, shallots, thyme and bay leaf and sauté for about 5 minutes.

Cover and sweat for a further 10 minutes. Stir in the flour and, stirring constantly, cook for a couple of minutes. Then pour in the stock, turn up the heat, bring to the boil and simmer for about 5 minutes.

Remove the partridges from the oven and, using a slotted spoon, transfer them to a suitable carving board. Carve and keep warm. Crush the carcasses by pressing on them firmly with a rolling pin or the flat of a large knife. Strain any juices back into the roasting pan.

Put the roasting pan over a medium heat and stir and scrape the bottom with a wooden spoon. Then pour in the wine, turn up the heat and boil to reduce it by about two-thirds.

Turn down the heat to medium, add the livers and cook for a couple of minutes. Then add the vegetables in their stock along with the crushed carcasses and, stirring continuously, simmer the sauce until it reaches boiling point.

Remove the pan from the heat, pick out the carcasses and bay leaf and pass the sauce through a mouli or a sieve, pressing down firmly to make sure that the livers are pushed through. Pour the sauce back into the pan, turn the heat down to low, add the brandy or Cognac and simmer for a couple of minutes.

Return the meat to the pan, season and simmer for a couple of minutes to reheat and serve.

Wood Pigeon

Unlike other feathered game, there is no close season for the pigeon. The best time to shoot them, however, is when they are at their plumpest and most succulent during the months from May to October when feeding from the crops in the fields. Pigeons should be hung by the legs for a day and, if you like their meat lighter and less pungent, cut at the neck and bled.

The older the bird, the tougher it becomes; so the

best way to cook pigeon is by stewing or braising. You can also bone out the breasts and roast these in an oven preheated to 220C/425F/gas7 for 10 minutes, or pan-fry them in a little oil and butter for a few minutes. Pigeons are so cheap that this is not as extravagant as it sounds. If you do want to roast a whole bird, you should first tenderize it by marinating it overnight in a strong red wine mixed with olive oil, chopped vegetables and a few cloves of garlic. Then cook it in an oven preheated to 200C/400F/gas6 for between 20–30 minutes. Allow one bird for every two people.

SQUABS, which are baby pigeons under four months old, are a much safer bet. Bred commercially, what they lack in flavour they certainly make up for in tenderness. Most squabs are sold dressed and oven-ready and, unless they are particularly large, one squab will feed a single person.

Winter means sparse feeding for woodland birds and animals.

Pigeon in a Hole

Hannah Glasse devised this intriguing way of presenting pigeon. It looks especially spectacular if the squabs are cooked in individual dishes — I find a small soufflé dish is an excellent fit — although on the other hand one large dish is easier to cope with. This is not — I had better warn you — a dish for delicate eaters, as the best way of coping with the birds is to pick at them with your fingers.

SERVES 4

30 g/1 oz raisins
450 ml/¾ pt plus 2 tbsp red wine
55 g/2 oz butter
225 g/8 oz smoked bacon, diced
1 carrot, chopped
1 leek, chopped
1 onion, sliced
2 garlic cloves, chopped
sprig of thyme
4 small squabs, plus their livers or 50 g/2 oz chicken livers, trimmed
zest of 1 lemon
225g/8 oz plus 2 tsp flour
2 size-1 eggs
450 ml/¾ pt milk
salt and freshly ground black pepper
sunflower oil, for greasing

Preheat the oven to 220C/425F/gas7 and lightly oil either 4 individual cocotte dishes large enough for the pigeons or one large deep-sided dish.

Put the raisins in a bowl with 2 tablespoons of the red wine and leave to soak for about 30 minutes, or until plumped up.

Melt half the butter in a sauté pan which has a tight-fitting lid over a medium heat. Sauté the bacon with the carrot, leek, onion, garlic and thyme until soft.

Meanwhile prepare the pigeons: spatchcock them by first cutting them along the backbone with a sharp knife, then open them up by gently pulling them apart and turn them over. Press them firmly on the breast to flatten them and then season them all over. Remove the livers, chop these finely and set aside.

Place the birds on the vegetables in the pan and add the lemon zest. Pour over the remaining wine, cover the pan and simmer gently for about 20 minutes or until the birds are tender.

Remove the pigeons and keep warm. Strain the contents of the pan through a sieve, reserving both the vegetables and the liquid.

Make a batter by sifting 225 g/8 oz of the flour into a bowl along with a pinch of salt. Break in the eggs and slowly beat in the milk. Whisk in 150 ml/¼ pt of the strained liquid from the pan along with the raisins in their wine and leave to rest for about 15 minutes.

Towards the end of this time, heat the oiled dish(es) in the oven for about 3–5 minutes until they are sizzling hot.

Remove the dish(es) from the oven and pour in the batter. Return to the oven and cook for about 15 minutes or until the batter is risen.

Place the pigeons on top of the batter and spoon over a little of the strained cooking liquid. Surround the birds with the reserved vegetables. Return the dish to the oven and cook for a further 5 minutes until the batter is golden brown.

Meanwhile make the sauce: melt the remaining butter in a clean sauté pan over a medium heat and cook the prepared livers for a couple of minutes.

Using a wooden spoon, stir in the remaining flour and scrape the bottom of the pan so the flour is well mixed in. Pour in the remaining strained liquid, turn up the heat and simmer, stirring constantly, until the sauce is thick and smooth.

Season and serve with the pigeons.

PIGEON IN A HOLE

Rabbit

Every farmer will tell you that the countryside is overrun with rabbits, but it is surprisingly rare to see rabbit from the wild on sale. Usually sold in fur, wild rabbit has a much stronger taste and darker flesh than those which have been commercially bred.

It is probably wise to avoid any wild rabbit weighing more than about 1.35 k/3 lb, as it may well be quite old, tough and powerfully flavoured. Another good way of ageing a rabbit is to inspect its ears, teeth and paws. Young rabbits have soft floppy ears which tear easily and smooth white teeth and claws: once the teeth and claws are blunted and rough, it is a sure sign of old age. If you are still not sure of the rabbit's texture and taste, to be on the safe side marinate it overnight in milk flavoured with herbs.

Commercially bred rabbit, on the other hand, is much milder and has paler milky-soft flesh, not unlike chicken. Most supermarkets sell jointed portions which may be roasted, casseroled or brushed with oil and grilled, fried or barbecued.

Rabbit with Chilli and Olives

SERVES 4–6

2 tsp sun-dried tomato paste
1 tsp chilli paste
1 clove of garlic, chopped
1 tbsp finely chopped fresh oregano
2 tbsp finely chopped fresh thyme
4 tbsp olive oil, plus extra for brushing
1 rabbit, weighing about 1.1 k/2½ lb, jointed or 8–12 rabbit thigh portions
4 whole heads of garlic
1 onion, finely chopped
6 large green olives, stoned and sliced
150 ml/¼ pt white wine
150 ml/¼ pt chicken stock (see page 106)
1 tbsp Greek-style yoghurt
small bunch of flat-leaf parsley, finely chopped
sea salt and freshly ground black pepper

Preheat the oven to 190C/375F/gas5.

In a bowl, mix the sun-dried tomato paste with the chilli paste, garlic, oregano, 1 tablespoon of the thyme, 2 tablespoons of the olive oil and salt and pepper. Using a stiff brush, paint the rabbit pieces with this paste. Leave to stand for about 10 minutes.

Meanwhile, using a pastry brush, paint the heads of garlic all over with olive oil. Then sprinkle them with the rest of the thyme and salt and pepper. Wrap them up in greaseproof paper and put them on a baking tray.

Heat the rest of the olive oil in a large ovenproof casserole over a medium heat. Add the onion and sauté for about 5 minutes until soft. Arrange the rabbit pieces on top and put in the preheated oven along with the prepared garlic clove parcels and roast for 30 minutes.

Remove the garlic and casserole from the oven. Unwrap the garlic and leave to cool. When cool enough to handle, peel the cloves and set aside.

Add the olives, white wine and chicken stock to the casserole. Bring to the boil over a low heat and simmer for about 30 minutes, or until the rabbit is tender. Using a slotted spoon, transfer the rabbit to a warm dish and keep warm.

Whizz the roasted garlic cloves along with about 1 tablespoon of the sauce from the rabbit in a food processor until smooth. Stir this into the sauce, turn up the heat and simmer the sauce to reduce it by about one-third. Stir in the yoghurt and parsley and season.

Pour the sauce over the rabbit and serve.

RABBIT WITH CHILLI AND OLIVES

Hare

Hare has no close season as such, but it cannot be sold between March and July. The best time to eat it is between October and January, before the animals are too thin and worn out from the winter. Leverets – hares under one year – are the most tender and, like rabbits, you can judge their age by their smooth white teeth, soft ears, claws and coat.

In Britain, we eat the common brown hare and the smaller Scottish or blue hare. Rather confusingly, the Belgian hare is actually a rabbit, and the American Jack rabbit is what we we call a hare. Hare has a far earthier, fuller flavour than rabbit. It should be hung for between three to seven days, depending on its size and the weather. Traditionally it is hung head-down and undrawn, over a bowl for catching the blood as it drips (which can then be used in the classic dish, Jugged Hare).

Hares are either sold whole or jointed. An average whole saddle will weigh 900 g–1.35 k/2–3 lb and serves two to four. The best way of cooking it is to roast it at 220C/425F/gas7 for 20–35 minutes. For extra flavour, lay it on sliced onions flavoured with thyme and rosemary.

Hare with Noodles

Based on an old Tuscan recipe from The Gastronomy of Italy *by Anna del Conte, this is an economical way of dealing with a whole hare. Only the legs are used in this rich full-bodied pasta sauce, which means that the saddle can be turned into a pâté (see Game Terrine, page 174) or roasted separately (see page 171).*

SERVES 4

2 tbsp olive oil
2 rashers of unsmoked streaky bacon
1 small onion, finely chopped
1 celery stalk, finely chopped
1 garlic clove, finely chopped
1 small sprig of rosemary, finely chopped
the legs of 1 hare
2 tsp flour
150 ml/$\frac{1}{4}$ pt red wine
150 ml/$\frac{1}{4}$ pt game stock (see page 106)
pinch of grated nutmeg
2 tbsp Greek-style yoghurt
sea salt and freshly ground black pepper

Heat the oil in a heavy-based saucepan over a medium heat. Add the bacon and sauté for 2 minutes. Then add the onion, celery, garlic and rosemary and cook until soft, stirring frequently.

Add the hare legs to the pan and sauté them until lightly browned.

Sprinkle in the flour and cook for about a minute, stirring constantly, until the flour is brown. Turn up the heat, pour in the wine and boil until it has reduced by about half.

Then add about half of the stock, the nutmeg and a pinch of salt and stir together. Turn down the heat to medium to low, half cover the pan and simmer for about 1 hour, checking occasionally. Add the remaining stock, a little at a time to avoid the pan catching, to make a thick sauce.

Using a slotted spoon, lift the legs from the pan. Bone them, cut the meat into small pieces and return these to the pan. Stir in the yoghurt, season and serve with large noodles.

A wild red deer stag.

Venison

Venison, the term for all deer meat, is in season at different times of the year, depending on the area and the type of deer from which it comes. In this country, there are three main types of wild deer: Red deer are large and their meat has a strong robust flavour; Fallow deer are milder-flavoured; and Roe deer are the smallest and most delicately flavoured.

Wild venison needs to be hung for a minimum of a few days. As with all game, it is difficult to age correctly and cuts from older tougher animals are best slowly casseroled or stewed.

Over the past few years venison farming has become increasingly popular and, whereas you can only get wild venison from licensed gamekeepers, most of that on sale in supermarkets is farmed. Sika is the most popular type and, as it is usually killed at about 18 months, it tends to be more tender and milder tasting, lacking the strong gamey flavour of its wild cousins.

All venison meat is incredibly lean, with a very low fat content. For this reason it must be carefully cooked so that it does not dry out. Sold ready-cut, the best joints are from the loin, leg, haunch and saddle. The shoulder is often cut into cubes and then sold as stewing meat.

When roasting a whole joint, either marinate it or bard it with bacon, and always remember to baste it while cooking.

Venison Saint-Hubert

SERVES 4–6

2 onions
2 carrots
1 celery stalk, chopped
2 sprigs each of marjoram, thyme and parsley, tied together in a bunch
3 juniper berries, crushed
3 black peppercorns, crushed
zest of 1 orange
3 tbsp red wine vinegar
450 ml/¾ pt red wine
1 boned and rolled haunch of venison, weighing about 900 g/2 lb
2 tbsp olive oil
170 g/6 oz salt pork, diced
30 g/1 oz flour
1 tbsp tomato paste
200 ml/7 fl oz game or chicken stock (see page 106)
3 tbsp brandy
75 g/2½ oz redcurrant jelly
salt and freshly ground black pepper

Chop 1 of the onions and 1 of the carrots, and in a bowl, mix with the celery, herbs, juniper berries, peppercorns and orange zest. Pour in the vinegar and red wine and stir together to make a marinade.

Place the venison in a glass or stainless steel bowl suitable for marinating, pour over the marinade and leave in a cool place for a minimum of 8 hours, turning it occasionally. (For a stronger flavour, you can leave the venison to marinate for as long as 3 days.)

Preheat the oven to 200C/400F/gas 6.

Remove the venison from the marinade, put it in a roasting dish and roast in the preheated oven for about 50 minutes, basting it occasionally with the marinade.

Meanwhile, start making the sauce. Chop the remaining onion and carrot and heat the oil in a pan over a medium heat. Add the salt pork along with the onion and carrot and sauté until brown. Then stir in the flour and tomato paste and cook for a further minute, stirring continuously. Strain the marinade and add to the pan along with the stock. Turn the heat down to low and simmer gently for about 30 minutes.

When the venison is cooked, transfer it to a warmed serving dish. Keep warm and leave to rest for about 20 minutes. Place the roasting dish over a medium heat and, using a wooden spoon, stir and scrape the juices in the pan. Then pour in the brandy, heat it and flame it to burn off the alcohol. Add the sauce from the pan to the roasting dish and stir in the redcurrant jelly. When it has melted, strain the sauce through a sieve into a sauce boat. Season and serve with the venison.

GAME TERRINE

Game Terrine

A game terrine such as this should be made two or three days in advance, so the flavours have plenty of time to mellow and blend. It needs a mixture of game meat along with pork and pork fat for flavour, moisture and texture. This recipe can be made with either hare, rabbit or venison or even, as here, wild boar.

At one time WILD BOAR did run free doing untold damage to the English countryside. However, unlike Italy, France and Germany where it is still hunted in the forests and hills, it has vanished in Britain. So what you buy as 'wild boar' in this country is, in fact, a farmed wild boar/pig cross. It has a more gamy flavour than an ordinary pig, but is milder and probably fattier than a true wild boar.

In France, only the marcassin *(a sanglier or wild boar from six months to a year old) and* bête rousse *(between one and two years old) are eaten in their entirety. They are easily recognizable, as a young boar has a striped back and, as he grows up, his coat changes to a rusty red. When even older the boar becomes tough and very highly flavoured, and by the time it has reached a ripe old age — some live as long as 30 years — and is known as an* ermite, *only its head is considered fit to eat.*

SERVES 10–12

450 g/1 lb wild boar, stripped off the bone
115 g/4 oz ham, diced
115 g/4 oz pork fat, diced
$\frac{1}{2}$ tsp allspice
pinch of cloves
pinch of nutmeg
$3\frac{1}{2}$ tbsp brandy
$3\frac{1}{2}$ tbsp Madeira
450 g/1 lb belly of pork
1 egg
15 g/$\frac{1}{2}$ oz truffle, finely chopped (optional)
350 g/12 oz rashers of streaky bacon
salt and freshly ground pepper

Cut half the wild boar into finger-size strips. Mix the strips in a bowl with the ham, pork fat, allspice, cloves and nutmeg. Pour in the brandy and Madeira, season and stir thoroughly. Cover the bowl and leave to marinate for 1 to 2 hours.

Preheat the oven to 180C/350F/gas4.

Put the remaining wild boar along with the belly of pork in a food processor and whizz until reduced to pieces about 2.5 cm/1 in thick. Strain the liquid from the marinade into this mixture. Break in the egg, add the truffle, salt and pepper and whizz again until reduced to pieces about half the previous size. (Be careful not to over-process or chop it too finely as this will result in a heavy and dense pâté.)

Line a suitable terrine with the bacon rashers, reserving 2 or 3. Spread one-third of the chopped mixture on the bottom and cover with half of the boar strip mixture. Repeat the process, and finish with a final layer of the chopped mixture. Cover the top with the remaining slices of bacon and lay a sheet of greaseproof paper on top.

Place the terrine in a roasting pan and half fill it with boiling water. Bake in the preheated oven for $1\frac{1}{4}$–$1\frac{1}{2}$ hours. To test whether it is ready, insert a skewer into

the pâté: if the juices that run out are clear, it is cooked.

Allow the terrine to cool slightly, then place a plate or a piece of wood on top and weight it with about 900 g/2 lb of weights to press down the terrine.

Wild boar is still hunted in some European countries.

Refrigerate overnight and keep for at least 2 days before serving, to allow the flavours to mellow.

Nuts

Nuts are the fruit of certain trees. Some, such as almonds, cashews, coconuts and pine nuts, are edible and contain a valuable source of fat and protein; others, like beechmast, oakmast (acorns) and horse chestnuts, were eaten in former times but have since been dropped from our culinary repertoire as frankly they do not taste very good. Peanuts and water chestnuts, strictly speaking, are not nuts; the former is the seed of a legume, the latter a bulb.

At the beginning of the season, you can often buy 'green' or immature ALMONDS and WALNUTS. These are young with a fleshy casing or 'shuck' and a soft underdeveloped kernel. Although too bitter to eat raw, they are ideal for pickling; simply prick the skin all

Walnuts are a speciality of South-West France.

over, soak them in a brine for a couple of days and then simmer them in a wine vinegar infused with spices and leave them for several weeks. They may then be eaten as a pickle.

As the season progresses, you can find 'wet' or fresh nuts. Wet walnuts from France are particularly juicy, with a fresh oiliness and a softer outer shell which you can crack with your hands. KENTISH COBNUTS, picked in August when the husks are still green, have a sweet and succulent milky white kernel. A seasonal speciality, these nuts do not keep and have to be eaten almost immediately.

Although often confused, the horse chestnut and the sweet chestnut trees are not related. It is the SWEET CHESTNUT that we know, love and eat, either roasted, in stuffings or as marrons glacés. In France, Italy and Switzerland, this most floury and least oily of all nuts is ground into a flour which is then used to make cakes and puddings.

Most of the nuts you buy in their shells are fully grown and sold dried so they will last for several weeks, provided you keep them in a loosely fastened plastic bag in a cool place. When choosing nuts, look for unbroken shells which have no traces of damp. Try holding them in the palm of your hand: a good nut will weigh heavy for its size.

Shelled nuts are sold loose or in packets or tins, raw or roasted and salted and sometimes further processed by chopping, blanching, flaking or grinding. If stored too long after being opened, they go rancid and bitter and develop an unpleasant sharp oily taste; so buy them in small quantities as you need them.

Chestnut Soup

Sweet chestnuts are in season from October through to the end of the year. Choose nuts with unbruised and undamaged skins, avoiding any which show any trace of damp or mould. If you buy whole nuts, they must be peeled before use. This can be done relatively easily by slitting their skins and roasting them in a hot oven for about 5–10 minutes or by boiling them (see below).

Although freshly peeled chestnuts do have a stronger, fuller flavour, peeling them is time-consuming. You may find it easier to buy them peeled and vacuum-packed in airtight jars or frozen in packs. For this recipe, use 350 g/12 oz, making sure they are unsweetened, and reduce their cooking time to about 30 minutes.

SERVES 4–6

450 g/1 lb fresh chestnuts
1 tbsp olive oil
1 onion, finely chopped
1 celery stalk, chopped
zest of 1 orange
1.1 1/2 pt chicken stock (see page 106)
1 tbsp Madeira
1 tbsp finely chopped fresh parsley
salt and freshly ground black pepper

To peel the chestnuts, use a sharp knife to make a couple of slits in the skin of each chestnut, put them in a saucepan, pour over enough boiling water to cover and bring to a simmer over a medium heat. Simmer for about 5 minutes, then take them out a few at a time, drain and refresh them under running cold water. Peel off their skins, which should now come off quite easily.

Heat the olive oil in a large saucepan over a medium heat, add the onion and celery and sauté gently for 5 minutes, or until soft. Add the orange zest and chestnuts and sauté for a couple of minutes.

Pour in the stock and bring to the boil. Turn down the heat to low, cover and simmer for about 45 minutes.

Whizz the soup in a food processor until smooth. Return it to the pan, stir in the Madeira, season and bring back to the boil.

Serve sprinkled with chopped parsley.

Aïllade or Walnut and Garlic Sauce

Aïllade is at its most pungent when made with wet walnuts (see page 176). However, by all means use ready-shelled nuts — the result is still superb and excellent for serving with cold meats.

In the walnut-growing area of South-West France, aïllade is one of the treats of late August. A couple of years ago, I visited one of the few farms in the region that still presses its own walnut oil and the owner passed on an invaluable tip: later on in the year, soaking the nuts overnight in hot milk gives the shells the glossy appearance of wet walnuts and revitalizes the meat.

MAKES 300 ML/$\frac{1}{2}$ PT

3 garlic cloves
115 g/4 oz walnuts
5 tbsp olive oil
100 ml/3$\frac{1}{2}$ fl oz crème fraîche or single cream
3 tbsp finely chopped fresh parsley
salt and freshly ground black pepper

Put the garlic cloves in a food processor along with a large pinch of salt and whizz until creamy. Add the walnuts and whizz again until they are finely chopped.

With the machine still running, gradually pour in the olive oil. When it is well amalgamated, pour in the cream and whizz for a few more seconds.

Fold in the parsley, season and serve.

Fungi

Most of the mushrooms we eat are cultivated and grown in the dark. The most usual is the COMMON MUSHROOM, sold in a variety of sizes from the small tight white buttons to the larger browny-beige open flat caps. When fresh, they are firm and unmarked with taut gills and an insipid flavour with a hint of chicken. The delicate, softly textured OYSTER MUSHROOM is also commercially grown and recently the more intensely – some would say almost overpoweringly – flavoured brown SHIITAKE MUSHROOM has been introduced and farmed on a commercial scale.

In spite of constant efforts, no one has yet succeeded in taming the hundreds of other edible wild mushrooms to be able to cultivate them. It is fair to say that once you have eaten the better wild mushrooms, the flavour of cultivated ones pales into insignificance.

I remember a couple of years ago I spent my holidays in early September in Tuscany, high up in the hills that surround Florence. My great treat was to go early in the morning to the Mercato Centrale, the covered food market. The streets were still empty, as the tourists had yet to make an appearance, but the market was already do a roaring trade. Built in the nineteenth century, it is a curious building a little like a Victorian railway terminus, with its cast-iron columns and glass sides; but it feeds all Florence and is known affectionately as 'the belly of the city'.

Luck was with me, I had arrived at prime mushroom time and there were mounds of *porcini*, the most treasured of all Italian mushrooms, freshly gathered and being carefully inspected by the Florentine housewives – the Italians, like the French and Poles, take their wild mushrooms very seriously. The *porcini* (*cèpe* in France and CEP or PENNY BUN in Britain), in season from early summer through to the autumn, has a densely meaty flavour and strange slippery – almost gelatinous – texture which are second to none. A fleshy mushroom with a thick white stalk and a rounded bulbous soft brown cap, it is excellent eaten on its own, lightly brushed with oil and grilled, or pan-fried with garlic and chopped parsley and finished with a little cream to be served with pasta. Dried *porcini* are sold throughout the year and add body and depth of flavour to stews, casseroles and sauces. If stored in an airtight jar with raw rice, they infuse it with a beefy flavour.

Throughout Europe there are hundreds of wild edible mushrooms. However, do let me give you a word of warning: until you are sure of what you are picking, always check with an expert before you even think of eating your bounty. In France and several other European countries, every pharmacist must, by law, be trained to identify mushrooms. Here we are not so lucky and have to rely on advice from knowledgeable friends, trained botanists, a well-illustrated reference book or a local nature club.

In Britain the season starts with the ST GEORGE'S MUSHROOM, thus named because it is traditionally found in grassy hedgerows, wood edges and pastures on and around April 23rd, St George's Day. The season progresses with the pitted head MOREL; then come dusky orange CHANTERELLES tasting a little of fleshy

As well as the large open flat caps and mottled chestnut mushrooms, soft grey and yellow oyster and orange chanterelle mushrooms are now also cultivated.

ripe apricots mixed with earthy mustiness, a prick of pepperiness and subtle sweetness, which grow any time between March to November depending on the country. The chanterelle year starts in March, with a first flush coming from Morocco; April sees a crop from Turkey, and by May and June there will be baskets from Southern France and Northern Italy; as summer heightens, supplies come from Poland, Yugoslavia, Germany, Austria and Scotland.

Late summer and autumn, before the serious frosts, is the time to go mushroom picking. You may find meaty FIELD MUSHROOMS, soft shaggy INK CAPS, giant PUFFBALLS, delicate wild OYSTER MUSH-ROOMS, CHICKEN-OF-THE-WOODS and FIELD BLEWITS with their stalks brushed with purple.

If the thought of picking wild mushrooms terrifies you, you can buy them in the shops. Although expensive, even a few cooked with cultivated mushrooms transform the taste. Do also remember that some edible mushrooms may be toxic unless cooked.

Italy and France are also famous for their truffles, underground tubers which are dug up by specially trained dogs or pigs. The Italian WHITE TRUFFLE is superb grated raw, using a special truffle grater, over a risotto; and the BLACK TRUFFLE from France is used in pâtés and stuffings, or even baked in batter like a miniature Yorkshire pudding and eaten whole. Black truffles are most readily obtained in this country either bottled or canned whole, or as pieces or shavings which can be used to great effect as flavouring ingredients.

Saffron milk caps are particularly appreciated on the Continent.

Mushroom Caviar

As this slow method of cooking down mushrooms develops and intensifies their flavour, ordinary cultivated mushrooms will do. However, do make sure that they are fresh, firm and dry — once they develop a wet, slimy skin it is a sign that they are past their peak. Clean them gently by wiping them with a damp cloth rather than using running water.

SERVES 4

1 tbsp olive oil
1 onion, finely chopped
350 g/12 oz firm button mushrooms
juice of ½ lemon
3 tbsp sour cream
1 tbsp finely chopped fresh chives
salt and freshly ground black pepper

Heat the oil in a sauté pan over a medium to low heat and cook the onion until soft.

Whizz the mushrooms in a food processor until very finely chopped and almost reduced to a purée.

Add them to the pan, season and cook over a low heat for about 8 minutes, until the mushrooms are soft and creamy-textured.

As the mushrooms give off a lot of juice while they cook, you will need to get rid of some of it. Simply turn up the heat to medium and stir the liquid and mushrooms together for a few seconds until the juices evaporate, then reduce the heat to low and carry on slow cooking. You will probably have to repeat the process at least 2 or 3 times.

Remove the pan from the heat and tip the contents into a bowl. Stir in the lemon juice, sour cream and chives, adjust the seasoning and chill for a couple of hours. Serve with toasted slices of Walnut Brioche (see page 196).

Mushroom Ketchup

Late on Saturday afternoon, my local market often sells off vegetables and fruits very cheaply, rather than having to keep them over the weekend. If I get a punnet of mushrooms, I am often tempted to make this ketchup as it is rich and juicy. No matter how much I make, it never seems to sit in my store cupboard for very long before it is all eaten up.

MAKES 450 ML/¾ PT

900 g/2 lb mushrooms, thinly sliced
2–3 anchovy fillets, chopped
2 garlic cloves, sliced
300 ml/½ pt port
½ tsp ground allspice
¼ tsp ground cloves
½ tsp ground mace
sea salt and freshly ground black pepper

Put the mushrooms in a large saucepan along with the anchovy fillets, garlic, port, allspice, cloves and mace, 5 tablespoons of water, salt and plenty of pepper.

Bring to the boil over a medium to low heat and simmer for about 10 minutes.

Pack into a warm dry sterilized jar and leave to cool. Seal and leave to stand for about 10 days for the flavours to blend and mature before use.

Risotto with Porcini

Use an Arborio rice for this risotto as the grains absorb just the right amount of liquid while retaining their texture. To lift the blandness of the rice you need the meaty flavour of the porcini.

SERVES 4

350 g/12 oz fresh ceps, sliced, or 325 g/11 oz fresh button mushrooms, sliced, plus 30 g/1 oz dried ceps
1.5 l/2½ pt chicken stock (see page 106)
3 tbsp olive oil
55 g/2 oz butter
1 onion, finely chopped
350 g/12 oz Arborio or risotto rice
55 g/2 oz freshly grated Parmesan cheese
salt and freshly ground black pepper

If you are using dried ceps, put them to soak in a small bowl of water for 15 minutes. Then drain them, reserving the liquid, and chop them. Put the stock to boil, strain and add the mushroom soaking water.

Heat the oil and half the butter in a large sauté pan over medium heat and sauté the onion until it begins to colour. Add the sliced mushrooms and cook for 2 minutes, stirring occasionally. If using the dried ceps, add to the pan and cook for a further minute. Stir in the rice and sauté for a minute or two, stirring continuously, until thoroughly coated with the oil and butter.

Add a ladleful of stock to the rice and as it absorbs the liquid, add another. Carry on stirring and adding stock until the rice is cooked 'al dente': it will take about 20 minutes and probably use up all the stock.

Remove from the heat, season and stir in the remaining butter and the Parmesan. Serve immediately.

RISOTTO WITH PORCINI left, MUSHROOM CAVIAR (SEE PAGE 181) right.

Plants from the Woods

Food for Free by Richard Maybe struck a chord when it was first published in 1972. It seemed that we had forgotten about all the wild edible foods growing in the countryside which were there for the picking.

Leaves from CHICKWEED, PENNYWORT and WATERCRESS (check first that the stream is fast flowing, otherwise there is the danger of liver fluke) make excellent salads; young BISTORT is boiled up with eggs and barley to be transformed into the Cumberland delicacy Easterledge Pudding. ALEX-ANDER STALKS, when boiled, are crisp and crunchy with a grassy taste; the tops of FIDDLE-HEAD FERNS may be steamed and served with melted butter – the list is endless and the possibilities exciting.

Whatever you use, however, do make sure the plants have not been sprayed. Also wash them thoroughly and, just to be on the safe side, carry a good reference book.

Dandelion and Lardon Salad

Cultivated DANDELION plants, grown for salads, are blanched to make their leaves soft and sweet. However, as wild dandelions are two a penny, it makes sense to put their leaves to good use. Pick only the tiny inner leaves, as the larger outer ones can be quite hairy and extremely bitter.

WOOD SORREL is another weed that grows in woods and in most people's gardens. Its vibrant green leaves are clover-shaped and, *as they have a soft succulent texture and the sharp lemon flavour of French sorrel, they make an interesting addition to salads.*

SERVES 4

140 g/5 oz tiny new potatoes, scrubbed
285 g/10 oz young dandelion leaves
55 g/2 oz wood sorrel or sorrel leaves
5 tbsp extra-virgin olive oil
1 tbsp hazelnut oil
170 g/6 oz piece of smoked back bacon, cut into 2.5 cm/1 in strips
2 shallots, very finely chopped
2 tbsp white wine vinegar
sea salt and freshly ground black pepper

Boil the new potatoes in lightly salted water over a medium heat for about 8 minutes, or until tender. Drain and keep warm.

Meanwhile, mix the dandelion leaves with the sorrel in a salad bowl, tearing any of the larger leaves with your hands. Sprinkle over a little sea salt.

Mix all but 1 teaspoon of the olive oil with the hazelnut oil and season with pepper. Add the potatoes to the bowl, pour the dressing over the salad and toss it thoroughly with your hands.

Heat the remaining oil in a frying pan over a medium heat and fry the strips of bacon, or lardons, until crisp. Add the shallots and fry for a further 2–3 minutes, or until they just begin to turn golden. Using a slotted spoon, lift the bacon and shallots out of the pan and scatter them over the leaves.

Turn up the heat to high, pour the vinegar into the pan and, stirring and scraping with a wooden spoon so the juices mix together, cook to reduce for about 1 minute. Pour this over the salad, give it a final toss and serve immediately.

DANDELION AND LARDON SALAD

The Granary

Cereals were man's first staple food, their importance
illustrated in their centuries-old role in harvest
festivities and as a symbol of plenty. And they remain
central to much country food — from breads and pies
to pastries and pasta.

In the West, most of the flour we use is milled from wheat. There are, however, a confusing number of different types of wheat flours, so the two most important points to bear in mind when buying flour are the type of wheat from which it is milled and its extraction rate – in layman's terms, this means the percentage of whole wheat grain left in after milling.

There are two basic types of wheat: 'strong', or 'hard', and 'soft'. Strong wheat has a hard grain with a high protein content. The more protein a flour contains, the more gluten there is in the dough; therefore STRONG FLOUR makes a dough which is more elastic and enables it to trap the bubbles of carbon dioxide produced by fermentation which cause the dough to rise. As strong or hard flour produces a large volume and open texture, it should be used for bread-making, all types of yeast cookery, some batters and pasta. Hard wheat grows best in warm dry climates, like those in the Canadian Prairies, Texas, North Dakota, Argentina, Australia and in Italy, where the local hard or DURUM WHEAT is used to make pasta.

SOFT FLOUR is milled from soft wheat which grows in temperate climates and has a soft grain, containing a higher level of starch than protein. It gives a small volume and is lighter and far more fragile than hard flour. When sold as PLAIN FLOUR, without any added raising agents, it is ideally suited for pastry-, cake- and biscuit-making etc. Bread can be made with soft flour, provided you do not use yeast, and it tends to have a much more crumbly texture and a more cake-like crust. Irish Soda and Scofa bread, for instance, are made with soft flour, but bicarbonate of soda rather than yeast is used as a raising agent. Although they can be made very quickly as you do not have to wait for the yeast to rise, the disadvantage of these breads is they do not keep well and go stale very quickly.

Flour also differs in the amount of wheat grain left after milling. WHOLEMEAL or WHOLEWHEAT FLOUR results from 100% extraction, meaning nothing has been taken away – or added – so all the goodness of the grain is intact. It can be coarse-, medium- or fine-ground and is heavier and denser than white flour, although far more nutritious. BROWN FLOUR results from 85% extraction and retains some wheatgerm and bran; MALTED BROWN or GRANARY FLOUR is also an 85% extraction flour to which malted wheat grains have been added to give it a distinct nutty flavour; WHITE FLOUR contains 75% of the wheat grain which means that most of the bran and wheatgerm have been removed in the mills (it is then bleached to make it a pure white); UNBLEACHED WHITE, a cream-coloured flour, is white flour which has received no bleaching. It is also worth remembering that by law, calcium must be added to all grades of flours, except wholemeal and self-raising, in an effort to restore some of its goodness.

Some flours are also sold as STONE-GROUND FLOURS; this means that the wheat is ground by the old-fashioned method between two stones rather than by the modern mass-production steel rollers. Stone-ground flour is usually more expensive but, because of the way in which the wheat is crushed at a cooler temperature and less harshly, more of the grains' goodness is preserved and it is thought to have a higher nutritional value. However, it usually has the disadvantage that it will not keep as long as milled flour.

SELF-RAISING FLOUR, used in certain cakes and pastry, is a soft, usually white, flour to which a raising agent has been added. The most common raising agent, baking powder, is a mixture of various simple chemical substances: the formulae vary, but the most common contains tartaric acid, or cream of tartar, and potassium tartrate. Some recipes call for plain flour and the addition of a raising agent, but in most cases the result is the same if you use self-raising flour.

Oats, wheat and barley are used in many forms – cooked whole, ground to make flours and even, in the case of barley, fermented to make alcoholic drinks.

Wheat is harvested in Gascony, South-West France.

used to make dense pancakes or soft chips, a speciality of Genoa.

The grain MAIZE, usually referred to as corn, is grown throughout the world and there are hundreds of different types, from the varieties used for popcorn to those grown for their huge cobs. Their colours range from white and yellow to red, blue and brown or even variegated. Yellow CORNMEAL is finely ground maize and used to make such fine American breads as cornbread and spoonbread. POLENTA is coarsely ground maize but the Italians also use the term for a traditional dish made from the maize meal boiled in water with butter or olive oil, sometimes with a little added grated Parmesan cheese.

HOMINY is hulled corn, made by soaking and boiling maize in wood lye (ashes and water) until the outer skin of the grain is soft enough to be rubbed off. When dried it can be ground into coarse granules, known as hominy grits.

All flour should be kept in an airtight storage jar in a cool airy place. As a general rule, plain white flour keeps for 4 to 6 months; self-raising for 2 to 3 months; and wholemeal and brown flours, because of their higher fat content, last for only about 2 months, tending to turn rancid if they are kept too long or at an incorrect temperature. I do remember one bread-making enthusiast, however, telling me that he always kept his wholemeal flour for months, most satisfactorily, in the freezer.

There are numerous other flours made from other grains, cereals, nuts or pulses, including barley, buckwheat, corn, rye, rice and soya. OATMEAL, for example, is obtained by grinding oats after the husk has been removed and comes in various grades from 'pinhead', the largest and the coarsest, to 'fine' which has a texture almost like flour. Chick peas, or *ceci* in Italian, are ground into a rich creamy flour which is

Thickening agents

Some flours also make effective thickening agents to be added to soups, stews and sauces etc. Plain flour, butter and milk make a roux, the basis of many a white sauce. ARROWROOT, made from a variety of tropical roots, is effective in clear meat and fruit sauces as it can be used raw and does not cloud the liquid because it is so fine. CORNFLOUR or CORN STARCH, on the other hand, should always be cooked: it is made by grinding and pulverizing the starch extracted from maize kernels and it can also be added to cakes and pastries to lighten their texture. POTATO FLOUR, made from dried and ground potatoes, should also be cooked but is particularly useful for anyone on a gluten-free diet and has the advantage of being almost completely tasteless.

Granary Bread

The simplest of all breads, granary bread is made from malted brown granary flour. For extra fibre, the bread can be further enriched by adding a teaspoon of fine wheat bran and then sprinkling it with a little more bran before baking. However, because of its higher bran and wheatgerm content, bread made with brown or wholemeal flour tends to have a denser texture and rises less than bread made with white flour.

MAKES TWO 450 G/1 LB LOAVES

2 tsp runny honey
350 ml/12 fl oz milk
30 g/1 oz fresh yeast or 15 g/$\frac{1}{2}$ oz dried yeast
675 g/1$\frac{1}{2}$ lb granary flour
2 tsp salt, plus more for glazing
1 tsp bran, plus extra for finishing
2 eggs
85 g/3 oz unsalted butter, melted, plus extra for greasing

Put the honey with 5 tablespoons of the milk in a saucepan and heat it over a low heat until lukewarm. Remove from the heat, mix in the yeast thoroughly, cover and leave to stand in a warm place for 15 minutes or until it bubbles.

In a large bowl, sift in the flour and salt. Add the bran, eggs and melted butter and pour in the yeast mixture with the remaining milk. Using a wooden spoon, mix until the dough comes together.

Knead on a flat, lightly floured surface for about 10 minutes, or until the dough is smooth. Cover with a cloth and leave to rise in a warm place until it has doubled in size.

Preheat the oven to 230C/450F/gas8 and generously grease a baking tray with some butter.

Knock back the dough by lifting it from the bowl and kneading it for a minute or so. Cut the dough in half and shape the pieces into two cigar-like loaves. Slash the tops with a knife.

Place the loaves on the prepared baking tray, cover with a cloth and leave to prove. When they have doubled in volume they are ready to be baked.

Using a pastry brush, lightly brush the loaves with a salt glaze made by dissolving a pinch of salt in 2 tablespoons of hot water. Sprinkle the tops with more bran and bake in the preheated oven for about 20–30 minutes, or until brown.

Remove from the tray and leave them to cool on a wire rack.

Hazelnut Bread

Traditional bread-making in France opposite.

Slices of hazelnut bread are particularly good served lightly toasted with a slice of goats' cheese melted on top. Instead of using bread loaf tins, I sometimes make fat column-shaped loaves in 10 cm/4 in unused clay flower-pots. The pots should first be soaked for a short while in water and this creates the effect almost of steaming the bread, making it particularly moist.

This recipe can also be adapted for a walnut bread: substitute the same quantity of walnuts for hazelnuts and use walnut instead of hazelnut oil.

MAKES TWO 450 G/1 LB LOAVES

1 tsp runny honey
150 ml/$\frac{1}{4}$ pt milk, plus more for glazing
15 g/$\frac{1}{2}$ oz fresh yeast or 8 g/$\frac{1}{4}$ oz dried yeast
225 g/8 oz strong unbleached white flour
225 g/8 oz strong wholemeal flour
1$\frac{1}{2}$ tsp sea salt
115 g/4 oz hazelnuts, roughly chopped
3 tbsp hazelnut oil, plus extra for greasing
30 g/1 oz rye flour

Put the honey with the milk in a saucepan and heat it over a low heat until lukewarm.

Remove from the heat, mix in the yeast thoroughly, cover and leave to stand in a warm place for 15 minutes, or until it bubbles.

Sift the white flour into a large bowl, add the wholemeal flour and salt and tip in the hazelnuts. Add the hazelnut oil and 150 ml/$\frac{1}{4}$ pt water to the yeast, mix together and pour into the flour. Mix until the dough comes together.

Turn the dough out on a flat lightly floured surface and knead for about 10 minutes, or until the dough is firm and elastic. Cover with a cloth and leave in a warm place for about 1 hour, or until the dough has doubled in volume.

Preheat the oven to 220C/425F/gas7 and lightly grease two 450 g/1 lb loaf tins with a little of the hazelnut oil.

Knock back the dough by kneading it again for a few seconds, divide it in half and shape each piece into a loaf. Scatter the rye flour on a clean work surface and roll the loaves in it until they are well covered. Reserve any unused rye flour.

Put the dough in the prepared loaf tins, cover and leave in a warm place for 30 minutes to prove for a second time. When it has doubled in volume it is ready to bake.

Using a pastry brush, paint the loaves lightly with a glaze made from 1 tablespoon of milk mixed with 1 tablespoon of water. Sprinkle the tops with the reserved rye flour and bake in the preheated oven for 35–40 minutes.

Remove from the tins and cool on wire racks.

Grissini or Bread Sticks

Until recently, I thought all bread sticks came in packets from huge industrialized bakeries. It was only when I visited Turin — the home of grissini — that I realized how wrong I was. There I found endless flavours and variations of these charming irregularly shaped sticks on sale in small local bread shops.

They are often made with semolina flour which, as it is such a hard flour, can be difficult to work unless mixed with wheat flour. SEMOLINA, a by-product of wheat, consists of the largest particles of the endosperm found when the outer skin, or bran, is stripped from the wheat berry. It is sold either as grains, ground into flour or as couscous, in which the grains are flattened, dampened and lightly rolled in a little fine flour.

MAKES ABOUT 20

15 g/½ oz fresh yeast or 8 g/¼ oz dry yeast
1 tbsp malt syrup
pinch of sugar
2 tbsp olive oil, plus extra for greasing and brushing
350 g/12 oz strong white flour
200 g/7 oz semolina flour
large pinch of sea salt

Pour 300 ml/½ pt warm water into a large mixing bowl and stir in the yeast, malt syrup and sugar. Cover and let stand in a warm place for about 10 minutes, until it is quite foamy.

Stir in the olive oil. Sift in the flour, 115 g/4 oz of the semolina flour and the salt and mix until the dough comes together. Turn it out on a lightly floured surface and knead for about 8–10 minutes, or until the dough is smooth, shiny and elastic.

Lightly oil a baking sheet. Shape the dough into a rectangle to fit the baking sheet and place it on the sheet. Using a pastry brush, lightly paint the top with oil. Cover and leave to rise in a warm place for about 1 hour, or until it has doubled in volume.

Preheat the oven 230C/450F/gas8.

Using a sharp knife, cut the dough into 20 equal pieces and, using the hands, roll each one on a board into long thin sticks about 30 cm/12 in long and 2 cm/ ¾ in wide. It does not matter if they are irregularly shaped as it makes them look really homemade. Sprinkle the remaining semolina flour on the board and then lightly roll the sticks in it to coat them.

Put the bread sticks back on the baking sheet so they are not touching and then bake in the preheated oven for 20 minutes.

Turn them out on wire racks and leave to cool.

Variations
Replace the semolina flour in which the bread sticks are rolled with 55 g/2 oz sesame seeds or poppy seeds or grated Parmesan cheese.

Olive Oil Bread

The taste of olive oil bread depends on the quality of olive oil used to make it: the best is an extra-virgin olive oil, with its defined flavour and low acidity.

The amount and quality of the salt is equally important. All bread needs salt for flavour and to help the yeast work properly. If you leave it out or do not mix it in thoroughly, the dough lacks springiness and rises in a misshapen fashion. I always use Maldon sea salt as it has a robust flavour and is also very easy to mix in as, unlike other sea salts, it is soft and crumbles into tiny particles when rubbed between the fingers.

MAKES 1 LARGE OR 2 SMALLER LOAVES

15 g/$\frac{1}{2}$ oz fresh yeast or 8 g/$\frac{1}{4}$ oz dried yeast
pinch of sugar
350 g/12 oz unbleached strong white flour or a mixture of 170 g/
6 oz wholewheat flour and 170 g/6 oz unbleached white flour
1$\frac{1}{2}$ tsp sea salt, plus extra for finishing
3 tbsp extra-virgin olive oil, plus extra for greasing and glazing

Dissolve the yeast and sugar in 250 ml/8 fl oz warm water, cover and leave to stand in a warm place for about 10 minutes until it froths.

In a large bowl, sift in the flour with the salt. Add the olive oil to the yeast, mix together and pour into the flour. Mix until the dough comes together.

Turn the dough out on a flat lightly floured board and knead for about 10 minutes, adding a little flour if necessary to prevent it from sticking. When the dough is smooth and shiny, place it in a clean lightly oiled bowl and turn it over on itself once. Cover and leave in a warm place to rise for about 30–40 minutes, until it has doubled in volume.

OLIVE OIL AND ROSEMARY BREAD top, OLIVE OIL AND GREEN OLIVE BREAD bottom.

Traditionally olive oil bread is very thin, so turn the dough out on a lightly floured board and, using a rolling pin, roll it into 1 large or 2 small ovals, about 1 cm/$\frac{1}{2}$ in thick.

With a sharp knife, make several diagonal cuts on the top of the ovals and then pull the cut edges apart slightly to open them up and give the loaves a latticed appearance.

Preheat the oven to 230C/450F/gas8 and lightly oil a baking sheet.

Place the dough on the prepared baking sheet. Brush the tops with olive oil and sprinkle with coarse sea salt. Cover and leave the dough in a warm place to rise for about 20 minutes.

Bake in the preheated oven for 20–30 minutes, or until golden brown.

Remove the bread from the tray and leave to cool on a wire rack.

Variations

1 Olive Oil and Green Olive Bread: after the dough has been rolled out into an oval, immediately put it on a baking sheet. Use the fingertips to make 24 holes over the surface of the dough, place a stoned green olive in each indentation, then brush with olive oil. Proceed as above, omitting the salt.

2 Olive Oil and Red Onion Bread: toss 1 thinly sliced red onion in a couple of tablespoons of olive oil and season with salt and freshly ground black pepper. When the dough has been shaped into ovals and placed on a baking sheet, spread the onions over the top and press them lightly into the dough. Brush with olive oil, sprinkle with salt and proceed as above.

3 Olive Oil and Rosemary Bread: add 1 tablespoon of finely chopped fresh rosemary to the bowl with the flour and proceed as above.

4 Olive Oil and Sun-dried Tomato Bread: add about 55 g/2 oz chopped sun-dried tomatoes to the bowl with the flour and proceed as above.

Brioche

Brioche is made from a yeast dough which has been enriched with eggs and butter.

A good unsalted butter is essential for brioche and those made in Gisors and Gournay, great French butter-producing centres, were particularly famous.

It may have have been in one of these towns that they dreamt up the brioche mousseline, a diet-defying concoction in which an extra 55 g/2 oz of butter is added to every 450 g/1 lb of dough, which is then baked in a tall mould further heightened by tying a band of buttered greaseproof paper around the top.

MAKES TWO 450 G/1 LB LOAVES

15 g/$\frac{1}{2}$ oz fresh yeast or 8 g/$\frac{1}{4}$ oz dried yeast
3$\frac{1}{2}$ tbsp sugar
400 g/14 oz strong white flour
a pinch of sea salt
5 size-1 eggs
115 g/4 oz unsalted butter, cut into small pieces,
plus extra for greasing

Put the yeast in a mixing bowl and stir in a large pinch of the sugar and 2 tablespoons of warm water. Cover and let stand in a warm place for about 10 minutes until it is quite foamy.

In another large bowl, sift in 375 g/13 oz of flour with the salt and remaining sugar. Beat 4 of the eggs into the yeast, mix together and pour into the flour. Mix until the dough comes together.

Turn the dough out on a flat lightly floured surface and knead for about 15 minutes. As the dough is very sticky, flour the hands every so often during the kneading process.

When the dough begins to come away from the fingers easily, place the butter, a few pieces at a time, on top of the dough and push them in. Squeeze the dough through the fingers to mix the butter in and then knead the dough with the palms of the hands. Carry on squeezing and kneading until all the butter has been incorporated.

Sprinkle some flour around the sides of the bowl and put the dough in. Cover and leave to prove in a warm place for about 2–3 hours, until it has doubled in size.

Knock back the dough by kneading it for a few seconds. Generously grease 2 brioche tins with butter. Divide the dough in 2 and then cut one-third off each piece. Roll all the pieces of dough into balls, put the larger balls on the bottom of the tins and, using the thumbs, make a circular indentation in the centre of each. Put a smaller ball on top of each and press it down firmly. Cover and leave them to prove again for about 1 hour.

Preheat the oven to 200C/400F/gas6.

Beat the remaining egg together with one tablespoon of water and, using a pastry brush, brush the brioches all over with the glaze. Bake in the preheated oven for 30 minutes, brushing them again with the glaze after 15 minutes.

Remove from the tins and turn them out on wire racks to cool.

Variation
Add 115 g/4 oz shelled and chopped walnuts to the flour before mixing in the yeast mixture, and then proceed as above.

BRIOCHE AND CORN MUFFINS (SEE OVERLEAF)

Corn Muffins

As well as the well-known cornbread, cheery yellow cornmeal is also used in such American favourites as hoecakes, pancakes and muffins, as below.

MAKES ABOUT 14

115 g/4 oz butter, melted and cooled, plus extra for greasing
255 g/9 oz fine cornmeal
150 g/5½ oz self-raising flour
75 g/2½ oz sugar
1 tbsp baking powder
1 tsp salt
2 eggs
300 ml/½ pt milk, warmed

Preheat the oven to 200C/400F/gas6. Generously butter some bun tins and line them with paper cases also greased with butter.

Sift the cornmeal, flour, sugar, baking powder and salt into a large bowl and make a well in the centre. In a separate bowl, lightly beat the eggs and stir in the melted butter and warm milk. Mix together and pour this into the centre of the dry ingredients. Using a wooden spoon, mix together until the batter is just smooth and blended.

Pour the batter into the prepared cases and bake in the preheated oven for about 20 minutes, or until well risen and golden brown.

Turn the muffins out on a wire rack and leave to cool slightly. Serve while still warm.

Variation
Dry-fry 115 g/4 oz of thinly cut slices of unsmoked streaky bacon until really crisp, drain them thoroughly on paper towels, crumble into small pieces and add to the flour. Proceed as above, cutting the quantity of salt by half.

Lincolnshire Plum Bread

This is actually more like a fruit cake than a bread. It will keep for several days, wrapped in foil and stored in an airtight tin.

MAKES TWO 450 G/1 LB LOAVES

225 g/8 oz unsalted butter, cut into small pieces, plus extra for greasing
350 g/12 oz plain flour
2 tsp baking powder
1 tsp freshly grated nutmeg
1 tsp ground cinnamon
1 tsp ground ginger
pinch of salt
55 g/2 oz blanched almonds, chopped
225 g/8 oz currants
225 g/8 oz sultanas
55 g/2 oz mixed peel, chopped
115 g/4 oz glacé cherries, chopped
225 g/8 oz soft brown sugar
4 eggs
a little milk, as necessary

Preheat the oven to 180C/350F/gas4 and generously grease two 450 g/1 lb loaf tins with butter.

Sift the flour with the baking powder, nutmeg, cinnamon, ginger and salt into a large bowl. Add the butter and, using a knife, cut it into the flour. Then, using the fingertips, rub it in lightly until the mixture is the texture of fine breadcrumbs.

Using a wooden spoon, stir in the almonds, currants, sultanas, mixed peel, cherries and sugar until thoroughly mixed.

In a separate bowl, beat the eggs lightly. Stir them into the mixture, adding a little milk if necessary, until it is smooth and of a dropping consistency.

Spoon the mixture into the prepared tins and bake in the preheated oven for about 1 hour. To test whether the loaves are done, insert a metal skewer into the centre: if it comes out clean, the loaves are ready.

Turn them out on a wire rack and leave to cool.

Shortcrust Pastry

This recipe made with plain flour results in a light biscuity pastry which is ideal as a base for savoury tarts. If you prefer using a brown or wholemeal flour, the pastry will be heavier. You must also remember that the higher the bran content, the more liquid the flour will absorb, so you will need to add more water.

MAKES 350 G/12 OZ

225 g/8 oz plain flour
pinch of salt
1 tsp caster sugar (for sweet pastry)
115 g/4 oz butter, cut into small pieces

If making the pastry by hand, sift the flour into a large bowl. Add the salt and sugar, if using, along with the butter and, using a knife, cut it into the flour. Then rub it in lightly with the fingertips until it is the texture of fine breadcrumbs. Slowly add 3–4 tablespoons of cold water and work the dough until it comes together.

Alternatively, put all the ingredients into a food processor and whizz for a few seconds until it has reduced to the texture of breadcrumbs. With the machine still running, slowly pour in the water and process until it comes together to form a ball.

Wrap the pastry up in film and leave it to rest in the refrigerator for 15–30 minutes before use.

Rich Shortcrust Pastry

This recipe creates an interesting base for open fruit tarts, particularly when it is enhanced with various flavouring ingredients as discussed on page 243.

MAKES 450 G/1 LB

255 g/9 oz plain flour
pinch of salt
1½ tsp caster sugar
1 size-1 egg
115 g/4 oz unsalted butter, cut into small pieces

Sift the flour into a large bowl with the salt and sugar. Make a well in the centre and break in the egg. Add the butter and slowly work the pieces in with the fingertips, drawing in the flour as you go.

When the dough is still crumbly, pour in 2–3 tablespoons of water and work the dough so it comes together to form a ball.

Alternatively, put all the ingredients in the food processor and whizz until crumbly. With the machine still running, pour in the water, a little at a time, and process until it comes together to form a ball.

Knead the pastry 2 or 3 times with the palm of the hand until it is completely smooth. Wrap it in greaseproof paper or a polythene bag and chill for several hours to allow it to rest before use.

If wrapped, it should keep for several days in the refrigerator.

Certosino or Italian Christmas Cake

The taste of this cake is far more aromatic than the traditional British Christmas cake. Instead of apples I have also made it with puréed quinces (see page 224), puréed pears or a mixture of the two and each time the spiced moist fruit flavour was superb. The cake matures and mellows with keeping so do make it at least a week before you want to eat it.

CERTOSINO

MAKES A 24 CM/9½ IN CAKE

55 g/2 oz unsalted butter, plus extra for greasing
75 g/2½ oz white seedless raisins
1½ tbsp rum
255–285 g/9–10 oz cooking apples, peeled and cored
juice of ¼ lemon
15 g/½ oz caster sugar
350 g/12 oz runny honey

1 tsp ground cinnamon
1 tbsp aniseed
375 g/13 oz plain flour
170 g/6 oz blanched almonds, coarsely chopped
75 g/2½ oz bitter chocolate, coarsely chopped
170 g/6 oz candied mixed orange and lemon peel
45 g/1½ oz pine nuts
1½ tsp bicarbonate of soda
3 tbsp apricot jam
candied fruit and walnut or pecan halves, to decorate

Preheat the oven to 160C/325F/gas3 and generously grease a large loose-bottomed 24 cm/9½ in cake tin or savarin mould with butter.

To prepare the fruit, put the raisins in a small bowl with the rum and leave to soak for 30 minutes. Meanwhile put the apples in a saucepan with the lemon juice, sugar, 15 g/½ oz of the butter and 2 tablespoons of water. Simmer gently for about 10–15 minutes until reduced to a soft purée. Pass the purée through a sieve, weigh out 170 g/6 oz and leave to cool.

Put the honey in the top part of a double boiler, or in a bowl set over a saucepan half-filled with warm water, and warm over a medium heat. Add the remaining butter along with 3 tablespoons of water and stir until the butter has all melted. Then stir in the cinnamon and aniseed and remove from the heat.

Sift the flour into a large bowl. Then slowly pour in the honey mixture, stirring vigorously with a wooden spoon until it is well blended. Stir in the apple purée, the almonds, chocolate, candied peel and the raisins with the rum. Carefully fold in the pine nuts so as not to crush them. Dissolve the bicarbonate of soda in a couple of teaspoons of water and stir this into the mixture also.

Spoon the mixture into the prepared tin and bake in the preheated oven for 1¼–1½ hours.

To test whether the cake is done, insert a metal skewer into the centre: if it comes out clean, the cake is ready. Turn it out on a wire rack and leave to cool.

To decorate the cake, melt the apricot jam in a saucepan over a low heat along with 1 tablespoon of water. Brush the top with the jam, then stud the walnut or pecan halves and candied fruit over the top and finally brush the cake all over with the jam to set the fruit in place.

As well as being used in many Italian and French cakes, candied fruits are a traditional gift at Christmas and New Year.

Chestnut and Orange Cake

Chestnut flour is made from dried and ground sweet chestnuts (see page 176) and is used frequently for baking in Italy, France and Switzerland. Unfortunately it is rather difficult to buy in this country, so I have adapted this recipe to use fresh chestnuts. This gives a less smooth, but more interesting texture, so even if you can buy the right flour, I still think the cake should be made with a mixture of chestnut flour and chestnuts: you can then be sure of deriving some of the benefit from the whole nuts.

MAKES A 22.5 CM/8½ IN CAKE

170 g/6 oz unsalted butter, plus extra for greasing
85 g/3 oz chestnut flour plus 85 g/3 oz chestnuts or 255–285 g/
9–10 oz chestnuts
115 g/4 oz caster sugar
2 size-1 eggs
zest and juice of 2 large oranges
85 g/3 oz self-raising flour
½ tsp salt
55 g/2 oz fresh white breadcrumbs
115 g/4 oz icing sugar

Preheat the oven to 190C/375F/gas5 and generously grease two 21 cm/8½ in sandwich cake tins with butter. Line them with discs of buttered greaseproof paper.

To prepare the chestnuts, use a sharp knife to make a couple of slits in the skin of each. Put them in a saucepan, pour over enough boiling water to cover and simmer for about 5 minutes. Take out a few chestnuts at a time, drain and refresh them under running cold water. Then peel off their skins, which should now come off quite easily. Return them to the pan with 2 tablespoons of water and simmer for about 10–15 minutes until soft. Drain, weigh out 55 g/2 oz (or 170 g/6 oz if not using chestnut flour) and chop them finely.

In a large bowl, cream 115 g/4 oz of the butter with the sugar until light and fluffy. In another bowl, lightly beat the eggs and then slowly beat them into the butter, a little at a time, taking care not to curdle the mixture. Stir in the orange zest, reserving about 1 teaspoon. Sift in the chestnut flour if using, the self-raising flour and the salt and fold them into the mixture along with the breadcrumbs and chopped chestnuts.

Pour the mixture into the prepared pans, smooth the tops and bake in the preheated oven for about 45 minutes. To test whether the cakes are done: insert a metal skewer into the centre, if it comes out clean the cakes are ready.

Allow them to cool for a few minutes in their tins. Then turn them out on a wire rack, peel off the greaseproof paper and leave to cool completely.

To prepare the icing: in a clean bowl, beat the remaining butter until soft and smooth. Sift in the icing sugar and fold it in with the remaining orange zest. Then beat in the orange juice, a little at a time, until the butter is soft, quite runny and easy to spread.

Spread the bottom of each cooled cake with a thick layer of the butter filling and sandwich them together.

Chill for about 15 minutes before serving.

Modern machinery makes harvesting much less strenuous than in previous centuries left. Sweet chestnuts right.

The Best-ever Chocolate Cake

This is not self-promotion, but a claim that I make on behalf of Josceline Dimbleby, whose recipe this is. Not only is this cake unrefusable but it is also incredibly easy. The secret, according to Jossie, is to make it with really fresh breadcrumbs, either from a white or brown loaf.

One of my two best friends is also a demon baker and she makes this cake at the drop of a hat, aided and abetted by her three sons: three-year old twins and their older brother, aged five. Last year they made it as my birthday cake and we all wolfed it down almost before the candles were blown out. You cannot get a better recommendation than that.

SERVES 8–10

225 g/8 oz unsalted butter, plus extra for greasing
225 g/8 oz plain dark chocolate, broken into pieces
225 g/8 oz caster sugar
6 eggs
225 g/8 oz ground hazelnuts (see page 64)
115 g/4 oz fresh breadcrumbs, brown or white
grated zest of 1 orange
2 tbsp marmalade

for the glaze:

115 g/4 oz plain dark chocolate, broken into pieces
2 tsp runny honey
55 g/2 oz unsalted butter, cut into pieces
30 g/1 oz white chocolate (optional), to decorate

Preheat the oven to 190C/375F/gas5 and generously grease two 21 cm/8½ in sandwich cake tins with butter. Line these with discs of buttered greaseproof paper.

Melt the chocolate in the upper section of a double boiler, or in a bowl set in a saucepan half-filled with water, over a medium to low heat and stir until smooth.

Remove from the heat and leave to cool slightly.

In a large bowl, cream the butter until smooth. Then whisk in the sugar, a little at a time, until the mixture is light and fluffy. Beat in the eggs, one at a time, beating well after each addition. If the mixture looks a little curdled, do not worry. Whisk the melted chocolate into the mixture, stir in the hazelnuts and breadcrumbs and finally stir in the orange zest.

Spoon the mixture into the prepared tins, smooth the tops and bake in the preheated oven for between 20–25 minutes, until the centre is firm to a light touch.

As these cakes are quite fragile, allow them to cool in their tins. Then loosen the edges with a knife, turn one of the cakes out on a serving plate and remove the greaseproof paper disc. Using a knife, lightly spread the cake with a layer of marmalade. Carefully turn the other cake out on a board, peel off the greaseproof paper disc and place it on top of the other cake.

To make the glaze: put the dark chocolate, honey and butter in the upper section of a double boiler, or in a bowl set in a saucepan half-filled with water, over a medium to low heat and stir until smooth. Remove from the heat and continue beating until it thickens. Pour over the cake and spread evenly all over with a spatula. Leave to set before serving.

If you want to decorate the cake: before the glaze has set hard, hold the piece of white chocolate over the cake and use a potato peeler to shave off thin slivers, allowing them to fall over the cake.

THE BEST-EVER CHOCOLATE CAKE

Thin Crackers

These crackers bear absolutely no relation to commercially manufactured cream crackers as they are far crisper and have a far more interesting taste.

In the 'good old days', they were rolled out using a 'biscuit break', a cunning invention consisting of a heavy adjustable roller attached to the pastry table. It could be rolled back and forth over the dough, thus relieving the cook of the hard work of flattening it. As this piece of equipment no longer seems to exist, you will just have to press extra hard on your rolling pin.

These biscuits have a short shelf-life and should really be eaten on the day they are made. If you do want to keep them, put them in a tin while still warm along with a sheet of greaseproof paper to prevent them from going soggy. You can always revive them by warming them briefly in the oven.

MAKES 15–20

55 g/2 oz butter, cut into small pieces, plus extra for greasing
225 g/8 oz strong white flour
large pinch of salt
1 tsp baking powder
6 tbsp single cream
ground sea salt, for sprinkling

Preheat the oven to 180C/350F/gas4 and generously grease a baking sheet with butter.

Sift the flour into a bowl, with the salt and baking powder. Add the butter and cut it into the flour with a knife. Then rub it in lightly with the fingertips, until it is the texture of fine breadcrumbs. Stir in the cream, then gather the mixture together to make a firm dough, adding a tablespoon of water if necessary.

On a lightly floured flat surface, roll the dough out very thinly, pressing down quite hard on it. Using a 7.5 cm/3 in biscuit cutter, cut it into rounds. Arrange the biscuits on the prepared baking sheet, prick them all over with a fork and sprinkle over a little sea salt. Bake in the preheated oven for 10–15 minutes, or until golden brown. Turn out on wire racks and leave to cool.

Pistachio Tuiles

Tuiles are light soft biscuits with a slightly sticky texture derived from their high egg white and sugar content. Classically they are made with ground almonds instead of flour, and scattered with flaked almonds. Whatever the content, they must be bent over a rolling pin to give them their characteristic shape of curved tiles or tuiles.

MAKES ABOUT 30

115 g/4 oz unsalted butter, melted, plus extra for greasing
4 egg whites
225 g/8 oz caster sugar
115 g/4 oz plain flour
55 g/2 oz pistachio nuts, peeled and roughly chopped

Preheat the oven to 190C/375F/gas5 and generously grease a baking sheet with butter.

In a large bowl, whisk the egg whites until soft and foaming. Whisk in the sugar, then add the melted butter, sift in the flour and mix together gently.

Bake the mixture in batches. Put a teaspoon of the mixture on the prepared baking sheet and, using the back of the spoon, spread it out into a thin circle. Sprinkle some chopped pistachios on top and repeat the process until the baking sheet is covered, allowing space between them for spreading.

Bake in the preheated oven for about 6 minutes, or until a pale golden brown. Remove the tray from the oven and immediately lift off the biscuits with a palette knife. While they are still soft and pliable, mould each one over a rolling pin so that they set in a curved shape. Leave to cool on a wire rack.

Repeat the process until all the mixture is used up. Store the tuiles in airtight tins until required.

Brandy Snap Baskets

Although the conventional way of serving brandy snaps is to curl them around the handle of a wooden spoon and then pipe them full of whipped cream, I like to mould them into individual small baskets and then fill them with fresh berries or an ice-cream or sorbet. Larger pieces of the mixture moulded over small bowls also make delightful serving dishes.

MAKES 20–30

115 g/4 oz unsalted butter, plus extra for greasing
115 g/4 oz golden syrup
115 g/4 oz granulated sugar
115 g/4 oz plain flour
pinch of salt
2 tsp ground ginger
1 tsp lemon juice

Preheat the oven to 160C/325F/gas3 and generously butter a baking sheet and several small cups or round moulds for pressing the brandy snaps over.

Put the butter with the golden syrup and sugar in the upper section of a double boiler, or in a bowl set in a saucepan half-filled with water, over a medium to low heat and stir until melted.

Remove from the heat, sift in the flour and salt and beat it in along with the ginger and lemon juice until the mixture is smooth.

Put teaspoonfuls of the mixture on the prepared baking sheet, placing them about 15 cm/6 in apart to allow room for them to spread. Bake in the preheated oven for about 8–10 minutes, or until golden brown. Leave to cool for a few moments (they should hold together but still be very pliable).

Using a spatula, lift the slightly cooled brandy snaps off the baking sheet and press them over the moulds. If you leave them to cool for too long, they will snap when you try to press them into shape; reheat them in the oven for a couple of minutes and try again.

Once shaped, leave them to cool and then serve filled with a sorbet or ice-cream (see page 247) or store them in an airtight tin until required.

Almond Biscuits

Cornflour added to flour lightens the texture when baked, so these biscuits are particularly rich and crumbly.

MAKES ABOUT 20

225 g/8 oz unsalted butter, plus extra for greasing
170 g/6 oz plain flour
30 g/1 oz cornflour
55 g/2 oz icing sugar
30 g/1 oz ground almonds
zest of 1 orange
1 tsp orange flower water
about 20 almonds

Preheat the oven to 180C/350F/gas4 and grease a baking sheet with butter.

In a saucepan, melt the butter over a low heat. Remove from the heat and sift in the flour, cornflour and icing sugar. Add the ground almonds, orange zest and orange flower water and beat the mixture to a smooth paste with a wooden spoon.

Break off small amounts of the paste and roll them lightly into balls between the palms. Put the balls on the prepared baking sheet and flatten them slightly with the thumb. Arrange an almond in the centre of each, pressing it down gently.

Bake in the preheated oven for about 20 minutes, or until a golden brown.

Turn out on a wire rack and leave to cool.

Bread and Butter Pudding

It takes a famous Swiss chef like Anton Mosimann to transform a stodgy traditional pudding into something light and wonderful. His recipe relies on a creamy flourless vanilla-scented custard and slices of fresh rolls, to make a British pudding of which we can all justifiably be proud.

SERVES 4–6

45 g/1½ oz unsalted butter, plus extra for greasing
300 ml/½ pt milk
300 ml/½ pt double cream
1 vanilla pod, split
3 eggs
125 g/4½ oz caster sugar
3 small soft bread rolls, cut into thin slices
30 g/1 oz sultanas, soaked in water and drained
2 tbsp apricot jam
2 tbsp icing sugar

Preheat the oven to 160C/325F/gas3 and generously grease an oval pie dish with butter.

In a heavy-based saucepan, put the milk, cream and vanilla pod over a low heat and slowly bring to the boil. Just as it is about to reach boiling point, remove from the heat.

In a large bowl, beat the eggs and sugar together until it is a pale yellow. Then slowly pour in the milk and cream mixture, stirring continuously.

Butter the slices of bread roll with one-quarter of the butter and arrange them on the bottom of the dish. Sprinkle over the sultanas, then pour over the milk and egg mixture through a sieve. Do not worry if the bread floats to the top. Dot with the remaining butter and cover with a sheet of greaseproof paper.

Place the dish in a deep roasting pan half-filled with hot water and bake in the preheated oven for 35–45 minutes, or until firmly set around the sides but still quite wobbly in the centre.

Remove from the oven and leave to cool for a short while. Then, using a pastry brush, lightly brush the top with a thin coating of apricot jam. Sieve over the icing sugar and serve warm.

BREAD AND BUTTER PUDDING opposite.

Buckwheat Pancakes

Like oatmeal, BUCKWHEAT or KASHA comes in fine, medium and coarse grades and can be used for making dumplings or for stuffing geese or carp. It may also be served to accompany Stroganoff instead of rice.

BUCKWHEAT FLOUR, a dirty grey in colour speckled with black, is ground from the seed. It is used primarily in Eastern Europe and Northern France, either plain or mixed with wheat flour for flat pancakes, galettes, or blinis — pancakes leavened with yeast which are usually served with caviar.

MAKES ABOUT 12

55 g/2 oz buckwheat flour
100 g/3½ oz strong white flour
½ tsp salt
3 eggs, lightly beaten
3 tbsp unsalted butter, melted
250 ml/8 fl oz milk
sunflower oil, for frying

Make the batter by sifting the buckwheat flour with the white flour and salt into a bowl. Beat in the eggs, then slowly beat in the melted butter, milk and 250 ml/8 fl oz water. Whisk until smooth.

Alternatively, put the milk in a food processor with the water and eggs and whizz together. Then, with the machine still running, slowly add the buckwheat flour, followed by the plain flour, salt and melted butter and whizz until smooth.

Either way, let the batter stand in a cool place to rest for about 1 hour before use.

To cook the pancakes: heat a heavy-based omelette or frying pan over a medium heat until very hot. Using a pastry brush, brush the inside all over with a little oil, then return it to the heat. Pour in about 1 tablespoon of the batter and swirl it around the pan until it is spread in an even thin layer over the bottom.

Cook it for 2–3 minutes, loosening the edges with a palette knife. Then, with a flick of the wrist, toss the pancake in the air and catch it as it lands, uncooked side down. Cook it for a further 2 minutes. (If the idea of tossing a pancake terrifies you, just use the spatula to flick it over.) Turn the cooked pancake out on a warmed dish and keep warm.

Continue cooking the rest of the batter in the same way. Fill each pancake with fruit compote (see below) and serve with crème fraîche.

Fruit Compote

MAKES 1.35 K/3 LB

225 g/8 oz dried apricots
115 g/4 oz prunes
115 g/4 oz dried figs
115 g/4 oz dried pears
115 g/4 oz raisins
1 tea bag
zest and juice of 2 oranges
1 cinnamon stick
large pinch of freshly grated nutmeg
pinch of ground cloves
pinch of ground ginger
115 g/4 oz demerara sugar
100 ml/3½ fl oz rum

Put the apricots, prunes, figs, pears and raisins in a large bowl along with the tea bag. Pour over enough warm water to cover and leave to soak overnight.

Remove the tea bag and put the fruit into a saucepan which has a tight-fitting lid. Add the orange zest and

After the harvest in Tuscany.

juice along with the cinnamon, nutmeg, cloves, ginger, sugar and rum. Stir together and bring to the boil over a medium to low heat. Just before it reaches boiling point, turn the heat down to low, cover and simmer for about 45 minutes, or until the fruit is soft.

Remove the cinnamon stick and serve with the buckwheat pancakes or use as a filling for Winter Pudding (see page 239) or with yoghurt for breakfast.

Savarin

The savarin is named after Brillat-Savarin, the celebrated French lawyer and gastronome. He supposedly devised the syrup used to soak the cake which is traditionally made in a large ring mould, now commonly known as a savarin.

SERVES 4–6

55 g/2 oz unsalted butter, melted, plus extra for greasing
125 g/4½ oz strong white flour
pinch of salt
15 g/½ oz caster sugar
2 eggs
8 g/¼ oz fresh yeast or 4 g/⅛ oz dried yeast

for the syrup:
250 g/8½ oz caster sugar
2 tsp rose water

for the filling:
225 g/8 oz mixed berries, including strawberries, blackcurrants, blackberries etc

Preheat the oven to 200C/400F/gas6 and generously grease a 20–22.5 cm/8–9 in ring mould with butter.

Sift the flour into a large bowl, along with the salt and sugar. Add one of the eggs and stir together with a wooden spoon. Dissolve the yeast in 1 tablespoon of lukewarm water and add to the flour with the remaining egg. Mix together thoroughly, knead it in the bowl until smooth and elastic, then beat in the melted butter.

Put the dough into the prepared mould, cover and leave to rest in a warm place for about 30 minutes. Bake in the preheated oven for 20–25 minutes. Turn out on a wire rack and leave to cool.

Make the syrup: in a pan over a low heat, put the sugar with 500 ml/16 fl oz of water and slowly heat until the sugar is dissolved. Turn up the heat and boil for about 5 minutes. Remove from the heat and stir in the rose water.

Balance the savarin on the rack with a bowl underneath and baste it with the syrup, leaving it to soak through to the centre.

Arrange the savarin on a serving plate, fill the centre with the berries and spoon over any remaining syrup.

SAVARIN

The Orchard and Soft Fruit Garden

Spring blossom heralds a rich harvest throughout summer and autumn. Few other foods provide such a spectacular range of intense tastes and colours as the fruits of the orchard trees, soft-fruit canes and bushes and the tangled branches of the hedgerows.

It has always struck me as a little curious that, although the supermarket shelves are filled all year round with mangoes, pineapples, bananas, mangosteens, pomegranates, kumquats, rambutans, tamarillos and just about every other exotic fruit you care to mention, you cannot buy much in the way of varieties of our home-grown top fruit, from trees, and soft fruit, from bushes. Where are the hundreds of varieties of apples that we boast? Or the range of plums, soft berries or pears? It is not that I have anything against foreign fruit, it is just that I wish the range of the varieties that we do grow was better represented.

Obviously, it would be ridiculous to restrict ourselves to home-grown fruit. For example, it would mean ignoring the treasures of the citrus fruits, as we just cannot grow them in our climate. The citrus family is enormous and members include the highly useful LEMON and the closely related, more acidic LIME; the astringent yellow-fleshed GRAPEFRUIT, and its sweeter ruby-red cousins; and, of course, the ORANGE, of which there are supposedly 2,000 varieties worldwide although in fact only 200 are grown on a commercial scale.

There are several basic categories of orange: the 'blond', the 'blood', the 'navel' and the bitter-sweet SEVILLE ORANGE, essential for a good old-fashioned sharp marmalade.

Another important group within the citrus family are the smaller, easier to peel and sometimes seedless MANDARIN ORANGE and its close relatives, like the SATSUMA, CLEMENTINE and the dome-shaped MINNEOLA. As citrus fruits can be crossed so easily, many hybrids have been developed – even hybrids from hybrids: new crosses are constantly being produced so it is quite difficult to keep up with all the latest developments.

When buying citrus fruits, choose fruit which weigh heavy in the hand as this is a sure sign of juiciness. The skin must be firm and it must look and feel as if it contains plenty of moisture, as once it starts to crinkle or shrivel the fruit is getting tired and old. Most of the citrus fruit we buy is grown in a Mediterranean-type climate, resulting in evenly coloured skins. However, fruit grown in the tropics may look dirty and somewhat discoloured: do not be put off by this as it is simply due to the lack of cold nights during the ripening season.

Oranges, lemons and limes are vital for cooking. Not only do you need their juice for flavouring but their zest can also be added to great effect as it gives a bitter-sweet fruity taste that adds subtlety to many a dish, ranging from soups to cakes.

Unfortunately most oranges and lemons are coated with an invisible wax containing toxic chemicals to protect them and prolong their life during transportation. So if you are going to use orange or lemon zest, make sure either to buy uncoated fruit or organically grown untreated fruit, or first scrub the skin with hot water and a tiny drop of washing-up liquid then rinse it thoroughly and pat it dry.

Particularly keen gardeners claim to be able to grow grapes, figs, apricots, peaches, nectarines and melons in our rather doleful climate. To my mind, however, to be successful they do need the help of a hothouse or, at the very least, the shelter of a glasshouse or verandah or the protection of a south-facing wall. All these fruits need remorseless sun to ripen and sweeten them and to allow them to develop their heady succulence.

It goes without saying that the best GRAPES come from the areas that boast a Mediterranean-type climate, such as the Mediterranean region itself, California and parts of South Africa and the Americas. Although generally thought of simply as either black or green, grapes can be any colour from a deep rich purple, through a ruby red to a pale creamy yellow. Table grapes, ie those for eating rather than making wine, come in endless varieties and choice must depend on preference and their taste and colour. Fortunately, as grapes are so small, it is often possible

Morello cherry blossom

to sample them before buying. My favourite variety of grape is the large richly scented muscat: sweet and heavy with a full flavour, these are one of the treats of autumn. If cooking with grapes, buying a seedless variety can save a lot of time and trouble. However, remember it is always possible to sieve a sauce to remove the pips and skins.

Depending on the variety, the skin of the FIG can range from a pale yellow, through a bright green to a deep purple; and their fleshy insides can be anything

from a pale pink to a deep scarlet. In fact it is the ripeness of the fruit rather than the colour which is an indication of flavour: for really ripe fruit look for soft figs which are just beginning to split at the bottom. Avoid any figs with spotted skins as this means that the fruit has turned sour. Fresh figs should always be eaten within a couple of days of purchase.

PEACHES with their soft downy skin, the smoother, more vividly coloured NECTARINES and smaller juicy APRICOTS all require a similar warm sunny climate to achieve perfection. Although far less easy to buy, it is worth trying the white-fleshed peach if you come across it; its flesh is softer and much more aromatic than the less-refined yellow-fleshed varieties.

The perfect MELON relies on the spring rains to swell its fruit and the summer sun to give it its ripe lusciousness and complex spiciness. Unlike most other fruits, however, melons do not carry on ripening once they have been broken from the vine. Broadly speaking, there are three principal groups of melons: 'winter' melons, with a smooth or slightly ridged hard skin, ripen late and the Honeydew is probably the best-known variety; 'musk' melons are also known as 'nutmeg', 'netted' or 'embroidered' melons; and Cantaloupes are those old-fashioned bumpy melons often looking more like pumpkins. The Charentais is a superb example of this last group. With its pale green shagreen skin and deep orange flesh, there is nothing quite like its heady sweetness, sharpened by a peppering of spiciness, and its unctuous juiciness.

The best way to choose melons is to cup one in each hand, weighing one against the other – always go for the heavier. Also gently press it and sniff it around the stalk; if it is slightly soft and has a perfumed scent, the chances are it is a winner.

Summer's bounty of luscious nectarines, cherries, peaches and plums.

Fruit from the Trees

During the summer and early autumn the orchards are heavy with fruit. First come the CHERRIES; then the cooking PLUMS swiftly followed by the eating plums, like the orangey red Victorias, the purplish-black Kirk's Blues and the pale, sugary GREENGAGES. The other members of the plum family, such as DAMSONS, BULLACES and SLOES, will not ripen until early autumn, when they are ready for bottling, turning into jams and jellies or used for flavouring gin – a traditional Christmas Day favourite.

Some APPLES are ripe for eating by mid-August, as are some PEARS; but you will have to wait until October to enjoy home-grown QUINCES. The hardier MEDLAR may ripen on the tree in the Mediterranean region, but here in our more temperate climate it cannot be eaten until early October, when it is picked from the branch 'bletted' ie soft, brown and half-rotten.

Apples

Apple-lovers from all over the world agree that Britain produces the finest apples, as – for once – our climate works to our advantage.

Ideal conditions for apples are plenty of rain to swell the fruit, comparatively low temperatures for slow ripening, weak sun to colour the fruit and cool nights to intensify the flavour; this pretty much sums up the British summer! So next time you sit shivering in August, you can console yourself with the thought that at least the apples are thriving and developing those well-rounded complex flavours for which they are justly famous.

In Brogdale in Kent, home of the British National Fruit Collection, there are over 3,000 named varieties of apple – heaven knows how many there are in the world! No two apple varieties are ever alike and no other fruit has such a wide range of tastes, aromas, textures, colours and shapes. Cox's Orange Pippin, with its crisp juiciness and nutty flavour, is perhaps one of the best known and Egremont Russet, Discovery, Katy, Granny Smith and Gala are other successful commercial varieties.

There are three basic uses for apples: making cider, cooking and eating. Cider apples are grown purely for their juice. You can, of course, eat them but you will soon find that it is not really a worthwhile experience. Their particular quality is that when pressed they juice easily; so, although on first bite you will find them moist and succulent, their flesh soon disintegrates as you chew and becomes pappy – giving an effect rather like sucking on blotting paper.

Cookers have a higher acid content and the best varieties include Howgate Wonder which tends to collapse to a fluffy heap and the Bramley which retains its shape much better. They are perfect for baking whole or cooking to a purée for apple sauce, an old-fashioned covered pie or crumble. The simplest way to make a purée is to peel and core a couple of apples and simmer them over a low heat with a little water or wine, a knob of butter, a stick of cinnamon, a couple of cloves and sugar to taste.

However, when I make an open apple tart or Tarte Tatin (see page 222) I prefer to cook with eaters as they will generally hold their shape better and they also have far more interesting complex flavours. Although just to be perverse, sometimes if I want to eat a particularly sharp apple I may well choose a cooker.

Eaters fall into four distinctive seasonal categories: 'early', ripening and ready for eating in August to early September, with a short shelf-life, like Discovery; 'mid', ripening in September to October, like James Grieve,

Cox's or Worcester Pearmain; 'late', ready for eating in October to December, such as Elstar; 'extra-late', ready for eating in December to March. Nowadays with controlled storage, of course, seasons can be extended and home-grown apples will last right through to May. The remaining gap is then filled with varieties imported from New Zealand, South Africa and the USA.

Experts look for several qualities in their apples: appearance, colour and shape; quality or toughness of skin; taste, the balance of sweetness and acidity and the complexity of aromas; length of flavour, ie how long it retains its flavour; texture of flesh, ie how juicy and succulent it is.

When buying apples avoid any with bruises, although a blemished, broken or wrinkled skin does not necessarily mean that it will not taste good. The size can be a controversial issue; some varieties produce smaller fruit, for example the natural size of the Cox, when it is at its best with a compact and less diluted flavour, is between 60–65 mm/$2\frac{1}{2}$ in; but, for reasons best known to themselves, the supermarket chains insist on larger apples. They think that a 70 mm/$2\frac{3}{4}$ in apple is ideal, so growers are then forced to comply with their specifications by stringent pruning.

Unfortunately we are also in danger of losing some of the old-fashioned and less well-known apples that are grown on too small a scale to satisfy the quantities which the supermarkets demand. Admittedly some may crop irregularly, do not travel well, bruise easily, make small fruit or have a short shelf-life, so they can be difficult for any ordinary wholesaler or retailer to handle. You can still, however, find these unusual varieties in farm shops and orchards and it is worth seeking them out: not only do some taste superb, but it is vital that we all make every effort to preserve what is, in effect, part of our culinary heritage. Have you ever eaten such old-fashioned apples as Worcester Pearmain, with its dense strawberry taste, the tiny Pitmaston Pine Apple, with its hint of pineapple, or Lady

Sudeley, which has been grown for well over 150 years? There are also the creamy Ribston Pippin; Tydeman's Late Orange; Orléans Reinette; Ashmead's Kernel, which reminds you of acid drops, and D'Arcy Spice, an East Anglian favourite with, as its name suggests, a hot spicy aroma. These are just a few of my favourites.

Old-fashioned varieties of apple often have more interesting, complex flavours.

Tarte Tatin

This dish needs a firm variety of apple which holds together well and preferably also one with a sweet dense flavour, so a cooker just will not do. When I can find them, I use the old-fashioned Orléans Reinette; otherwise the nutty Egremont Russet or a well-ripened yellow-skinned Golden Delicious are more than acceptable.

It is up to you whether you peel the apples. Frankly I don't bother, as I like the contrast of the soft flesh and the skin. However, as you start cooking the apples on top of the stove, you must use a heavy-based flameproof pie dish that will not buckle under direct heat. I find a cast-iron skillet is ideal.

SERVES 4–6

85 g/3 oz butter, plus extra for greasing
55 g/2 oz caster sugar
675 g/1½ lb apples (see above), cored
½ tsp ground cinnamon
225 g/8 oz rich shortcrust pastry (see page 199), rested

Preheat the oven to 200C/400F/gas6 and heavily grease a flameproof dish or thick-based cake pan with butter. Sprinkle the bottom with about 30 g/1 oz of the sugar.

Depending on the size of the apples, cut each half into 2 or 3 slices about 1 cm/½ in thick. Arrange the slices of apple overlapping around the dish, sprinkle them with cinnamon and sugar, dot with butter and then repeat the process until all the apple, butter and sugar are used up.

Put the pan over a medium to high heat and cook for about 10–15 minutes until the sugar has caramelized, taking care not to let it burn. If a lot of liquid is produced, as sometimes happens if you are using very juicy apples, simply pour some of it off into a small saucepan (hold a lid against the apples to keep them in place while draining) and boil the liquid over a high heat to reduce it until it is thick and syrupy, then pour it back over the apples.

Meanwhile, roll out the pastry into a circle about 6 mm/¼ in thick and slightly larger than the pan. Fold in the edge of the dough to make a border, press it flat and crimp the edge and pierce the pastry all over with a fork to make tiny holes through which the steam can escape.

Lay the pastry over the apples, folded side down, and bake in the preheated oven for about 25 minutes, covering the pastry with foil if it begins to get too brown. Remove the tart from the oven and unmould it by placing a serving plate over the pan and carefully turning it the right side up.

Serve hot or warm with a huge bowl of cream or crème fraîche.

TARTE TATIN

Apple and Quince Soufflé

The QUINCE *is a subtly fragrant fruit with a heady honeyed perfume. The type most familiar in Britain is similar to the pear in shape and it can be easily distinguished by its golden yellow skin covered with a dusty down.*

Quince is the one top fruit that cannot be eaten raw as it is too hard and acid. When cooked with sugar, however, the flesh turns a delicate soft pink and makes wonderful jam, jelly or paste. Interestingly, the Spanish name for the fruit is marmelo *and it is thought that marmalade was originally made with quince, the use of Seville oranges being a later adaptation.*

In season from September to November, few quinces are actually grown in this country as the fruit prefers a warmer climate. So if you are tempted by this recipe and cannot find the right fruit, try it with pears instead, adding a little lemon juice to the poaching water.

SERVES 4–6

30 g/1 oz butter, plus extra for greasing
3 tbsp caster sugar
225 g/8 oz quince, peeled and cored
225 g/8 oz aromatic eating apples, peeled and cored
2 cloves
1 tbsp Calvados
3 size-1 eggs, separated
1 tsp icing sugar

Wicker baskets hang ready for apple-picking.

Preheat the oven to 200C/400C/gas6 and grease a soufflé dish with butter. Put a tablespoon of the caster sugar into the dish and turn it round and round to coat it evenly with the sugar.

Chop the quince into small dice and put them into a heavy saucepan with 5 tablespoons of water. Chop the apples into slightly larger pieces and scatter them on top along with the cloves.

Cover the pan and simmer over a medium to low heat for about 10–15 minutes until the juices run and the fruit softens. Remove the lid, turn up the heat and simmer rapidly for a further 5–10 minutes until it has reduced to a soft but dry consistency.

Purée the fruit in a food processor or by passing it through a sieve. Stir in the butter, Calvados and caster sugar to taste (make the purée on the sweet side as the sweetness will be diluted by the beaten egg whites) and beat in the egg yolks while it is still warm.

In a separate bowl, whisk the egg whites until they form stiff peaks. Using a metal spoon, carefully fold them into the fruit purée. Pour the mixture into the prepared soufflé dish and put the dish on a baking tray. Place in the preheated oven and bake for 20 minutes.

Half open the oven, carefully draw out the baking sheet just far enough to be able to reach the soufflé and sprinkle the top with icing sugar. Close the door gently and leave for another 5 minutes. Serve immediately.

Spiced Crab Apples

Once the countryside was full of wild crab apple trees bearing tiny sour fruit. Because of their high acidity these apples were never eaten raw but were used to great effect in cider or in pickles and jellies. It is their very astringency which makes them ideal for pickling, as their sharpness counteracts the vinegar and spices and their flavour is never overpowered. The pickle is delicious with roast goose (see page 117) or Homemade Sausages (see page 150).

Contrary to popular belief, our native wild or crab apple trees are a different species to our eating apples. The latter come from an eastern strain which were cross-bred to produce the cultivated variety. The term crab apple has also come to cover the ornamental non-edible varieties introduced from China and Japan which grow in many gardens.

I am particularly fond of this recipe as, although you almost never find them on sale, crab apples are often grown as propagators in orchards and, as I hate to see anything going to waste, this is the ideal solution for coping with the fiddly sour fruit.

MAKES 2 K/4½ LB

1 k/2¼ lb crab apples
300 ml/½ pt white wine vinegar
225 g/8 oz demerara sugar
3 cloves
½ tsp freshly grated nutmeg
6 allspice berries
15 g/½ oz fresh root ginger, peeled and coarsely chopped
½ cinnamon stick, crushed

Put the apples in a large preserving pan or saucepan along with enough water to cover, bring to the boil over a medium heat and simmer for about 5 minutes, or until the apples just begin to soften.

Using a slotted spoon, transfer the apples to warm dry sterilized jars and reserve the liquid.

In a clean saucepan over a medium heat, put the vinegar with the sugar, cloves, nutmeg, allspice, ginger and cinnamon. Bring to the boil and simmer for 10 minutes. Add 300 ml/½ pt of the liquid in which the apples have cooked, turn down the heat and simmer for another 5 minutes.

Pour the syrup over the apples and leave to cool before sealing the jars.

Store in a cool place for about 7 days to allow the flavours to mellow before eating.

Pears

The perfect dessert pear is juicy with a buttery texture and a mellow, sweet flavour. They should be eaten on their own or accompanied by shavings of a hard strong cheese, like Parmesan. During the late summer in France and Italy, you can buy tiny bright-yellow pears which look as if they might be straight out of a still-life, with skins lightly russeted and brushed with a watercolour pink. If you see them – and I must confess I cannot name the variety – do buy them: their melting tenderness and honey sweetness almost defy description.

In this country we are not so lucky. Almost on the edge of pear country, most of our commercially grown pears are picked when still unripe. You can ripen them at home by keeping them in a cool place wrapped in brown paper. However they are never the same; their texture is mealy and they never attain that full rounded perfection given by lots of sun.

Like apples, there are several varieties of pear and each one has a distinctive flavour and a natural season which, also like apples, has been extended by controlled storage. The best known and most widely grown in this country is the Conference. Sharp and firm with a slightly gritty texture, it is easily distinguished by its long tapered shape and heavily russeted green skin: it is a good all-rounder and may be cooked or eaten raw. The Doyenne de Comice is fatter, more conically shaped and far sweeter, as is the Williams Bon Chrétien which is pale-yellow, sometimes flushed with red, and has a particularly soft, yielding flesh. Real connoisseurs favour the Beurre Hardy, which as its name suggests, melts like butter in the mouth.

The trouble with buying pears is that, unless you know your varieties, you can never be sure of what you are buying. Their texture may be mealy or dryly fluffy and they may have gone 'sleepy', or started rotting from the inside out. The colour of the skin, which ranges from a deep green to a waxy yellow, and the shape, which varies from round to conical, are also no indication of the taste. If you can, try to get your greengrocer to cut one up to allow you to sample it and see what condition they are in.

Pears Poached in White Wine with Cassis

In Victorian days, a distinction was made between stewing and eating pears. The former had a firm almost hard texture, lacked flavour, were long keeping and were ideal for cooking as they kept their shape; the latter were softer, buttery, acid but sweet and had to be eaten as soon as they were ripe.

Nowadays this distinction has disappeared, but only certain pears really cook well. Conference, Packham's Triumph and the small Comice are ideal for poaching. If you can't find any of these, however, choose any pear with an even shape that has yet to soften.

Once cut, all pears discolour readily; so it is a good idea to soak them in water acidulated with lemon juice or to rub their flesh with the cut half of a lemon.

SERVES 6

170 g/6 oz caster sugar
300 ml/$\frac{1}{2}$ pt white wine
zest of 1 large orange
cinnamon stick, broken into pieces
6 firm pears, peeled and cored
2 tbsp crème de cassis

Make a simple sugar syrup in a saucepan just large enough to stand the 6 pears upright. Put the sugar in the pan along with 575 ml/1 pt of water. Stir over a low heat until dissolved. Turn up the heat and bring to the boil, then boil to reduce by about one-third. Stir in the wine, orange zest and cinnamon.

Put the pears in the pan, turn the heat down to low and poach for about 15 minutes, or until they are just beginning to soften.

Using a slotted spoon, lift out the pears. Then turn up the heat, stir in the crème de cassis and boil to reduce the liquid by about two-thirds, or until it is quite thick and syrupy.

Turn down the heat to low and lift out the cinnamon pieces. Return the pears to the pan and simmer for a further 3–5 minutes, spooning the liquid over the pears so they become streaked with the syrup.

Transfer the pears to a serving dish, pour over the syrup and leave to cool before serving.

PEARS POACHED IN WHITE WINE WITH CASSIS

Pears in a Brioche

I once tried this recipe with perry pears, the descendants of the wild pear introduced to this country by the Normans and which are still grown especially for their juice. The result was a bitter-sweet pudding with a more pungent, woodier flavour than you normally find from a dessert pear.

SERVES 4

30 g/1 oz unsalted butter, plus extra for brushing
450 g/1 lb firm pears, peeled, cored and sliced
1 tbsp sugar
1 tbsp eau-de-vie de Poire Williams
250 ml/¼ pt double cream
1 brioche (see page 196)
15 g/½ oz flaked almonds

Preheat the oven to 180C/350F/gas4.

Melt the butter in a sauté pan over a low heat. Put in the pears, sprinkle with the sugar and gently cook them, turning them occasionally, for about 5 minutes or until tender.

Stir in the Poire Williams and cream, turn up the heat and boil briskly to reduce the syrup to a reasonably thick coating consistency. Remove from the heat and keep warm.

Meanwhile, cut out a wide circle in the top of the brioche and make a hollow deep enough for the pear slices. Brush the whole thing all over with melted butter.

Put it on a baking tray with the almonds scattered around it and toast in the preheated oven for about 10 minutes, or until the almonds turn golden.

Remove the brioche from the oven. Spoon the pears into the hollow (most of them should fit in with a few overflowing on top), dribbling some of the sauce down the sides, and scatter over the toasted almonds.

Serve immediately, cutting it in slices like a cake.

Plums

Many a child has, at least once during a long summer, hidden under a plum tree away from the watchful eyes of grown-ups and crammed themselves fit to burst with the brightly coloured juicy treasures from the tree.

You can always tell a fresh plum by its firm skin, tautly stretched over the succulent flesh, and its gentle bloom giving it a look as if it has been lightly smeared with chalk. The trouble with ripe plums, however, is that they spoil and bruise so easily; so usually those on sale in shops just do not match the juicy fleshiness of those picked from the garden.

Pears range in colour from bright green to deep scarlet opposite. The Victoria plum is one of the best-known varieties below.

Plum and Pear Jam

Ripe plums are full of natural sugar and pectin, so they can be used in one of the few jam recipes that needs absolutely no added sugar. You must, of course, use very soft ripe plums and pears in this recipe to achieve the right sweetness and set. It is therefore an ideal way of coping with a windfall, provided you cut out any bruises or damage from the fruit. This recipe is more like a purée than a true jam in texture, but it will keep for months provided you store it in the refrigerator or in a very cool place.

MAKES 1.35–1.8 K/3–4 LB

900 g/2 lb ripe eating plums, stoned and halved
zest and juice of 1 orange
stick of cinnamon, crushed
2 cloves
900 g/2 lb pears, peeled, cored and roughly chopped
zest and juice of 1 lemon
2 tbsp honeyed sweet dessert wine, such as Beaumes-de-Venise or Vin Santo (optional)

Put the plums in a preserving pan with the orange juice and zest, the cinnamon, cloves and 250 ml/8 fl oz of water. Over a low heat and stirring frequently, simmer for about 20 minutes or until the fruit is quite soft.

Add the pears along with the lemon zest and juice and sweet wine, if using. Simmer, stirring occasionally, for a further hour, or until the fruit has reduced to a thick pulp. Add more water if necessary at any time to prevent the fruit sticking to the bottom of the pan.

If you like jam very smooth and more like a purée or paste, pass it through a sieve; otherwise bottle it as it is in warm dry sterilized jars. Leave it to cool before sealing the jars and store in a cool place.

BLACKBERRY AND SCENTED GERANIUM LEAF JAM left (SEE PAGE 244), PLUM AND PEAR JAM left. The cherry-picking period in orchards is a short one, generally no more than a week above right.

Cherries

MORELLO or SOUR CHERRIES are one of the few fruits that can successfully be grown on a north-facing wall. Their use is admittedly rather restricted as they are far too bitter to eat; but they can be pricked all over with a needle and left to soak for months in vodka to make a fiery, fruity drink, or they can be turned into a sharp sauce to accompany roast duck.

SWEET CHERRIES need plenty of sun to ripen and they are best grown in warm sunny climates. They should be juicy with a good ratio of fruit to stone. The way to judge their freshness is to look at their stalks: if they are still green it means they have been recently picked, but after a few days the stalks start to dry up and turn brown.

The cherry season starts in early May with imports from Turkey and Southern California. As the summer progresses, the more northerly ones from Italy and France — and eventually England — ripen. Apparently the most popular varieties are the fat red and juicy Bigarreaux, as the paler White Hearts have the disadvantage of bruising easily, although it is fair to say that few people buy a specific variety.

Clafoutis

For a clafoutis, or cherry cake, choose the plumpest firmest cherries you can find. If they are slightly bitter, simply add a little extra sugar to the recipe.

Some recipes suggest using unstoned cherries for a stronger flavour. However, I find the stones irritating and, providing you choose plump fleshy fruit with a good flavour, it should not be necessary.

SERVES 4

3 eggs
200 g/7 oz plain or self-raising flour
85 g/3 oz caster sugar
pinch of salt
250 ml/8 fl oz warm milk
1 tbsp rum
45 g/1½ oz unsalted butter
450 g/1 lb fresh cherries, pitted
1 tsp icing sugar

Separate one of the eggs, put the egg yolk with the two whole remaining eggs in a large bowl and lightly beat them. Sift in the flour, sugar and salt and stir together. Pour in 2 tablespoons of the milk and beat until the mixture is smooth. Then, gradually stir in the remaining milk and rum. Beat the batter until it is smooth and shiny and leave it to rest for 1–2 hours in a cool place.

Preheat the oven to 220C/425F/gas7 and use about half of the butter to grease thoroughly a 23 cm/9 in round ovenproof gratin or quiche dish.

Whisk the remaining egg white until it forms stiff peaks and fold it into the batter. Pour the batter into the prepared dish, drop the cherries in (don't worry if they sink down because they will rise to the top during cooking) and dot the top with the remaining butter.

Bake in the preheated oven for 35–40 minutes, or until the batter is puffed up and golden brown.

Remove from the oven, sift over the icing sugar and serve immediately.

Fruit from the Bushes

Late June to September is the season for soft fruit. There is a profusion of BLACKCURRANTS, RED-CURRANTS and WHITE CURRANTS; tiny iridescent cooking GOOSEBERRIES and the full-blown 'levellers' or 'eaters'; STRAWBERRIES in all their juicy glory; the softer subtler RASPBERRY; and the larger, darker LOGANBERRY with its sharper taste. Finally comes the BLACKBERRY which may be picked from the hedgerows right up to mid-October, although according to an old country superstition blackberries should never be touched after the old Michaelmas Day, October 10, as on this day the Devil is said to spit on the fruit to spite his rival, the Archangel Michael.

Sweet cherries left

As they damage so easily, soft fruits are best left unwashed, although you can always gently wipe firmer fruit with a damp cloth. As they are so fragile, treat them carefully; never squash them under the weight of heavy shopping and keep them in the refrigerator until they are required.

The range of soft fruit seems to multiply every year as keen gardeners and nurserymen busy themselves cross-pollinating. BLUEBERRIES and BILBERRIES are well known, but have you even ever heard of, let alone tasted: TAYBERRIES, a raspberry-blackberry cross; tart JOSTABERRIES, bred from the blackcurrant and gooseberry; or the MARIONBERRY, with its logan-berry flavour and blackberry appearance?

Most soft fruits make excellent fruit vinegars, which may seem to be just a current fad but have actually been made for centuries. Simply put a handful of lightly mashed fruit in a jar and cover them with a good wine or cider vinegar and leave to infuse for a week. Then strain through a jelly bag or muslin-lined sieve, measure equal quantities of liquid and sugar (use less sugar to make a sharper vinegar for adding to savoury sauces), boil it for 10 minutes and store in bottles until needed.

Another excellent use for soft fruit is to purée them into a coulis or fruit sauce. Choose very ripe fruit, such as raspberries, strawberries and loganberries, and just press the fruit firmly through a sieve or food mill. The sauce can then be left plain or flavoured with a little sugar or sweet wine and served with ice-cream, slices of fruit or meringues.

Strawberries

Strawberries herald all the joy of summer. Tradition-ally served with lashings of rich double cream, they take pride of place at summer parties and picnics — and, of course, at events like Wimbledon.

It is not that I am old-fashioned, but I do not approve of the fact that nowadays strawberries are flown in from all over the world throughout the year. Not only does this year-round availability spoil the pleasure of anticipation but, more importantly, the imported fruit does not taste particularly good.

The juicy ripe bright-red strawberry, with its perfect balance of sweetness and acidity, is a fruit to be treasured. The tiny wild, or alpine, strawberry has a heady, intense flavour, but I still prefer the larger, more luscious fruit of our cultivated varieties. They come in all shapes: from round or pendulous to globular and even irregular. At one time Cambridge Favourite was the most commonly grown variety on the grounds that it was prolific, disease-resistant and a regular cropper. Its serious disadvantage was that it had very little taste, but growers soon realized the error of their ways and started planting more fully flavoured fruit such as my favourite, the Gorella.

The best way to buy strawberries is to go to pick-your-own farms; you can then be certain that the fruit is in peak condition. They should be slightly soft, yielding to the gentlest of squeezes and highly and evenly coloured. If their colour fades away to white or, worst still, the palest of greens, they are not ripe. When choosing them in the shops, look out for signs of bruising or squashing and check that their calyx and stalk are still a fresh green.

Ideally, strawberries should never be washed and certainly not under a running tap as this literally drowns their flavour. However, as you can never be certain whether or not they have been sprayed (unless of course you buy organic fruit), just wipe them gently with a damp cloth. Strawberries are best eaten raw and the laziest way to serve them is to pile them into a dish without even hulling them and then leave your friends to pick them up by the calyx and dip them into a bowl of crème fraîche or lightly whipped double cream.

Marinated Strawberries

Strawberries at their peak cannot be improved on and need nothing more than cream. Unfortunately it is all too rare to be able to buy them at their best, so a sweet marinade will improve their flavour.

SERVES 4

900 g/2 lb fresh strawberries
115 g/4 oz caster sugar
zest of 1 and juice of 2 large oranges
5 tbsp Grand Marnier
1 tbsp chopped fresh mint leaves (optional)

Hull the strawberries and put them in a large bowl, allowing plenty of room so they are not overcrowded or they will bruise. If they are quite large, cut them in half with a sharp knife. Sprinkle over the caster sugar and orange zest, add the juice and Grand Marnier and stir them together carefully so as not to crush them.

Cover the bowl and leave to macerate in the refrigerator for about 2 hours, stirring carefully from time to time. Serve chilled, accompanied by lightly whipped double cream flavoured with a few chopped mint leaves, if liked.

Strawberry Tarte Brulée

When choosing the strawberries for this tart, it is better to buy very firm, slightly under-ripe fruit. If they are too juicy and squashy, they will not retain their shape or texture while cooking.

SERVES 4–6

15–20 large firm strawberries
1 tbsp brandy
55 g/2 oz caster sugar
225 g/8 oz rich shortcrust pastry (see page 199)
450 ml/¾ pt double cream
4 egg yolks
butter, for greasing

Preheat the oven to I90C/375F/gas5 and lightly grease a 25 cm/I0 in tart or shallow pie dish with butter.

Using a sharp knife, cut the strawberries in half and put them in a large bowl. Pour over the brandy and sprinkle with half of the sugar. Stir gently so as not to crush or bruise the strawberries and leave them to macerate for I hour.

Roll out the pastry to a thickness of about 6 mm/¼ in and line the dish with it. Trim the edges of the pastry and prick the bottom with a fork. Cover the dish with a sheet of greaseproof paper weighted down with some baking beans and bake blind in the preheated oven for I5 minutes.

Meanwhile pour the cream into a saucepan. Warm it over a medium heat for I minute. Put the egg yolks into a suitable bowl and beat in the warmed cream.

Set the bowl over a pan of boiling water and, stirring constantly, cook the egg and cream mixture for 5 minutes. Then pass it through a sieve into a clean bowl and leave to cool.

Drain the strawberries and arrange them flat side down in a single close-fitting layer on the pastry. Stir their drained juices into the cream mixture, pour it over the fruit and chill for 2 hours.

Preheat the grill.

Sprinkle the top of the tart with the remaining sugar, set under the preheated grill and grill until the sugar caramelizes into a golden brown, turning it from time to time so that it browns evenly.

Serve either hot or chilled.

Strawberries and roses are synonymous with summer.

Raspberries

With their velvet texture and a bloom like a soft kid glove, raspberries are very definitely a fruit for eating raw. Always choose them when slightly soft but without a blemish or bruise and try to check the bottom of the punnet for any tell-tale stains.

Although keen fruit-growing gardeners recommend the yellow raspberry and insist that it is even more delightful than its soft wine-red cousin, this is not much use to those of us who do not have the luxury of a fruit cage, as they are rarely to be seen in the shops. However, if you find them, snap them up.

Recently re-reading Elizabeth David's *Summer Cooking* I came across what has now become my definitive recipe for raspberry jam – the only exception I ever make to not cooking the fruit. It preserves almost intact the fresh flavour of the fruit and, if you can resist eating it, it will last for up to a year. All you do is put equal quantities of raspberries and sugar in a large dish in a medium oven for 20–30 minutes; then break the fruit down to a purée with a wooden spoon and bottle it in warm dry sterile jars and seal with a round of waxed paper dipped in brandy.

Raspberry and Hazelnut Shortbread

SERVES 4

350 g/12 oz unsalted butter, chilled and cut into small pieces, plus extra for greasing
170 g/6 oz hazelnuts
255 g/8 oz plain flour
55 g/2 oz semolina
115 g/4 oz caster sugar
pinch of salt
250 ml/8 fl oz whipping cream, whipped
450 g/1 lb fresh raspberries
1 tsp icing sugar

Preheat the oven to 190C/375F/gas5 and lightly grease 2 baking trays with butter.

Scatter the hazelnuts on a baking tray, roast them in the preheated oven for 10–15 minutes, or until golden brown. While they are still warm, rub them in a dry cloth to remove the skins.

Put them in a food processor and whizz until they are the texture of coarse breadcrumbs. Sift in the flour, semolina, sugar and salt. Add the butter and whizz again until the mixture comes together to form a ball. Wrap this pastry in a polythene bag and put it in the refrigerator to chill for about 30 minutes.

Divide the pastry into 3. Roll out each piece into a round about 6 mm/¼ in thick and, using a large biscuit cutter or the base of a cake tin, cut each into identical circles. Put the rounds on the prepared baking trays and bake in the preheated oven for about 15–20 minutes.

Leave them to cool slightly on the trays before transferring them to a cooling rack. When they are quite cool, assemble them into triple layer sandwiches by spreading some of the cream on one of the rounds

Scotland is known for its fine-flavoured raspberries.

and then arrange half of the raspberries on it. Spread these with a little more cream and place a second round on top. Repeat the process, using the remaining cream and raspberries and finishing with the remaining shortbread round.

Sift the icing sugar on top and serve chilled.

Variation

You can, if you prefer, divide the pastry into 12 pieces to make 4 individual shortbreads.

Summer Pudding

This is truly one of the great treats of summer and can be made with most soft fruits in any combination — the mixture is up to you. Be sure that all the fruit is ripe and fresh and pick it over thoroughly first, discarding any bruised or mouldy berries as even the slightest blemish can ruin the flavour of the pudding.

SUMMER PUDDING

SERVES 8–10

450 g/1 lb raspberries
225 g/8 oz caster sugar
225 g/8 oz blackcurrants
225 g/8 oz redcurrants
225 g/8 oz white currants
1 tablespoon crème de mure
2 tablespoons white wine
1 loaf of day-old white bread
double cream, lightly whipped, to serve

Put the raspberries in a bowl and cover with about 30 g/1 oz of the sugar. In a separate bowl, put the blackcurrants, redcurrants, white currants and the rest of the sugar. Leave both bowls to stand for about 3–4 hours, or until the juices start to run.

Tip the bowl containing the mixed currants into a saucepan along with the crème de mure and white wine and bring almost to the boil over a medium heat. Simmer for 2–3 minutes to cook the fruit lightly, remove from the heat and, when cool, mix in the raspberries.

Meanwhile, trim the crusts from the loaf and cut it into slices about 6 mm/$\frac{1}{4}$ in thick. Cut a circle out of one of the slices to fit the base of a 1.1 1/2 pt pudding basin and then cut wedges of bread to fit snugly round the sides – there should be no gaps. Spoon in the fruit and juice and cover the top with two slices of bread, trimming the edges to make a neat finish.

Cover the bowl with a plate small enough to fit just inside the rim, place a couple of weights on top to press it down and leave it to stand overnight in a cool place.

To serve the pudding, put the blade of a sharp knife under running hot water and then ease the blade round between pudding and basin. Place a serving dish upside down on top and turn the whole thing over quickly, giving it a short sharp shake.

Serve the pudding cut in slices with lashings of lightly whipped cream.

Variation

You can also make a Winter Pudding using the Fruit Compote (see page 210) and very thinly cut slices of wholemeal bread.

Blackcurrant Leaf Sorbet

Light, delicate and refreshing, this sorbet is made with the leaves of the edible blackcurrant plant (the ornamental species does not have the same flavour). Blackcurrant leaves are curiously aromatic and when soaked in a sugar syrup, they infuse the liquid with a heady perfume which is not dissimilar to the muzzy taste of elderflowers. Be sure to pick young tender leaves free from frost and insect damage, and wash and refresh them in ice cold water before use.

SERVES 4

140 g/5 oz granulated sugar
3–4 handfuls of young blackcurrant leaves
zest of 2 and juice of 3 lemons

In a saucepan over a low heat, dissolve the sugar in 575 ml/1 pt of water. Then turn up the heat, bring to the boil and let it simmer for 5 minutes.

Remove the pan from the heat, add the leaves, cover the pan and leave to stand to infuse for about 4–5 hours (or overnight if you wish, for a stronger scent and a deeper green sorbet).

Turn the freezer compartment to its lowest setting, if using.

Strain the liquid through a sieve, pressing down quite hard on the leaves to extract their flavour and all the syrup, stir in the lemon zest and juice.

Then make the mixture into sorbet in a sorbetière or ice-cream maker, according to the instructions.

Alternatively, put the mixture into a shallow freezer tray and freeze until the sides are firm but the centre is quite runny (the actual time will depend on the efficiency of your freezer).

Remove it from the freezer, pour it into a chilled bowl, beat it thoroughly until smooth and return it to the freezer in the tray and freeze until almost solid.

Blackcurrants

Open Fruit Tarts

Most fruit can be used in an open fruit tart. Rhubarb needs a special treatment (see overleaf); some, such as plums, greengages, apricots, gooseberries, blueberries, blackcurrants, redcurrants or white currants, peaches, cherries and figs, can either be poached first in a sugar syrup (see Pears in White Wine page 226) or baked in the oven in the tart or, if they are very ripe, they may simply be stoned, sliced and arranged in the cooked pastry case; others, especially strawberries and raspberries, should never be cooked.

The best pastry to use is a rich shortcrust (see page 199) and you can subtly alter its flavour by including ground nuts or other flavourings (see page 243).

Once the pastry case has been baked blind it should be cooled and the base spread with a confectioner's custard (see page 243) or a jam of your choice, and then baked with the fruit; if it is not going to be cooked again you could also use a whipped cream or a fruit coulis (see page 233).

Finally the fruit should be glazed. Either sprinkle the fruit with sugar and pop it under a preheated grill until it starts to caramelize; or heat a jam or jelly and reduce it slightly and then paint this over the fruit.

The important thing to remember is to choose ingredients and flavours to complement each other (see overleaf for suggestions).

OPEN FRUIT TARTS: from left to right, STRAWBERRY, RASPBERRY, GOOSEBERRY, REDCURRANT, CHERRY.

Rhubarb and Marmalade Open Tart

Rhubarb tends to collapse into a 'mush' when cooked and can spoil the pastry in a tart. To prevent this, dry-fry it first in sugar, just long enough to let its juices start to run but keeping it firm enough to stand the pieces upright in the tart.

SERVES 4–6

15 g/½ oz unsalted butter, plus extra for greasing
225 g/8 oz rich shortcrust pastry (see page 199), chilled and rested
450 g/1 lb rhubarb
2 tbsp caster sugar
4 tbsp coarse marmalade
1 tbsp whisky

RHUBARB AND MARMALADE OPEN TART

Preheat the oven to 190C/375F/gas5 and generously butter a 20 cm/8 in tart tin or 4 individual tart tins with removable bases.

Roll out the rested pastry into a circle about 6 mm/¼ in thick and slightly larger than the tin. Line the tin(s) with it, trim the edges, prick the bottom(s) with a fork and cover with greaseproof paper weighted down with some baking beans. Bake blind in the preheated oven for 15 minutes. Remove from the oven and leave to cool slightly. Turn up the oven to 230C/450F/gas8.

Meanwhile cut the rhubarb into 5 cm/2 in lengths. Put them into a saucepan with the sugar and cook gently over a low heat for about 5–7 minutes, shaking the pan occasionally, until the rhubarb releases some of its juices but is still firm enough to handle. Strain, reserving the juices and leave to cool.

When the pastry is slightly cooled use a pastry brush to paint the base(s) and sides with 2 tablespoons of the marmalade. Stand the pieces of rhubarb upright in the tart(s), packing them in tightly, dot the top(s) with the butter, cover with greaseproof paper and bake in the preheated oven for about 15 minutes. Remove from the oven and leave to cool slightly.

To make the glaze: in a saucepan boil the rhubarb juices over a high heat to reduce to about 1 teaspoon. Stir in the remaining marmalade and the whisky and, stirring constantly, continue boiling to reduce by about half. Using a pastry brush, paint the glaze over the top of the fruit and allow to cool before serving.

Open Tart Variations

1 Replace 55 g/2 oz of the plain flour with ground almonds when making the pastry, use a confectioner's custard (see right) for the base, fill with 675 g/1½ lb raw halved and stoned plums, bake in an oven preheated to 200C/400F/gas6 for 20 minutes and glaze with apricot jam.

2 Add a teaspoon of orange zest when making the pastry, use a confectioner's custard (see right) for the base, fill with 675 g/1½ lb halved and stoned greengages poached in a sugar syrup for 5 minutes, glaze with sugar then brown under the grill.

3 Add a teaspoon of cinnamon when making the pastry, use whipped cream for the base, fill with 675 g/1½ lb stoned and sliced apricots poached in a sugar syrup for 3 minutes and glaze with apricot jam.

4 Replace 55 g/2 oz of the plain flour with ground hazelnuts when making the pastry, use a confectioner's custard (see right) for the base, fill with 450 g/1 lb mixed blackcurrants, redcurrants and white currants poached in a sugar syrup for 5–7 minutes, glaze with sugar then brown under the grill.

5 Add a teaspoon of chopped mint when making the pastry, use an apricot jam for the base and fill the tart with halved figs dotted with 30 g/1 oz butter and sprinkled with sugar. Bake the tart in an oven preheated to 200C/400F/gas6 for 15 minutes and glaze with apricot jam.

Confectioner's Custard

2 egg yolks
2 tbsp caster sugar
300 ml/½ pt milk
vanilla pod

In a bowl thoroughly whisk the egg yolks with 1 tablespoon of caster sugar until they become pale and form a light ribbon.

Slowly bring the milk to the boil in a saucepan with the vanilla pod and the remaining caster sugar. Remove from the heat, pour the milk over the egg yolks and stir together well.

Remove the vanilla pod and return the mixture to the saucepan over a low heat. Using a wooden spoon, stir until the mixture thickens and begins to coat the back of the spoon. Do make sure not to let it boil. Pour the custard into a cold bowl and cover with greaseproof paper to prevent a skin forming. Leave to cool until needed.

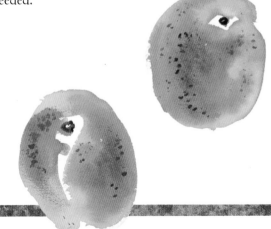

Blackberry and Scented Geranium Leaf Jam

The basis of a good jam is ripe fruit with a high sugar and pectin content. So choose, or pick, the ripest and sweetest blackberries possible and discard any broken or bleeding ones. If you must wash them, do it very gently to avoid damaging the fruit any further.

Scented geranium leaves, with their content of volatile oil, add an extra dimension of flavour to the jam. The best variety to use here is lemon verbena. Geranium or peppermint leaves can also be effective when added ahead of time to the sugar in a jar to infuse it with their flavour.

900 g/2 lb ripe blackberries
3 scented geranium leaves
caster sugar (see below)

Put the blackberries in a preserving pan with the geranium leaves and 175 ml/6 fl oz water, or just enough to prevent them from sticking to the pan.

Stew the fruit over a low heat, stirring frequently, until they are very soft. Pass them through a sieve to get rid of their pips, pressing down very hard to extract all the juice and pulp.

Measure the pulp and return it to the preserving pan. For every 575 ml/1 pt of pulp, add 450 g/1 lb of sugar. Stir over a low heat until the sugar is dissolved. Turn up the heat to bring to the boil and cook rapidly, stirring continuously, until setting point is reached. This stage can take anything from 10 to 30 minutes, depending on how fiercely the jam is boiling and how ripe the fruit was, but you must stir continuously otherwise it can catch and burn in the pan.

To test whether setting point has been reached, put a small amount on a saucer and cool it in the refrigerator; after 5 minutes it should have the right consistency, or set, of a jam.

Bottle it in warm dry sterilized jars and cover.

Honey

Honey comes from nectar collected by bees from flowers on plants, shrubs and trees. No two nectars are the same as they vary in the quantity and type of sugar and other trace elements. For this reason the taste, aroma and colour of honey change according to the nectar from which it is made.

Beekeepers often move their hives around the countryside: in the spring they may hire out their bees to pollinate the orchards or crops in the fields; then, depending on the time of the year, they will move the hives to the moors, woods, fields or meadows so the bees can concentrate on a particular herb or blossom. Even then such plans can be thwarted as bees are known to travel up to two miles for food.

Most of the honey we buy is 'blended' or made from mixtures of different types and flavours of honey from several countries. The advantage of such blending is that it produces a consistent, if bland, taste; it is like buying a generic wine which cannot possibly offend anyone as all its characteristics and idiosyncrasies have been ironed out. Blended honeys are the cheapest of all the honeys and fine for using in cooking. Like most honeys they are sold either in a cloudy, fairly solid form or runny and clear. The latter have usually been heat-treated to remain liquid.

Bee hives are often moved from site to site so that the bees can collect nectar from specific flowers or herbs.

'Polyfloral', or mixed flower, honey is produced from a mixture of flowers or blossoms from one particular part of the country, such as the MIXED BLOSSOM HONEY from most of the Mediterranean countries or the nutty CHESTNUT AND SYCAMORE HONEY from Scotland.

'Monofloral', or single flower, honey is made of nectar from the flowers or blossom of a single species. At their best, these honeys can be superb, with a unique flavour and aroma that can range from delicate to strong, depending on the flower source. The best known are THYME HONEY or ORANGE BLOSSOM HONEY from the Peloponnese in Greece, LIME HONEY from Northern France, LAVENDER HONEY from the South of France, CHESTNUT HONEY from Northern Italy, HEATHER HONEY from Devon and RASPBERRY HONEY from the raspberry fields in Blairgowrie, Scotland. These honeys are like estate-bottled wine; they each have a distinctive character and taste, which varies from year to year according to the climate. They also cost quite a lot more than most other honeys.

Should your honey crystallize in storage or if it is a solid variety, it is worth remembering that it can always be made runny for cooking by simply standing the jar in a bowl of hot water for a few minutes.

Honey and Lavender Ice-cream

For the most exciting honey ice-cream, use a monofloral honey with a distinctive well-rounded flavour.

SERVES 6

170 g/6 oz lavender honey
450 ml/¾ pt whipping cream
2 tsp lavender flowers, lightly crushed

Turn the freezer to its lowest setting, if using.

If the honey is set rather than clear and runny, melt it in a saucepan over a low heat and set aside. Whip the cream lightly until it forms soft peaks and fold in the honey and lavender flowers.

Make the mixture into an ice-cream in a sorbetière or ice-cream maker according to the instructions.

Alternatively, put the mixture into a shallow freezer tray and freeze until the sides are firm but the centre is quite runny (the actual time will depend on the efficiency of your freezer). Then remove it from the freezer, pour it into a chilled bowl and beat it thoroughly until smooth. Return it to the freezer in the tray and freeze until solid.

You could just let this ice-cream freeze without even beating it; it will not be quite as smooth but, because it has quite a high sugar and fat content, it should not form any of the large ice crystals which ruin the texture of ice-cream.

Variations
1 Use lime blossom honey with 2 teaspoons of lime zest.
2 Use an orange blossom or acacia honey with 2 tablespoons of grated orange zest.
3 Use a thyme or herb honey with 1 teaspoon each of lemon zest and finely chopped lemon thyme.

HONEY AND LAVENDER ICE-CREAM IN A BRANDY SNAP BASKET (SEE PAGE 207) left. Lavender fields in Provence below.

Seasonal Menus

Spring

Light Lunch

Roulade with Asparagus (page 129)
Poached Cod with Capers (page 81)

Lunch for Friends

Liver Parfait with a Basil and Tomato Sauce (page 108)
Roast Salmon with Stewed Cucumbers
(page 72 and page 30)
Gooseberry Tart (page 240)

Simple Supper

Fishcakes with Hollandaise Sauce (page 82 and page 128)
Pears in a Brioche (page 229)

Vegetarian Supper

Pasta with Spring Vegetable Sauce (page 34)
Tarte Tatin (page 222)

Dinner

Terrine of Lemon Sole with Prawns (page 89)
Navarin of Lamb (page 145)
Rhubarb and Marmalade Open Tart (page 242)

Summer

Brunch

Mirror Eggs (page 127)
Grissini (page 192)
Blackcurrant Leaf Sorbet in Brandy Snap Baskets
(page 239 and page 207)

Seafood Supper

Fish Soup (page 86)
Mixed Poached Seafood with Samphire (page 95)
Savarin (page 212)

Vegetarian Lunch

Soufflé Omelette with Sorrel and Crème Fraîche (page 131)
Globe Artichokes with Broad Beans (page 39)
Olive Oil Bread (page 195)
Summer Pudding (page 238)

Dinner

Lettuce and Chervil Soup (page 41)
Turbot in Rock Salt (page 88)
Paper Bag Potatoes (page 21)
Honey and Lavender Ice-cream with Pistachio Tuiles
(page 247 and page 206)

Picnic

Chicken in a Loaf (page 113)
Spinach, Curd Cheese and Raisin Tart (page 61)
Marinated Strawberries (page 234)

Autumn

Light Lunch

Game Terrine with Onion Marmalade
(page 174 and page 23)
Toasted Brioche (page 196)
Pears Poached in White Wine with Cassis (page 226)

Simple Lunch

Jambon Persillé with Granary Bread
(page 155 and page 191)
Warm Red Cabbage Salad (page 27)

Supper

Hare with Noodles (page 172)
Buckwheat Pancakes with Fruit Compote (page 210)

Dinner for Friends

Chestnut Soup (page 176)
Pheasant with Celery (page 165)
Apple and Quince Soufflé (page 224)

Harvest Supper

Courgette and Corn Chowder (page 30)
Braised Pork with Wild Mushrooms and
Juniper Berries (page 147)
Plum Tart (page 243)

Winter

Brunch

Homemade Sausages with Onion Marmalade and Coarse-grain
Mustard (page 150, page 23 and page 159)
Kedgeree (page 101)
Scrambled Eggs (page 131)
Corn Muffins (page 198)

Lunch

Oxtail with Grapes (page 138)
Bread and Butter Pudding (page 209)

Fireside Tea

Blackcurrant and Scented Geranium Leaf Jam (page 244)
Granary Bread (page 191)
Chestnut and Orange Cake (page 203)
Lincolnshire Plum Bread (page 198)

Dinner

Curried Parsnip Soup (page 16)
Roast Loin of Pork Studded with Ham (page 148)
Roast Vegetables with Thyme (page 38)
Buckwheat Pancakes with Fruit Compote (page 210)

Christmas Dinner

Tartare of Salmon with Cucumber Salad (page 70)
Roast Goose with Spiced Crab Apples
(page 117 and page 224)
Henrietta's Roast Potatoes (page 21)
Certosino or Italian Christmas Cake (page 200)

Index

Page numbers in *italic* refer to illustrations

Acknowledgements

There are so many people whom I would like to thank for their help with *New Country Kitchen*: Gwen White for the hours spent on her word processor and, with her chef/husband Colin, for their generous contribution to the recipes; Denise Bates, my editor, for her tireless coaxing and patience; Lewis Esson for his eagle eyes and strivings for exactitude; Andrew Hewson, my agent; Rebecca Delegano and Rebecca Morley for their patience in the kitchen while testing; Paul Welti for his splendid designs; Jess Koppel and Lyn Rutherford for, respectively, photographing and recreating my recipes; the endless farmers, growers, producers and retailers who have generously given of their time and expertise; and finally, all my friends who have manfully stayed the course and eaten up the food.

Recipe acknowledgements

Claiming a recipe as my own can be a moot point, as so often it may be a classic which I have absorbed into my repertoire. Some may come from more recent acknowledged sources, but in cooking them several times I may have changed the balance of flavours with a twist here, a tweak there and made them my own. Others I have reproduced in their entirety and would therefore like to thank: Raymond Blanc for *Tartare of Salmon with Cucumber Salad*; Anna del Conte for *Chicken Breasts with Orange* and *Hare with Noodles*; Elizabeth David for *Oxtail with Grapes* and *Grilled Calves' Liver Kebabs with Lettuce Sauce*; Josceline Dimbleby for *The Best-ever Chocolate Cake*; Peter Graham for *Whiting with Curd Cheese*; the late Jane Grigson for *Curried Parsnip Soup* and *Eels in Green Sauce*; Ian McAndrew for *Liver Parfait with a Basil and Tomato Sauce* and *Breast of Guinea Fowl with Lentils*; Patricia Lousada for *Corn Muffins*; Deborah Madison for *Courgette and Corn Chowder* and *Green Tomato, Raisin and Mint Chutney*; Anton Mosimann for *Bread and Butter Pudding*; Rick Stein for *Terrine of Lemon Sole with Prawns* and Mary Taylor Simetti for *Chicken in a Loaf*. Other writers to whom I owe a particular debt are Marcella Hazan, Joy Larkcom, Marie-Pierre Moine, Roger Phillips and Claudia Roden. Thank you one and all.

The publishers would like to thank the following photographers and organizations for their permission to reproduce photographs in this book:

10–11 J. Ducange/Agence Top; 12 J.-P. Couderc/Agence Top; 13 Mike England; 14 Michael Boys/Boys Syndication; 23 P. Hussenot/Agence Top; 26 Michael Boys/Boys Syndication; 29 Michelle Garrett; 33 Michelle Garrett; 36 Lucy Mason; 40 Jess Koppel; 46–7 Debbie Patterson; 49 Michael St Maur Sheil/Susan Griggs Agency; 53 Robert Harding Picture Library; 58 S & O Mathews; 62 F. Jalain/Explorer; 64 Jacqui Hurst; 66–7 Michelle Garrett; 70 Anthony Blake Photo Library; 72 Zefa Picture Library; 75 Gary Rogers; 76 Anthony Blake Photo Library; 87 S & O Mathews; 90 S & O Mathews; 92 Glyn Satterley; 98 Glyn Satterley; 99 Jacqui Hurst; 101 Glyn Satterley; 102–3 Michael Busselle; 104 Nicholas/Pix; 106 S & O Mathews; 114 Zefa Picture Library; 116 Anthony Blake Photo Library; 119 Anthony Blake Photo Library; 125 J.M. La Roque/Explorer; 132–3 Michael Busselle; 135 Glyn Satterley; 140 S & O Mathews; 142 Mike England; 148 Edward Parker/Hutchinson Library; 152 P. Hussenot/Agence Top; 158 R. Tixador/Agence Top; 160–1 Zefa Picture Library; 162 Zefa Picture Library; 167 Landscape Only; 172 Glyn Satterley; 175 Zefa Picture Library; 176 Laurence Delderfield; 180 Anthony Blake Photo Library; 186–7 John Miller; 190 Laurence Delderfield; 193 Jerrican; 201 Timothy Winter/Robert Harding Picture Library; 202 Michael Busselle; 203 Linda Burgess/Insight Picture Library; 211 Enrico Rainero/Robert Harding Picture Library; 214–5 F. Jalain/Explorer; 217 Jacqui Hurst/ Boys Syndication; 221 George Wright; 224 Linda Burgess/Insight Picture Library; 228 Hank Delespinasse/Image Bank; 229 John Lewis Stage/Image Bank; 231 Anthony Blake Photo Library; 232 Jacqui Hurst; 235 Jacqui Hurst/Boys Syndication; 237 Lucy Mason; 239 Lucy Mason; 244–5 Bansse/Pix; 245 J.N. Reichel/Agence Top; 247 Catherine Bibollet/Agence Top.

Special photography by Jess Koppel: 2, 19, 20, 24–5, 31, 35, 39, 43–4, 50–1, 56, 60, 63, 65, 68, 71, 74, 77, 79, 81–3, 88, 91, 94, 96–7, 108, 111, 117, 118, 121, 122, 126–30, 137, 143–4, 149, 151, 153–4, 164, 169, 171, 174, 179, 182–5, 189, 194, 197, 200, 205, 208, 213, 218, 223, 227, 230, 238, 240–2, 246.